THE COLLAPSE OF BARINGS

Also by Stephen Fay

Measure for Measure: Reforming the Trade Unions
The Great Silver Bubble
The Ring: Anatomy of an Opera
Portrait of an Old Lady: Turmoil at the Bank of England
Power Play: The Life and Times of Peter Hall
The Zinoviev Letter (with Lewis Chester and Hugo Young)
The Death of Venice (with Phillip Knightley)
Hoax (with Lewis Chester and Magnus Linklater)

Please renew/return this item by the last date shown.

So that your telephone call is charged at local rate, please call the numbers as set out below:

	From Area codes 01923 or 0208:	From the rest of Herts:
Renewals:	01923 471373	01438 737373
Enquiries:	01923 471333	01438 737333
Minicom:	01923 471599	01438 737599

L32b

The Collapse of
BARINGS

STEPHEN FAY

RICHARD COHEN BOOKS · London

British Library Cataloguing in Publication Data:
A catalogue record for this book is available from the British Library

Copyright © 1996 by Stephen Fay

ISBN 1 86066 037 1

First published in Great Britain in 1996 by
Richard Cohen Books
7 Manchester Square
London W1M 5RE

3 5 7 9 8 6 4 2

Design by Margaret Fraser

Typeset in Linotron Sabon by
Rowland Phototypesetting Ltd,
Bury St Edmunds, Suffolk

Printed in Great Britain by
Clays Ltd, St Ives

Contents

Acknowledgements   vii

Dramatis Personae   ix

Prologue   1

1   A Family Story   5

2   Red Braces, Lace-Up Shoes, Big Cigars   21

3   Big, Swinging Dicks   36

4   The Stabbath   51

5   The Education of Nicholas Leeson   70

6   The Game Begins   79

7   Why It All Happened   102

8   Miracle-Worker   120

9   Scissors and Paste   147

10   Too Much to Bear   178

11   Have I Bought Barings?   202

12   In Denial   223

13 Hung Out to Dry   235

14 Witch-Hunt   242

15 Panic, Ignorance, Greed   253

16 'I Am Guilty, Your Honour'   271

17 The Bitterest of Tastes   289

    A Note on Sources   298
    Bibliography   300
    Photographic Section Acknowledgements   302
    Index   303

Acknowledgements

Everyone to whom I spoke in the course of my research for this book asked if I had met Nick Leeson, but he decided to keep his thoughts for the ghost of his own book, and declined to talk to me. This ban was extended to members of his family. But Leeson's authentic voice does appear in this story, thanks to the transcript of Sir David Frost's television interview with him in jail in Frankfurt in September 1995, about half of which was broadcast. I am most grateful for Sir David's permission to quote from it.

In the summer of 1995, Patrick Masters held my hand in Companies House, and was my first guide to the futures-and-options markets.

Roger Geissler continued my education in these markets and corrected errors in my description of them.

Margaret Allen helped me to understand financial markets, and the politics and people of Singapore, where Sylvia Tan, Irene Hoe, and Mary Lee continued my education.

For their advice and encouragement, I should like to thank Chris Bailey, Stephen Cohen, John Clitheroe, Christopher Fildes, John Footman, David F. Gallacher, William Gleeson, Tony Gray, Joanna Lafeber, Sir Kit MacMahon, Sir Derek Mitchell, John Murray, Helen Parry, Stephen Pollard, Piers Pottinger, Fiammetta Rocco and Anthony Sampson.

I am grateful to the past and present employees of Barings who took time to explain their roles in the collapse. Many who spoke openly are credited in the text. I am especially grateful to them, but I should also like to thank those who, for one reason or another, chose anonymity.

David Galloway read the manuscript, and made various helpful suggestions. Any errors are my own.

As usual, Prudence Fay read and edited the manuscript with great insight and precision.

Stephen Fay
London
1 February 1996

Dramatis Personae

Barings

[BIB = Baring Investment Bank; BFS = Baring Futures (Singapore) Pte Ltd; BSS = Baring Securities Singapore; BSJ = Baring Securities (Japan) Ltd; BSL = Baring Securities Ltd]

James Baker	Internal auditor, BSL
Ron Baker	Head of Financial Products Group, BIB
Peter Baring	Chairman, Barings plc
James Bax	Managing Director, BSS
Andrew Baylis	Former Deputy Chairman, BSL
Gordon Bowser	Risk Manager, BSL
Geoffrey Broadhurst	Group Finance Director, BIB
Andrew Fraser	Head of Equity, Broking and Trading, BIB
Tony Gamby	Settlements Director, BIB
Brenda Granger	Manager Futures and Options Settlements, BIB
Fernando Gueler	Head Proprietary Equity Derivatives Trading, BSJ
Norhaslinda Hassan	Senior Settlements Clerk, BFS
Tony Hawes	Group Treasurer, BIB
Christopher Heath	Former Chief Executive, BSL
Lynn Henderson	Former Assistant Director, Finance, BIB
Ian Hopkins	Director and Head of Group Treasury and Risk, BIB
Simon Jones	Director BFS; Finance Director, BSS
Diarmaid Kelly	Deputy Head of Equity Broking and Trading, BIB

Mike Killian	Head of Global Equity Futures and Options Sales, BIB
Nick Leeson	General Manager/Assistant Director, BFS
Ian Martin	Former Financial Director, BSL
Peter Norris	Chief Executive Officer, BSL
Tony Railton	Futures and Options Settlements Senior Clerk, BIB
Miles Rivett-Carnac	Chairman, BSL
Sajeed Sacranie	Personal Assistant to Peter Norris
Andrew Tuckey	Deputy Chairman, Barings plc
Mary Walz	Global Head of Equity Financial Products, BIB
Dr Edmund Wong	Independent systems consultant to BFS
Rachel Yong	Financial Controller, BSS

Bank of England

Michael Foot	Deputy Director, Supervision and Surveillance
Eddie George	Governor
Rupert Pennant-Rea	Former Deputy Governor
Brian Quinn	Executive Director, Banking Supervision
Carol Sergeant	Head of Major UK Banks Supervision

SIMEX

Ang Swee Tian	President
Soo Yu Chuan	Senior Vice-President, Audit and Review Dept.
Elizabeth San	Chairman of Exchange

Singapore Inspectors
Michael Lim
Nicky Tan

Prologue

The picture of Nick Leeson in custody, with his rueful smile and back-to-front baseball cap, will become one of the enduring images of the 1990s. At the age of twenty-eight, Leeson established a niche for himself in the history of finance as the man who lost £869 million and broke Barings, the Queen's bank. As one of the great losers of all time, he achieved the status of an anti-hero. The plasterer's son from Watford became a contemporary Ned Kelly, or the City of London's Lucky Jim.

Leeson's improbable celebrity said plenty about the nineties. Familiar themes exposed raw nerves about conflicts between pushy youth and insecure old age; between the children of the suburbs and comprehensive schools and the privileged minority from public schools and the shires. From the subtext, more conflicts emerge: between computer nerds and computer illiterates, for whom the future is a closed book; between the dreamlike world of the City of London, where the streets are paved with golden bonuses, and the real world of post-industrial Britain – early retirement, redundancy and unemployment.

But the collapse of Barings was not a parochial matter. It happened in the bursting, turbulent derivatives markets that had caused more excitement than anything in world finance in the past decade. Huge sums of money had been changing hands; Leeson's losses revealed for the first time to a general audience the size of the stakes.

Everyone had an opinion about Leeson, and one of the most commonly expressed was that he was the scapegoat, the man who took the blame for his greedy and incompetent bosses at Barings. These expressions of sympathy for Leeson sometimes took extraordinary forms. One young man compared him with the former chancellor of the exchequer, Norman Lamont, who had himself lost a billion or so pounds in 1991 trying vainly to keep sterling in the exchange-rate mechanism.

This confusion about Leeson's real role was only one of the strands in this story that caught my imagination. I had first learned about futures markets when the Texan billionaire Bunker Hunt tried to corner the silver market in 1979. Futures were then still obscure, options were virtually unheard of, and no one had yet thought up the word 'derivatives' for these markets. Later in the eighties, I had become interested in the Bank of England's status as the regulator of the City of London. The combination of these various themes in one story made it irresistible.

The collapse of Barings involves cover-ups and accusations of conspiracy; it reveals gross defects in the way a legendary City bank was run, and examples of office politics and incompetence of a sort that would seem beyond belief if they hadn't actually happened. The Bank of England, too, made a mess of regulating Barings. Indeed, it was the City's incompetence that provided the pretext for Leeson's main line of defence: that he was the true victim of the affair because he had been allowed to get away with fraud and forgery. This image of the criminal as exploited figure inspired popular music in Germany and an opera in London (so far unperformed). The South China Brewery created a Leeson lager. His ghosted book fetched a packet at the Frankfurt Book Fair, and was serialised, at no expense to the newspaper, so it claimed, by London's *Daily Mail*.

This autobiography, entitled *Rogue Trader*, is illustrated by a photograph of Leeson wearing his trader's jacket and a nice smile. It conveys the flavour of one of the dictionary definitions of 'rogue': 'a playful, mischievous child'. The less sympathetic definition is 'swindler'. I realised, eventually, that even that term does not do justice to the crimes that Leeson began to commit in July 1992 and continued to commit until February 1995.

He was sentenced to six and a half years in a Singapore prison, but, because he pleaded guilty, only a few isolated details of his crimes were revealed in public. Two official reports on the Barings collapse were produced. They are rich mines of information, but neither makes light reading. Despite the huge volume of words written to explain and excuse Leeson, the full case for the prosecution has never been heard.

This case is the principal theme of this book. But it is a story, not a court case, and, like all good stories, it deserves to be told from the beginning. It starts with Barings.

I

A Family Story

A distinguished member of the Baring family, who remains anonymous – for he would not have spoken at all had he thought he might be identified – recalls Baring Brothers' image of itself during the banking crisis of 1974. A number of fringe banks that had lent unwisely to property speculators had failed, and the virus spread so fast that the Bank of England had to reassure the City about the soundness of even the National Westminster Bank. But at number 8 Bishopsgate, Baring Brothers was untroubled. It had never been tempted to plunge into the property business. The nameless Baring places the fingers of both hands together, and smiles. 'We felt we weren't clever enough,' he says.

He was expressing, simultaneously, the instinctive conservatism and complacency of recent generations of Barings, their Olympian detachment and the discretion one would expect from the Queen's bankers. All these attributes play a significant part in this story, because they help to explain why it is that, while individual Barings can be delightful company, their name stirs strong feelings but excites little sympathy.

Picture the start of a meeting between Baring Brothers and one of its corporate clients. The clients are present, but there are no Barings. Barings always arrive late. This act of self-conscious arrogance is intended to suggest that the clients are lucky to be in their company. It is part of the Baring inheritance, along with experience, occasional flashes of ruthlessness and an inherent sense of superiority. These qualities created a mystique about Baring Brothers, and without it the name would not have inspired the confidence it did. Indeed, a merchant bank is always a confidence trick of a kind: its greatest single asset is never its balance sheet but its name. When confidence in the name declines, so does the bank.

By 1974, the year in which Barings remained untouched by a bout of property speculation, the name had become associated with a conservatism that was deep and inert. The Barings who had made it a great bank would not have recognised the place.

It was the Duc de Richelieu who, in 1817, is reputed to have made the best-known remark about Baring Brothers & Co. when he listed the six great powers in Europe: 'England, France, Prussia, Austria, Russia – and Baring Brothers.' Philip Ziegler, who entitled his elegant history of the bank *The Sixth Great Power*, concedes in a footnote that he has not actually been able to find any proper reference to the Duc's flattery dated earlier than 1912. But he adds loyally that even if the Duc de Richelieu did not say this, he should have done. Ziegler sees in it a poetic truth, for it accurately reflects not only Barings' opinion of itself but the world's too – at least for 125 years or so, until the bank suffered the first of two terrible self-inflicted wounds.

In banking terms, the family history begins in 1762, when Francis Baring set up a merchant's business in Mincing Lane, in the City of London. Francis was the son of Johann or John Baring, who came from Bremen to Exeter to learn the wool and linen trade. His family, originally from Gröningen in Friesland, had produced a solid line of pastors, civil servants and professors ('The Barings were not Jews,' is the unforgettable first sentence of Ziegler's family history). Indeed, trade was nowhere to be found in the family tree before Johann Baring's mother, the daughter of a Bremen wool merchant, took her place in it. Johann was brought up in his mother's parents' house, an environment which, presumably, influenced the direction he took.

Johann proved to be good at trading. He decided to stay in Exeter, changed his name to John and married well, into a local merchant family. When he died in 1748 he was one of the richest merchants in the West Country, and one of only three men in Exeter who kept a carriage, the others being the bishop and the recorder.

Francis Baring was John's third son. In London, he soon realised that there was more to a merchant's life than serge cloth and linen. He traded exotic commodities like cochineal, copper and diamonds. He had an original mind, and was one of the first bankers to appreciate that financing trade could be a more reliable way of making money than trading itself. By guaranteeing that the supplier would be paid by the buyer, he provided the credit that oiled international trade. Banks involved in this business were called 'acceptance houses', and Barings was one of the first in London. This mixture of trading and banking later became known as merchant banking.

The adjectives Ziegler used to describe Francis Baring are reliable, strong, sensible and self-reliant; but he adds two more traits: 'a strain of adventurousness, sometimes even of recklessness'. These characteristics led Francis Baring to a disastrous speculation in soda ash in 1774, which nearly put him out of business. Then, in 1787, in league with Hope & Co. of Amsterdam, the richest and most powerful merchant house in Europe, he tried to corner the market in cochineal, and fared no better.

Being paid commission to raise money to finance war and peace proved a better risk. Barings helped the British government to fight first the Unites States, then France. When the United States wanted to buy Louisiana in 1802 it turned to Barings. Despite the fact that Britain was at war with France, and the sale would help Napoleon to finance his war, Barings obliged. Francis's second loyalty was to his country; his first was to international finance.

By the time Francis died in 1810 his bank was the most splendid in Europe. He himself was described as 'unquestionably the first merchant in Europe – first in knowledge and talent, and first in character and opulence'. Byron celebrated this power in a verse in *Don Juan*:

> Who keeps the world both old and new, in pain
>   Or pleasure? Who makes politicians run gibber all?
> The shade of Buonaparte's double daring?
>   Jew Rothschild and his fellow, Christian Baring.

When it came to arranging loans for foreign governments, 'Emperors and kings, prime ministers and ambassadors anxiously awaited their decisions, that might make or break a throne,' wrote Joseph Wechsberg. He wasn't exaggerating. Alexander Baring, Francis's second son, outlined the philosophy that was to propel Baring's banking business through the nineteenth century: 'Every regulation is a restriction, and as such contrary to that freedom which I have held to be the first principle of the well-being of commerce.' Margaret Thatcher would have loved him.

Not many of their descendants were as clever as Francis or Alexander, but they all had 'a profound belief in themselves, in their family, and in their country ... [they were] not subtle or mentally agile, but endowed with that curious combination of character which lends authority even to doubtful decisions.' The family was shrewd enough to realise when its own resources were limited, and to let an outsider run the bank for a while. The first of these was Joshua Bates, an American, who was not always able to resist speculation (he tried to corner tallow in 1830). But Bates, who ran the bank for thirty years, understood, as good bankers must, the delicate balance between boldness and prudence: 'By being too liberal we lose our money, and being insufficiently liberal we lose our business.'

The basic business was still financing trade. It was common knowledge that a man in Boston could not buy a cargo of tea in Canton without getting credit from Messrs Matheson or Messrs Baring. But the bank was sufficiently liberal in the mid-nineteenth century to speculate on its own account (an activity that later became known as proprietary trading) in English,

French, Russian, and Austrian stocks, Panama bonds and American railroad shares. Barings was easily London's biggest 'American house', raising $500,000,000 for United States and Canadian government loans between 1860 and 1890.

Marrying rich women and collecting paintings were two family habits. Francis commissioned Sir Thomas Lawrence to paint his portrait along with his brother and son-in-law (the original 'brothers'). He had a taste for Dutch paintings, concentrating on Rembrandt, Rubens and Van Dyck ('the first must not be too dark, nor the second too indecent'). Alexander bought a Titian and a suspect Giorgione, and more Dutch paintings, but the most distinguished collector was Thomas who, in the middle of the nineteenth century, also bought Italian Renaissance art, and added substantially to the Dutch collection. Barings also collected Hampshire, and various members of the family still own large tracts of it. Walter Bagehot described them as 'men who inherited wealth, power and culture, and combine the tastes of the aristocracy with the insight and verve of businessmen'.

The family accumulated peerages steadily throughout the nineteenth century. Alexander was created Lord Ashburton (motto: Fortitude Under Difficulties) in 1835. The second Sir Francis, a former chancellor of the exchequer, became Lord Northbrook in 1866, and Evelyn Baring, the great Egyptian pro-consul known as 'Over-Baring', became Earl of Cromer in 1892.

Only one Baring received a peerage principally because he was a banker: Edmund, otherwise known as Ned. The others had been politicians or public servants. Ned became Lord Revelstoke in 1885, when London was the undisputed financial capital of the world. Revelstoke father and son ran Barings for fifty years, and Ziegler describes them as a formidable pair. 'Both were intelligent and cultivated, self-confident to the point of arrogance. They were dignified in manner and imposing in appearance, men accustomed to demanding the deference of their inferiors, putting into that category the generality of mankind.' But Ned Baring also had a streak of recklessness inherited from his grandfather, and a gambler's instinct (his father won his Mayfair house at a game of cards). He was a generous man, and he could afford to be: his annual income was £100,000, worth £6,100,000 today.

Revelstoke's enthusiastic embrace of Victorian capitalism red in tooth and claw was best illustrated by the flotation of Guinness shares in 1886. So over-subscribed was the issue of £4.5 million of ordinary and preference shares that the price of £10 ordinary shares rose to £16 10s when the market opened. No fewer than one-third of these shares had been allocated by Baring Brothers to members of the family and their intimates; £800,000-worth was reserved for the bank itself; and another £800,000-worth was allocated to partners, their friends and close contacts in the City. The profit attributed to the house and the partners alone was in excess of £500,000. 'Even among insiders who had benefited from the operation, there was a feeling that it had gone too far,' said Ziegler.

Revelstoke's Guinness triumph misled him. He came to believe that public confidence went so deep that Barings' name on a share issue was enough to guarantee its sale. Revelstoke took an enormous punt in Argentina, and it went badly wrong. Tom Baring, one of the partners in New York at the time, wrote: 'Verily, "a great Nemesis overtook Croesus." The line has never been out of my mind since the Guinness success.'

What Revelstoke did was to underwrite a £2 million share issue by the Buenos Aires Water Supply and Drainage Company. That meant that Barings sent the money to Argentina before it had sold the shares, and the shares subsequently proved virtually impossible to sell. Much of Barings' capital was tied up in South America, and since the continent was going to pieces, questions of confidence in the bank were raised. It was committed to paying bills amounting to millions of pounds, and there was not enough money to meet the debt. Moreover, interest rates were rising and money was tight. This was a classic recipe for a bank failure.

But this crisis was not about one bank. David Kynaston says it could have shaken international confidence in the City.

There was no getting away from the almost unthinkable consequences if Barings did go down: not only would the failure of the City's leading acceptance house inevitably bring down a host of other firms, including all the discount houses, but the very status of the bill on London would be threatened, and thus the pre-eminence of the City as an international financial centre.

Because the stakes were so high, Barings was bailed out in November 1890 by a consortium organised by the governor of the Bank of England, William Lidderdale. The consortium drew on money from the bank itself and from the government of the day. Once the government was committed, Rothschilds joined in, the rest of the City followed, and a fund finally amounting to £17,326,000 – worth more than a billion pounds 100 years later – met Barings' commitments. But it had been a close-run thing. Ziegler believes that, had the governor of the Bank of England been less courageous, Barings would have failed.

Although it was the end of Lord Revelstoke's career and the partnership was wound up, the bank survived as Baring Brothers & Co. Ltd, with a paid-up capital of £1 million. Since the individual partners were responsible for all its debts, everything had to go: lands, houses, pictures, horses. Revelstoke's country estate at Membland in Devon (which had a special larder big enough for 2,000 head of game) and his Mayfair mansion at 37 Charles Street both had to be sold, along with the French furniture and *objets d'art*. Even the children's nanny went.

The episode was known to later generations of Barings as the 'Deca-Dance'. It could be treated fairly lightly because the recovery from the debacle was quick and complete: by 1896, the bank had been repossessed by the family. But, like a person surviving a bad car crash, Baring Brothers was never quite the same again. One of the inherited characteristics that had made the family so special had been lost. Barings remained reliable and honest, arrogant and contained, but they were no longer risk-takers. As bankers they had lost their nerve. An advantage of this new demeanour was that it made Barings the perfect City representative of the British establishment. John Baring, the second Lord Revelstoke, soon took his place on the court of the Bank of England – its board of non-executive directors – and became the closest financial adviser to George V, a link between the bank and the monarchy that remains unbroken.

After 1890, family peccadillos took a different form. John Revelstoke's younger brother, Cecil, who had sat in the bank reading Homer throughout the crisis, was sent to New York, where he eloped with a partner's wife. During the exile that followed this embarrassing misdemeanour, Cecil bought Lambay, an island off Dublin. He commissioned Sir Edwin Lutyens to improve the house, Gertrude Jekyll to design the garden, and built a real tennis court on the quayside.

Because Barings never regained its earlier entrepreneurial drive, it slipped from the first rank of City merchant banks to the second. It was not at the cutting edge of finance before or after the First World War. Conservatism, though, did have some blessings: other London merchant banks plunged into Germany to finance the economic recovery in the late 1920s, and were badly burned when the great Depression began. Barings did not take that risk.

When the second Lord Revelstoke died in 1928, the succession at the bank was divided between an outsider, a Canadian named Edwin Peacock, and Edward Reid, a Revelstoke nephew. They were utterly responsible, perfectly reliable, but deeply conventional in their attitude to investment. Caution by now had become a way of life. Some clients who were getting a poor return would have preferred a less reverential approach to their money. Take, for example, the case of Calypso Baring, the daughter of Cecil Baring of Lambay, who became the third Lord Revelstoke on his brother's death. When war broke out in 1939, Calypso was married to one of Britain's spymasters, Guy Liddell, who was MI5's man in charge of internal intelligence. Calypso wanted to spend the war years in the United States, and, despite the fact that her husband was in charge of security at all sea ports, she managed to set sail without his noticing. Arriving in New York, she declared that Barings had managed her money so poorly that she intended to sue. Prudently, Barings settled out of court.

Reid and Peacock were both knighted for their loyalty to the City and to Barings, and the family still turned out City grandees. Rowland, known as Rowley, the third Earl of Cromer, was the first Baring to become governor of the Bank of England. He was appointed in 1961 at the age of forty-three by Harold Macmillan, who subsequently discovered that a senior partner, Evelyn B. Baring, was quite underwhelmed by the decision. Cromer's wife Esme reported later: 'On receiving the news, Evelyn Baring rather churlishly replied: "All right, we'll let Lord Cromer go, but after you've finished with him we can give no assurance that we will take him back."'

When Labour won the General Election in 1964, Cromer saw it as his patriotic duty to save sterling from Harold Wilson. He got no thanks from the prime minister for that, and did not seek re-appointment at the end of his first term in 1966. Returning to Barings, he finally took over the bank as senior partner from his distant cousin, now Sir Edward Reid.

Once in charge, Cromer set about securing the future of the partnership. There are two views of Cromer's motives. One is held by outsiders: that Cromer was in a funk about socialism, and took desperate measures to avoid a wealth tax. The second, held by the Barings, is that he was sensibly protecting his fellow directors from death duties. Ever since 1891, the bank's equity capital had been held by a partnership of the bank's directors. When a director retired, his share passed to his successor. But if a partner were to die suddenly in office, his liability for death duties would mean a value had to be put on the shares, and ruinous death duties might force the dead director's estate to put his Barings shares on the market. Anyone might then buy them.

Cromer's solution was to give the directors voting shares that paid no dividends, and to transfer 74 per cent of the equity to the Baring Foundation, set up to carry out good works. (In 1986 the remaining 26 per cent of the shares was also transferred to the foundation, which, in 1994, gave grants of, or spent, £14,041,751 to aid welfare, health and the arts in Britain and abroad.) Whatever Cromer's real motive, the directors' income from Barings shares was much reduced after 1969. After 1985, when there was no longer any share income, they relied on their bonuses to bolster their salaries. The way the directors got rich after 1985 was by awarding themselves spectacular bonuses.

In 1971, Cromer was recalled to public service: the prime minister, Edward Heath, asked him to become ambassador to Washington. After a discreet power struggle within the bank, John Baring emerged as the new senior partner. Known as 'Basher Baring' because he had demolished most of Stratton Park, one of the finest Neo-Classical buildings in the country, John was the first of the Ashburton branch of the family to rise to the top of the heap for some generations. While Cromer had been blocking his way, John Baring had contemplated a career in politics; with Cromer gone, he relished his position as senior partner. When Cromer's term as ambassador ended in 1974, Barings decided not to take him back.

The family rule about working in the business was a common one in the City's merchant banks. If a Baring wanted a job, one would be made available, automatically. The new boys started, like clerks, sorting the post. In the 1960s they still sat on high stools and wrote cheques in longhand. John Baring thought it a suitable introduction to the bank. 'It was pretty dull work, but if a man can't get through dullness he won't get places. It is a sort of negative test,' he once said.

One of the Barings who passed the test early in John Baring's chairmanship was Leonard Ingrams, a great-grandson of the first Lord Revelstoke (and brother of Richard, formerly editor of *Private Eye*). Ingrams had taught a bit at university before seeking a position in the family business, and, shortly after taking his place in the mail-room, asked if he might not have lunch with some of the directors. They were his cousins, after all. He was invited, but to remind him of his presumption was told that no one else had ever asked himself to lunch. Ingrams was a good banker – he made money for Baring Brothers in Saudi Arabia, where he went to live for five years, helping to recycle the oil money when the Saudis had more of it than they knew what to do with.

When Ingrams returned to London in 1979, he felt he knew a thing or two about international finance and deserved a senior position in the international capital-markets department. Unfortunately, a charming and plausible young man called Andrew Tuckey was already sitting in the chair Ingrams wanted. Ingrams regarded Tuckey as less qualified than himself – 'He'd never smelled a bill' – but nepotism seemed suddenly out of fashion. 'My cousins were leaning over backwards not to be seen to be fair to the family,' Ingrams recalls. He quit, returning to Riyadh and making money for himself instead of the bank. He made enough to purchase Garsington, the manor house on the fringe of Oxford where the members of the Bloomsbury Group had misbehaved at weekends, and to start his own summer opera festival there.

The most conspicuous change at Barings in the 1970s was the forced demolition (for road-widening) of the fine Victorian office building at number 8 Bishopsgate, with its pleasing façade by Norman Shaw, its interiors by William Cubitt and Edwin Lutyens, and its archaic system of moving papers about in a basket hung from a balcony by a pulley. It was replaced by a twenty-five-storey glass box of little architectural merit. Sir Thomas Lawrence's portrait of Francis Baring and brothers, a second Lawrence of Francis Baring and the Dutch paintings seemed uncomfortable and out of place hanging there, and indeed the re-developed building was quite out of character with the bank John Baring ran.

John Baring took over a bank which had only 300 employees. 'It was a very traditional, very nice, quite straightforward banking business,' says Miles Rivett-Carnac, who had joined Barings in 1970 on leaving the navy. John Baring had gravitas, a quality known as 'the silence of a banker' – you are not supposed to know what he is thinking, and certainly not to question whether he is thinking at all. He was considered a melancholy man: his wife Susan left him as soon as their children had grown up.

John Baring was rumoured to have coveted the governorship of the Bank of England when it became vacant in 1982. As a member of the Bank's court, he felt he had established the necessary stature, and when he turned down a couple of prestigious posts, colleagues guessed it was so as to leave himself free to assume the governorship. If that was his wish, it was not to be. But as one of the last grandees of the old City of London, he secured Barings' reputation for discretion, loyalty and conservatism. The bank had no bad debts: it took no risks.

Just how conservative Barings was can be appreciated from reading Sir John Baring's valedictory remarks in the annual report for 1988. He recalled the early 1950s when he had first joined the bank. The fax had not been invented, and telex was primitive and slow. Barings had acquired calculating machines, but computers were still unheard of. Transatlantic crossings were made by ocean liner. The sterling area, embracing dominions and colonies, still provided London with a steady international business.

In the 1950s the cost of money (interest) was less than the yield from shares (dividends). Barings borrowed the money to buy the shares, and the difference between the cost of borrowing and the dividends was pure profit. But there wasn't very much of it – profits were a modest 2 to 3 per cent a year: sufficient for Barings, but not nearly enough to satisfy more thrusting and ambitious merchant banks such as S. G. Warburg.

The comfortable life, Sir John records, ended with the bonfire of regulations, including exchange controls, lit by the Tories in 1979, and by Big Bang in 1985. Competition changed everything, including the values of banking.

> We are without any doubt more professional than we were, with the result that standards of performance are noticeably higher. At the same time, however, sheer competitiveness, as in the field of sport, has sadly brought about somewhat more obvious lapses of

behaviour. There is no point in harking back to the old days; they are rightly and inevitably gone. But we do have to do everything in our power to ensure that personal values are not lost, and that our behaviour as businessmen is no less upright than we would expect of ourselves as private individuals.

The firm grew, and by 1986 Sir John had to stop making his Christmas tour round the office because he found he could no longer address every employee by name. Barings was probably best known for being banker to the Queen, although Sir John never said a word about that, even to senior colleagues. It was good at issuing sterling loans; it was building a strong investment business; and it had not ignored corporate finance, organising new issues of stocks and bonds for British business. Indeed, it had advised the winner in the seminal City takeover battle in 1962, when Courtaulds fought off a bid by ICI. Barings celebrated, but first it went to St Michael's, Cornhill, to give thanks.

One of the promising young corporate financiers at this time was Andrew Tuckey, the young man who had squeezed out Leonard Ingrams. Good-looking, with an engaging manner, Tuckey is one of three sons of a post-war emigrant to southern Rhodesia who prospered in the tobacco industry. He educated the three boys at Plumtree, a private school in Salisbury. They all left Rhodesia, Simon to read law, James to go into the property business and Andrew Marmaduke, born in August 1943, to study accountancy. Each of them has done remarkably well: Andrew's elder brother Simon is the Hon. Mr Justice Tuckey of the Queen's Bench division of the High Court; James is chief executive of MEPC, the property company.

Joining Barings after spending a couple of years with British American Tobacco, Andrew was fiercely ambitious. The Barings thought it must be something to do with being born in Africa, and not having gone to university. But Tuckey made good friends in the City – Eddie George, the man then most likely to succeed as governor of the Bank, among them. He was socially ambitious, joining White's, the gentleman's club in St James's, and making his mark as a member of the board of the Royal Opera House. By the time Sir John Baring was preparing for mandatory retirement in 1988 at the age of sixty, Tuckey, while not himself in a position to succeed him, was in a position to influence the succession.

There were two candidates, brothers who traced their ancestry to the first Lord Revelstoke. Their father, Francis Baring, was the son of Hugo, Revelstoke's youngest son. Nicholas Hugo was born in 1934 and Peter in 1935. In 1940, Francis Baring was killed in action, and their education at Eton and Magdalene College, Cambridge was taken care of by family trusts. Both availed themselves of the family privilege and took jobs in the bank.

Both prospered, but Nicholas made the greater mark. He was tall and slim, more cheerful and outgoing than Peter, and an intellectual with the family passion for painting. He became a trustee of the National Gallery, eventually taking over as chairman. Like Sir John, he loved the privileges of merchant banking – the car with its engine running at the front door, the visits to the Bank of England, and the lunches at the Palace. The arduous work of administration, seeing to details like settlements in the back office, was left to the people that Barings still thought of as clerks.

Nicholas concentrated on the bank's overseas business – 'Nicholas liked South America,' a colleague remembers. However, he became chairman of Henderson–Baring, a joint venture in investment management which did well in Japan and the Far East. And it was Nicholas rather than Peter whom John Baring had chosen to become vice-chairman of Baring Brothers. Some members of the family, in fact, thought Nicholas a more likely candidate than Sir John for the Bank of England governorship.

Peter Baring made a less vivid impression on his contemporaries. He was truly conservative, by nature as well as by training. When he rejected any suggestion that he might be a bit more adventurous with his own investments, his colleagues knew he meant it. Peter was invited to become chairman of the Glyndebourne Opera House Trust, but he was no champagne-drinker – indeed, he had given up drink. Many friends of the family found his wife Theresa the more challenging of the pair. She had taken a degree in sociology and was a dedicated member of the Rowntree Trust, chairing a committee investigating inequality of income in Britain, something of which she had first-hand experience. Her refusal to punish their three sons, even when they were rude to visitors, was attributed by the family to the degree in sociology.

Inside Barings, then, Nicholas seemed to have the edge; but there were three strokes against him. He had had a severe fight with cancer in the mid-1980s, though he had made a remarkable and complete recovery. He was liked and admired as a banker (he was chairman of the City's capital markets committee between 1983 and 1987), but as an administrator he was considered indecisive. And Andrew Tuckey was thought to be opposed to him. This is one of those Barings stories that is hard to check because the principals refuse to talk about it, but Leonard Ingrams says quite confidently that Tuckey told Sir John Baring that if Nicholas Baring took over, he would resign.

Tuckey, who was certainly one of the people consulted by Sir John, has spoken to friends about a consensus emerging in support of Peter Baring, but story of his threat to leave remains current, and, significantly, senior colleagues at Barings believed it to be true. The other version, perhaps more credible, is that Sir John had decided that Nicholas was too 'flashy' – an astonishing adjective to apply to his stately vice-chairman – and that he chose Peter Baring to succeed him in 1989 because he thought he had more gravitas than Nicholas, and a safer pair of hands. It was the last decision Sir John took; as usual, it was the conservative option.

The retirement age at Barings is strictly enforced, so Peter faced a term of six years that would end in 1995. The younger generations had produced no suitable candidates, so it was understood that when he went control of Barings would pass out of the hands of the family, probably for ever.

Some clients found Peter Baring's style chilly, but he was well liked by his peers in the City and was one of the last gentleman bankers. But his grasp of details was sometimes tenuous. Even when he was finance director, he occasionally got lost among the figures. Barings' management committee and departmental heads met for dinner twice a year to discuss prospects, and when one of them asked the chairman what the overhead for the group worldwide would be in the current year, Sir John deferred to Peter. One participant recalls the scene. 'Peter Baring's answer bore no relationship to the group's revenues. He made it sound as though Barings was going to lose £25 million or so, and when his figures were questioned, Peter had to get up from the table and go to his office to get his budget papers. When he returned ten minutes later, he said he was sorry, he had made a mistake. The figure was wrong by £100 million.' This performance did not inspire confidence among his colleagues, who naturally tended to turn to the vice-chairman, Andrew Tuckey, rather than to Peter Baring for guidance about the bank's future. Peter was the new chairman; Tuckey was the power behind the throne.

But Peter Baring's inheritance was very different from Sir John's or the Earl of Cromer's. When the City had transformed and deregulated itself in 1985, Barings had not plunged in, buying up a stockbroker and gilts dealer, as S. G. Warburg had done. It was almost by accident that Barings would be as profoundly affected by Big Bang as any bank in the City. The bank Sir John was handing on to his distant cousin was not the bank that Peter Baring and Andrew Tuckey were going to run. Big Bang affected Barings in ways that no one could have foreseen, and managing it was going to be a challenge. 'Not being clever enough' would no longer do.

2

Red Braces, Lace-Up Shoes, Big Cigars

The City of London had been utterly transformed in the last years of Sir John Baring's chairmanship of the bank by the reformation known as Big Bang. Until the early 1980s, the City had been a quintessentially English place, reflecting a class system in which the schooling of a young man was considered to be of more consequence than his intelligence, and young women were considered to be of no consequence at all. Directors went to public school; clerks went to state school. The old-boy network operated effectively. The style was in the dress: top hats were still worn in the gilts markets, and a chap who worked for a merchant bank was expected to wear lace-up shoes. Since the City reflected a caste system, its business was based on rules, not laws, and the rule was that a gentleman's word was his bond. If discipline were required, the governor of the Bank of England would raise an eyebrow.

The encrusted traditions began to break down in the 1970s when the fringe-banking crisis (the one Barings was not clever enough to take part in) led to the beginning of the end of informal regulation, and to the introduction of the first laws to regulate City behaviour. New information technology was making international business speedier and more profitable, but the biggest single change was the sudden demolition of restrictive practices in 1985. Previously, business on the stock exchange and in the gilts market had been neatly divided between brokers and jobbers, and anyone who did not belong to the club was effectively excluded.

Merchant banks like Barings, which had had a comfortable niche business raising capital for clients, managing assets and running a modest treasury and trading operation, now had to decide whether to compete with the Wall Street investment banks and offer clients a complete range of financial services, not just in corporate finance, but as brokers in the gilts and stock markets as well.

In 1985, the City of London began to transform itself into a global financial centre, one of the three legs of the world's financial system, the others being New York and Tokyo. Banks and securities houses from all over the world now needed a London presence, and they poured in. From the United States came firms like Salomon Brothers, Goldman Sachs, Morgan Stanley and Bankers Trust, who moved into new buildings; Nomura and Daiwa came from Japan, and restored old buildings. German and French banks had no choice: if they wanted to be players in international finance, they needed to be in London. The City's brokerage houses became much sought after, and many were taken over by foreign banks at inflated prices.

Since many more people were needed to work this vast new machine, the City became a magnet for clever young men – and now also women – from Oxford and Cambridge, who could earn more than their professors in their first year on the job, and for young school-leavers from London and the Home Counties, who could make more money in a year than their fathers made in ten. They soon learned how to spend it too. What was unheard of in 1985, when the City was populated by phalanxes of men in suits, some of them still wearing bowlers, was no longer remarkable in 1995: it was not uncommon, for instance, to see two or three well-dressed young women sitting under a sunshade in Royal Exchange Court, sharing a bottle of champagne, shortly after midday.

The London merchant banks reacted to Big Bang in a variety

of ways. S. G. Warburg decided it wanted a place in the top international league, providing a complete range of financial services to clients at home and abroad. Rothschilds was more modest, confirming a significant place in the City simply by buying into Smith New Court, the stockbrokers. Morgan Grenfell, afflicted by problems of its own making, sold out to the Deutsche Bank of Frankfurt.

Barings' directors, however, refused to join the clamour for expansion and takeovers. Barings concentrated on earning fees by advising banks which were buying from brokers or brokers who were selling to banks, but it made no flamboyant purchases. Sir John and Nicholas thought that prices were beyond reason. And no one could take Barings over: the Baring Foundation offered guaranteed protection against unwelcome predators. The family might no longer own the shares, but their grip on the foundation allowed them to retain control.

Nevertheless, the one modest little purchase Baring Brothers did make turned out to be the City's most profitable deal of the decade. In 1984, while everyone elsewhere was paying enormous prices in the run-up to Big Bang, Barings bought a fifteen-man dealing and research team specialising in Far Eastern stocks from the stockbrokers Henderson Crosthwaite. It was headed by a clever young broker named Christopher Heath. After much discussion, dithering and due diligence, the price was fixed at £6 million. It is said by junior members of the family that Sir John opposed the purchase, though he evidently did not veto it. Sir John neither confirms nor denies stories of this kind, but opposition would have been his instinctive reaction: nothing ventured, nothing lost. (There is another explanation: Heath and some of the senior people in the team they bought were Roman Catholics, and the older Barings had inherited a profound dislike of Catholics.)

Barings' commitment to the Far East was a legacy of that illustrious past when a man in Boston could not buy tea in Canton without credit from Barings. They had begun to sell Japanese yen bonds in European markets, and saw Japanese business as promising enough to justify a modest purchase to boost Barings' presence in the Japanese market. Shortly after the acquisition, Andrew Tuckey was talking to John Craven of Morgan Grenfell, who was interested to know how this new team would fit into Baring Brothers' strategy. 'Oh, it's only a small thing,' replied Tuckey. Not a lot was expected of it. But Andrew Tuckey had reckoned without Christopher Heath.

Heath soon achieved notoriety as the most highly paid man in Britain. In 1986 Barings paid him £2,515,595, yet no one outside the City had ever heard of him. Nor was there any indication as to exactly why he should be worth so much money. He wasn't even a director of the main board of Barings plc. But Heath was a brilliant salesman who had chanced upon a product before it became fashionable and cashed in when it did. He became rich because of Japan's amazing stock market, which went on and on going up and up, and especially because of a little-known instrument called Japanese warrants. This might, to a contemplative and vengeful sort of person, have seemed ironic.

Heath was the second child of the second family of Sir Lewis Macclesfield Heath, a lieutenant-general in the British army, who was stationed in Singapore in February 1941. He waited there for his replacement before taking up a new post in the Middle East, but the Japanese army arrived instead, and the general and his wife were interned in Changi prisoner-of-war camp, where their daughter was born. Starved and exhausted, the parents survived, but their daughter died in Changi. Immediately after the war, the general retired from the army and moved on to Kenya, where Christopher was born in 1946. The Mau Mau uprising forced the family to move again, to Cornwall, where Sir Lewis died only four years later. Christopher and his mother were provided with a grace-and-favour apartment in Hampton Court, and his mother worked as a school matron.

Christopher did not distinguish himself at Ampleforth, his Roman Catholic boarding school in Yorkshire. He even repudiates the one achievement that was credited to him: that he discovered an aerodynamically efficient way of cross-country running. (The trick was to lean backwards, but it didn't win him any races.) Ampleforth was full of clever boys bound for Oxford and Cambridge, but while his contemporaries were dutifully studying for their entrance exams, Heath was already in business, as an order clerk for ICI's plastics division.

By the 1970s Heath had moved into the City, as a stock-broker with a medium-sized company called Henderson Crosthwaite, selling this and that. He looked the part: red braces, lace-up shoes, big cigars. He was already exhibiting the quality that became his selling point: phenomenal energy. He could sell all day (which made him attractive to his colleagues) and dance all night at smart nightclubs like Annabel's (which made him attractive to women). Moreover, he could keep up this demanding regime year after year. All that was missing was the product that would enable him to maximise his talents and his income.

He got the Big Idea from James Nelson, who, with his wife Lucy, was a special friend. Nelson, a fund manager with Foreign and Colonial, suggested one day in 1975 that Heath specialise in Japanese stocks. The Japanese stock market, having failed to weather the oil-price crisis of 1973 and 1974, had just reached rock bottom, and it looked like a good moment. Heath armed himself with a list of five good reasons for buying Japanese stocks, and urged them on any fund manager who would listen. He got into the office earlier than anyone else, to study the closing prices on the Tokyo stock exchange, and by the time the fund managers arrived at work, Heath would have put together packages of shares to suit them. But he saw that studying the prices in London was no substitute for visiting Japan and researching the strengths and weaknesses of its companies at first hand.

Heath, who is not especially contemplative or vengeful, makes a joke of his relationship with the Japanese. He went there, he says, armed with a piece of advice from an old friend. 'You've just got to remember that from the very first moment a Japanese is in his perambulator, he's irredeemably shifty. As long as you remember that, you won't go far wrong.' Heath never had any illusions about Japan. He made some good Japanese friends after a while, but adjusted easily to the fact that most Japanese don't like foreigners. Heath was not going to allow that to interfere with business. 'I loved it from that point of view,' he says.

He worked at a fierce pace, learned at speed, and found it incredibly exciting. 'I'd pick a list of twenty-four companies across a wide range of industries and in two weeks I'd visit them all, to sort out the wheat from the chaff. I'd write reports on them in Hong Kong, presenting them personally to clients there, before doing the same thing in the UK.' The competition was distributing elegant research papers on Japan to clients; Christopher Heath was going out and telling clients what he had seen and heard.

James Nelson was delighted by the results. 'Christopher started off as the chap fiddling in the corner with those funny foreign people, and lo and behold, it worked. He became an important source of profits to the firm.' By the early 1980s, Heath was bringing in about 65 per cent of Henderson Crosthwaite's profits, and was already earning £500,000 a year.

By the time Heath discovered Japanese warrants in 1983, he was perfectly prepared to exploit one of the great bonanzas of the 1980s. He had learned about warrants on the grapevine, from a pal at Schroders. In 1982 Japanese companies raised money in the Eurobond market in London for the first time, and, to help sell these bonds, warrants were attached, giving the holder the option to buy some of the company's shares. 'The warrants were a bell and a whistle to make the bonds more attractive,' Heath says. To take an example: warrants issued on a bond sold for Fuji Photo Film Co. would entitle the bearer to buy, say, 150 Fuji Photo Film shares for 3,000 yen each at any time before June 1992. At the time of the sale, the Fuji share price could have been 1,000 yen, but as long as there was a chance that it might rise above 3,000 yen before 1992, there would be a market in such warrants. Heath was in a position to make that market.

He recalls: 'I had a look at them and thought that, on a long-term basis, they looked good value. We bought a few at $15, although it didn't seem like the cleverest move after three months when we had watched them sink to $1. Then I started educating clients and they began to go up.' And up. And up. Warrants he had bought at 15 subsequently sold at 140. A client could buy a warrant at 25 which might eventually give him the right to buy a share at 100 points less than its market price. In a rising market, warrants were a good bet – and the Japanese market did not stop rising.

The phenomenon caught the interest of some people at Barings, who were already big clients of Heath's, and in November 1983 he was asked if he would explain over lunch how it worked. Learning that Heath controlled the Far East group within Henderson Crosthwaite, Barings asked him to think about working for them instead, bringing his trading team with him.

This was not the first approach that had been made to Heath. A Brazilian bank was interested, but he thought it too obscure. Jacob Rothschild had talked to Heath too, but a partnership with him would have put Heath on the Arab League's banned list and his second-biggest client was the Kuwait Investment Office – 'In those days, they operated like that.' Barings were cautious. They took their time. Heath was inspected by Sir John and by Nicholas, who asked for a business plan and received just two pages of foolscap. 'My business was exceedingly simply in those days,' Heath explains.

So in June 1984 Barings bought Heath's profit share at Henderson Crosthwaite and hired the Far East team at the price of £6 million. It was an attractive deal all round. Henderson Crosthwaite realised that Heath's business must expand, and knew they could not afford to finance it. Barings was glad to bolster its Far East operation. Heath and his close associates got 25 per cent of the equity, a 25 per cent share of the profits and a free hand. They would be known as Baring Far East Securities, but left to their own devices. Though not all his colleagues were quite as enthusiastic as Heath – one thought

27

that he had been flattered by the aura of the Barings – they were all swept along.

Heath's independence was confirmed by the premises he took. Staying clear of the head office at number 8 Bishopsgate, and even of the fund-management group further up the street, he rented two floors in Lloyds Chambers in Portsóken Street. His style was hands-on, and frenetic and casual at the same time. His place was either in the field selling, or in the dealing-room selling. It was straightforward broking, matching the buyer with the seller of shares and warrants. But since there were so few competitors in the field, he could make big profits on the spread between the bid and offer prices; in other words, they generally bought cheap and sold dear. Baring Securities were market-makers, so they always had a stock of warrants ready to sell. As the price of warrants rose, so did the value of that inventory.

The profits were so breathtaking that the prose in the annual reports of Barings plc came close to being exuberant. In 1985, the first year in which Heath's operation is mentioned, Sir John Baring wrote: 'I am happy to say that the results of the first eighteen months have greatly exceeded our expectations.' That was putting it mildly. Submitting his two-page business plan, Heath had calculated the profits he expected to make in his first seven years with Barings. He had met that target in those eighteen months.

In the following year's annual report, Sir John trumpeted: 'Baring Securities, which has established an important position in the specialised international equity market, had an outstanding year of achievement ... [and made] a substantial contribution to profits.' No hint of the salary and bonus paid to Heath appeared in the annual report; since he was not a director, there was no requirement that it should. But Baring Securities' own annual report, lodged at Companies House, shows that Heath's take-home pay was £2,515,595.

In 1987, the annual report stated: 'Baring Securities continued to grow strongly ... Its contribution to group earnings rose substantially.' But it had not been such a good year for

Heath; his earnings had fallen to £1,338,219 – and £1.2 million of that was his share of the profits. After that, the company's solicitors decided not to disclose how much Heath earned. But his lifestyle made it clear that the money was still flowing in.

On Black Monday, 19 October 1987, when stock markets round the world slumped, Baring Securities were slow off the mark in Hong Kong. Their book showed a loss, at closing prices, of £1 million. Heath was furious with his lieutenant, Andrew Fraser, whom he blamed for the loss; but he also used to boast that it was the only time the firm did not make money in the 1980s. The million pounds was regained in a few days, and the Tokyo stock market also recovered quickly. Baring Securities, whose application for full membership of the Tokyo stock exchange had been accepted, went on milking it.

The top managers at Baring Securities all seemed to get on so well together that one of them turned their relationship into a management theory. Ian Martin, who had joined Heath in 1987 as finance director, believed the firm was run in a uniquely democratic manner by a top echelon of five men: Heath and Andrew Fraser, himself, Andrew Baylis (vice-chairman and Heath's top henchman) and Diarmaid Kelly. After the five had discussed a proposal, so Martin's theory ran, opposition from a single one of the five had veto power. It is an interesting notion, but it appears unsupported by actual practice. 'With all due respect to Ian Martin, I ran Baring Securities,' says Christopher Heath – and Baylis, Kelly and Fraser support his view.

Until it became physically impossible, Heath used to conduct every job interview himself. This went on for five or six years, during which he concedes only one error (it was not he who hired Nick Leeson).

> I gave everybody lots of responsibility, but everyone was accountable. Because we had an extremely limited amount of capital, no one was allowed to exceed their limits. People who did were watched like hawks. I sat on the desk, talked to clients, dealt

myself. I was right in the thick of it, in an open trading-room in a tiny building in a back street, and it was immense fun. We were making money. When I handed out the bonuses to the six girls in the general office, and they got £5,000 on top of £8,000 to £10,000 a year, they kissed me.

We had tremendous loyalty and affection – it was a real family atmosphere. No headhunter ever persuaded our people to leave. The money was an incentive, but we enjoyed being together, working hard. It was non-bureaucratic, very client-driven, and we were always on the look-out for new things to add on. That was our culture. Richard Greer in Tokyo used to say that the securities industry is like riding a bicycle. If you stop pedalling, you fall off.

Heath's know-how was legendary. When he began selling Japanese stocks, he did his own research. Now he had teams of clever analysts to do it for him, but the principles were the same. The analysts were not disinterested parties; they were there to help the salesmen. Documents were written overnight and presented in beautiful packages to the clients the following morning. The information was so copious, and the presentation so glossy, that one Australian journalist remembers thinking of Barings as a publishing house first and as a broker only second.

An analyst in Tokyo might cost the firm half a million pounds a year, but damn the cost. What Barings did was to tell the client more about Asian markets than anyone else in London, or any foreign broker in Tokyo. If a client wanted to know what was in the accounts of an Indonesian company, Barings was the place to go. It was an agency business, buying and selling stocks: if the client then wanted some obscure Indonesian stock, Barings was the place to buy it. The saying in Barings was that client was God, but the enthusiastic young salesmen and analysts at Baring Securities were the Masters of the Universe.

William Daniel, a linguist who had taught in the Far East, joined Heath's team in 1988, and started work on the Hong Kong equity-sales desk, which was relegated to a corner of the trading-floor while the Tokyo equity brokers took centre stage.

Daniel observed straight away: 'People were driven. Being associated with success was critical, and Christopher was able to lock in their loyalties. But he had had to keep them happy.' And Heath was good at that.

Like many people who themselves enjoy eating and drinking, talking and dancing, Heath felt better about it if he could encourage his colleagues to do the same thing. Clients had to be entertained in the best restaurants, and if there were no clients around at the end of a hard day at the screen, they still liked to entertain themselves. Judith Rawnsley, who joined the research department in Japan in 1988, writes with genuine affection about their Tokyo days and nights; about drinking a £1,000 bottle of wine, using Dom Perignon champagne in a cocktail (such a waste!), and flying in Nick Faldo for a round of golf with some of the clients. Good salaries and staggering bonuses were spent on five-star, first-class travel; eccentric hobbies were cherished (one colleague collected Russian tanks, in working order). Their punishments were bizarre (one trader was Sellotaped into an office chair and left in a glass-walled elevator, riding up and down, bound and gagged, until rescued by charitable person in a neighbouring office). 'Such high jinks ... were merely the result of a combination of boisterousness and stress that manifested itself in such childish pranks as water-pistol fights between the trading and research departments,' Rawnsley writes. 'Although inherently silly, these school-room antics demonstrated the excellent morale among the employees, who felt very much part of a family, rather than just a company.'

They were not all Hooray Henrys in Tokyo in the late 1980s. There were nerds as well, who spent their leisure time drinking beer and talking earnestly about computer software. The nerds were Americans mainly, while the Henrys and Henriettas were mostly English. But they still belonged to the same tribe.

William Daniel, who had some experience of primitive societies, detected a form of tribalism at Baring Securities: strong leadership exerting firm discipline and rewarding loyalty. This tribe was united by a shared passion for making a lot of money.

But there were two tribes inside the Barings Group as a whole. There was Heath's, and there were all those Barings. Each came to regard the other as the enemy within.

Andrew Baylis understates it when he says that Baring Brothers & Co. found Heath's tribe 'a bit of a burr under the saddle'. The bankers knew that the bonuses earned at Baring Securities were better than theirs: that was why the brokers were better and more expensively dressed. The bankers were left open-mouthed by the brokers' extravagant lifestyles, but were unable quite to decide whether to hold them in contempt or apply for membership. The trouble was that the bankers were not so passionate about making money. They did not belong with the securities crowd. Promising recruits at Baring Brothers were taught law, insurance and economics by university professors, whereas at Baring Securities they were given spelling tests and taught how to order in a Japanese restaurant.

Baylis believes that, although Baring Securities' business was not particularly complicated, the bankers never really understood it. 'It wasn't so much an intellectual failure as a psychological one. It was a matter of differences in attitude between bankers and brokers. Broking is essentially a short-term activity, and brokers are more gung-ho, wanting to get something done today. The banker is, by nature, more cautious, more measured, more conservative.'

The gulf between the two tribes was not unbridgeable. In Hong Kong, Baring Securities' man, Willie Phillips, began to collaborate on deals with a young man called Peter Norris, who had been sent to run Baring Brothers' corporate-finance department. Norris's people would structure the corporate finance and Phillips' brokers would sell the shares. 'We did some wonderful deals together. It really put Barings on the map in Asia,' says Norris. The only problem arose over the division of the revenues: that influenced bonuses, so it always led to a row.

Heath's case for independence within the firm had been based on the instinctive differences between brokers and bankers. For the first few years the brokers had been left, as promised, to their own devices. John Dare, the chairman, was a Baring Brothers man, and Andrew Tuckey had a seat on the board from the start, but they all soon agreed that the monthly board meetings were a waste of time. 'John Dare would ring up and take the temperature, particularly after the market had been volatile, but it was arm's-length stuff,' says Heath. Tuckey wanted Baring Securities to expand in Europe, because the bank had no specialist research in Europe and no salesmen. But when Heath decided to go ahead with offices in Frankfurt and Geneva, he did so of his own accord. Independence also meant a kind of freedom from office politics, and Heath boasted that his team was far too busy for such things. However, Peter Norris, working in Hong Kong, observed: 'Whatever pleas-antries were exchanged at the senior level, it was completely different below that. Everyone else had to fight their own battles.'

In 1988 Sir John Baring delightedly announced that Baring Securities had won a Queen's Award for Export. He had a personal reason for taking pleasure in its success: in 1985 his salary had been £293,920; in 1988, with the profits from the securities business, Sir John took home £398,540. It was small beer compared to Heath's earnings, but still a tidy sum. For his part, Heath did not discourage the feeling among his own tribe that they paid the bonuses of a bunch of second-rate bankers from a 'pisspot, third-rate bank'.

The growth of Baring Securities was a sensation. It had begun in 1985 with overseas offices in Tokyo and Hong Kong. New York opened in 1986; Frankfurt and Singapore in 1987; in 1988 Geneva, Los Angeles, Melbourne, Sydney, T'ai-pei and Bangkok. The next phase was Osaka, Kuala Lumpur, Manila, Jakarta, Paris, Karachi and Seoul. Five years after its inception, there were nineteen offices, and the staff, which had numbered fifteen at the start, was now 995. In 1989, Baring Securities contributed over half of the group profit of £65.9 million, with Japan still bringing in 85 per cent of Heath's profit.

It was a golden time for Heath. Having worked so hard to earn his fortune – the *Independent on Sunday* calculated his net worth at £25 million in 1990 – he had begun to spend it lavishly. He took time to talk on the telephone to his racehorse-trainer and the boatyard as well as to clients: one of his horses, The West Awake, was quite promising, winning a couple of races at Cheltenham. He had a shoot at his house in Hampshire. Although he was not a director of Barings plc, the holding company, he was now better known in the City than most of those who were. The only uncharted reef was his pride; it looked as though he might be in danger of believing his own publicity. Baring Securities had done marvellously well in the Japanese market, especially selling warrants, but the muscular New York securities houses like Morgan Stanley and Goldman Sachs had done even better. Having beaten the British competition, Heath started to turn his thoughts to combating the giant American firms. One or two of his colleagues thought uneasily about hubris.

Andrew Fraser, believing that Asia had a more promising future than Japan, wanted to start diverting resources away from Tokyo to the emerging markets in places like Jakarta and Bangkok. Andrew Baylis had also started to worry about the Tokyo stock market. The bull run that had begun in 1975 had bulldozed prices upwards for fourteen years. It was as if the most basic rule of markets – that what goes up must come down – had been suspended. Even though the Nikkei index of Tokyo shares had risen to 39,000 by the end of 1989, in October that year Baylis had advised his colleagues that he proposed taking out an insurance policy, in case the great big Tokyo bubble burst.

Because they were brokers doing an agency business, most of Baring Securities' sales and purchases took place within a day's trading. They had not needed to use the clever new financial instruments in the futures and options markets to hedge against losses on shares they themselves were holding, but these frontiers of international finance were becoming more densely occupied, and Baring Securities now had to be able to sell futures and options to clients who wanted them. The firm thus became a player in these new markets for the first time in

1988, operating in London, Tokyo, New York, Hong Kong and Sydney.

In October 1989, Baylis bought an over-the-counter 'put' option on the Nikkei 225 for £500,000. If the Tokyo stock market continued to boom, all well and good; but the option meant that in the unlikely event that the Nikkei index started to fall sharply, Baring Securities would still be in the money and the next year's bonuses would be safe.

3

Big, Swinging Dicks

When Andrew Baylis bought an option to sell futures contracts on the Nikkei 225 for Baring Securities in 1989, he was being shrewd, fashionable and daring. By the late 1980s options were a fast-growing item in a new market known as derivatives. Baylis's option, based on a stock-market index, was *derived* from the prices of equities bought and sold on the Tokyo stock exchange. Contracts derived from interest rates are known as swaps, and those from currency markets as financial futures. This is the cutting edge of the global markets.

In the olden days, let's say before 1980, there were markets in shares or equities on the stock exchange. There were markets in gilt-edged securities, the bonds issued by governments and large reputable companies. Lastly, there were markets for commodities, everything from pork bellies to platinum, tin to tea.

The reason the new markets in options, swaps and financial futures are called derivatives is that the prices at which they are bought and sold are derived from these three basic markets. It's a simple concept. The complicated part is explaining what derivatives are for and how they work. Even people who earn their crust in the City of London or on Wall Street wipe away a thin film of sweat when they are asked to explain derivatives. It is a white-knuckle ride, but there is no avoiding it. Derivatives markets play a central role in the story of Barings' crack-up, and before we go any further we need to know why Andrew Baylis risked £500,000 on a trend on the Tokyo stock exchange, and what made Nick Leeson plunge into futures and options markets in Singapore and Osaka.

Some years ago I learned about commodity futures markets in gold and silver, a wonderful world in which speculators sell what they don't own and buy what they don't want. But options were hardly heard of then, and played no part in that story. To find out about them, I returned to the traders in New York City who had taught me about the bullion markets. One of them is a high-profile figure named Dr Henry Jarecki. If you measure a trader's skill by his fortune, Jarecki is very successful indeed. He had taught psychiatry at Yale before spotting a way of making money by converting dollar bills into silver, the technical term for which is arbitrage. Now Dr Jarecki is said to be worth hundreds of millions of dollars.

Although Roger Geissler is worth a few millions himself, he does not care too much about making money. What he loves best is the markets. Slim, intense and energetic, he has such a lightning-quick mathematical mind that he can calculate most sums faster than the computers in the trading-rooms. Jarecki admires his skills extravagantly. They have worked together on and off; nowadays, Geissler trades for one of the leading hedge funds in New York.

I was sitting in Jarecki's board-room early one morning when he swept in, looking tanned and pear-shaped, issuing instructions to his secretary and his driver. He asked what I was doing in town. I explained that I had come to learn about options. 'You've come to the right place,' he said, radiating confidence. 'I invented them.' He plunged straight into a lecture on option trading.

Purchasing an option gives the buyer the right, but not the obligation, to buy or sell in the market at a later date, he explained. Seeing a look of uncertainty on my face, he gave an example: when the price of silver is $6 an ounce, our man purchases an option to buy 100,000 ounces in ninety days' time at $6.10 an ounce. The option has been priced at 6 cents an ounce, or $6,000. If the price of silver does not rise higher than $6.10 after ninety days, it will not be worth the while of the purchaser to exercise the option, and the dealer will have earned the buyer's $6,000 premium – the price of the option.

Now, say silver has risen to $6.35 an ounce after ninety days. In that case, the client will exercise his option and buy 100,000 ounces of silver at $6.10. He will then immediately liquidate his position. This gives him a net profit of 19 cents an ounce (the difference between $6.35 and $6.10, minus the 6 cents an ounce premium). The client risked $6,000 and made $19,000. When he bought the option it was 10 cents 'out of the money'. When he exercised it, the option was 25 cents 'in the money'.

This transaction will have satisfied both participants in the options market. If the purchaser was a trader in silver, he will have managed his risk by insuring against flunctuations in price that would have upset his production costs. If he was a speculator, he will have made three times his original stake.

The underlying contracts on which options are granted can be from bullion (like silver); or on individual shares (like British Petroleum); on share indices (like the FTSE 100 – the 'Footsie' – or the Nikkei 225); on municipal bonds and treasury bills; on mortgages (like Fannie Mays); on currencies (like the dollar and the Deutschmark); and on commodities of any kind (orange juice to bismuth).

There was, Jarecki told me, nothing really new about options. Options had been written in the Chicago grain market in the early 1930s, when they were known as privileges. But there had been a falling-out between the farmers and the speculators, and those options were prohibited by the US federal government in 1934.

In the thirty years or so after the end of the Second World War, there was no pressing need for them. Currency values were fixed, exchange controls were the rule rather than the exception and the foreign-exchange market was for commercial customers only. That changed utterly in 1973, when the dollar was set free to float and the value of currencies in relation to one another began to change daily. The immediate effect of this was chaos. International businesses intending to trade in foreign currency some months ahead had no idea what they would be paying – or receiving – for it. This is the kind of risk competent financial directors prefer to avoid. They needed a way of hedging it.

Soon after currencies started to float, enterprising traders at the Chicago Mercantile Exchange started a financial futures market in currencies like the dollar, sterling, the Deutschmark and yen. They enabled clients of foreign-exchange markets to guarantee the price of the currency they wanted when they wanted it. They bought currency ahead of time at a known price, and would pay only that sum for it, no matter if the price rose in the intervening months.

Through their brokers, these commercial hedgers became participants in a derivatives market, as buyers and sellers of financial futures contracts. It was better than risking price movements unprotected, but it was not free. They were required to put up margin payments, and to meet margin calls when the price moved against them. And if the markets went haywire, they could get burned; they might, for instance, end up losing money if the cost of a currency was lower by the time they wished to use it than it had been when they bought it. The advantage of buying an option rather than a futures contract was that, while it eliminated risk like a futures contract did, it cost no more than the purchase price of the option. It never cost the full contract price.

One more advantage of options is that the buyer is not asked to meet margin calls. Margin payments are like insurance policies. To make sure they can meet any losses, clients in the futures markets are required to deposit with the exchange a proportion of the value of the contracts they buy or sell. But this initial margin is continuously re-calculated to take account of price changes. When more insurance is required, the exchange makes margin calls. These are made, usually, on a daily basis, though some exchanges – the Chicago Merc and SIMEX in Singapore, for example – sometimes make margin calls during the day when the markets are particularly active. Margin calls mean that cash is always on hand to protect the exchange against unpredictable price changes, and against reck-less gamblers. They also keep the traders on their toes, because, when a margin call is made, they have to stump up the money on the spot – terms are cash only.

The derivatives market soon spread to interest-rate futures (known as swaps) for the exchange of fixed and floating rates, and to equities. Since these 'underline' mortgages and pensions funds, building societies and pension funds also use derivatives as a hedge. Without knowing it, then, most people with money invested anywhere have a small stake in the derivatives market.

Options also attract speculators, who provide the liquidity in the market. Their presence means that there is always a buyer when a hedger is a seller, and vice versa. Compared to the potential for profit, the game is cheap to play. The relationship between potential profit and cost is known as leverage. To go back to our example in which our man purchases an option priced at $6,000 to buy 100,000 ounces of silver for $6.10: this enables him to control an asset worth $600,000 for only $6,000. The leverage, therefore, is 100:1.

The questions that preoccupied Jarecki in the early 1970s, before the market existed, were 'What is the value of an option?' and 'How do you price it?' And the lecture he gave me began with the name of a nineteenth-century French math-ematician called Bachelier, and proceeded by means of the Socratic method.

Question: imagine you leave a friend in a field. While you are away your friend moves about. When you return, where will you find him?

I reply that I don't know.

Jarecki answers the question. Three factors will influence his position. The first is time. 'The longer you are away, the more likely he is to be further from where you left him.' The second is that his movements are most unlikely to be in a straight line. The third is volatility. 'The faster he moves, the further away he is likely to be.'

This exercise in probability told Jarecki that, to price an option, he needed to know about the timescale involved; to remind himself that no one can know whether the price would go up or down; and to judge how volatile the market was. 'The judgement call is about volatility,' says Jarecki.

While Jarecki was contemplating the prudent methods and the legality of trading options, an economist called Fischer Black, working with two MIT economists, produced the mathematical formula for pricing them in 1973. This was the intellectual basis for the derivative markets, and it made Black, who died in 1995, the most influential economist never to win the Nobel Prize. Though there was still some question about the legality in the US of options-trading, Jarecki tested it successfully even earlier, in 1972. He didn't exactly invent options, as he claims, but he is important in their history because he made the first reliable two-way market in them, so that clients could sell as well as buy.

That market, once in place, grew fast. Visitors to the Mercantile Exchange in Chicago are presented with some stunning facts. In the whole of 1964, 249,601 contracts were traded; in 1994, 2,371,878 contracts were traded on a single day (4 February). The value of contracts traded on an average day is $712 million (and the weight of the trash swept from the trading floor on a average day is more than a ton). Turnover in the global market is now measured in trillions of dollars a year.

One reason for Jarecki's success as a trader is his great reluctance to lose money. His system of options-trading was designed to reduce risk to a minimum. This, too, is complicated to explain, but what basically happens is that each time there is a movement in the price of our silver – from which the option to buy or sell silver in ninety days is derived – he hedges his position, buying or selling more futures contracts to manage the risk.

In the language of options-trading, he is computing the 'delta'. This is a mathematical concept which measures the probability of an option ending up 'in the money'. Roger Geissler, the brilliant trader, calculated that when our client bought silver at $6.00, the delta – the measure of the change in the option price as a result of a movement in the price of the underlying contract – would be approximately 40 per cent; when silver had risen to $6.10, the delta would have risen to 50 per cent. Another of these measures is the 'gamma', which tracks changes in the delta. The gamma is the most important of all risk measures because it tells a trader about volatility, or how fast the delta is moving relative to the price. Needless to say, a market has sprung up in trading volatility.

Conducted properly, options-trading requires an expensive computer operation and constant vigilance. 'It's tweaked all day,' says Roger Geissler, who never stops glancing at the screen on his computer to monitor prices, checking on more measures of risk, such as the 'theta', the effect on the price of the time remaining before the option can be exercised; and the 'vega', which measures the impact of changes in volatility. The third group in the market, after the hedgers and the speculators, are the volatility traders, who spot options that are wrongly priced. Options-trading is not for amateurs.

Geissler now took me in hand. We sat in the dealing-room by a screen (all trading instructions are transmitted simply by touching the relevant area of the screen – the keyboard is now redundant). He was showing me how to price an option on the Nikkei 225 share index in Tokyo. We needed first to know the strike price – the price at which the option would be exercised – and the current price. Next he fed in the rate of interest, and then the relationship between the spot price and the forward price, or the 'contango', which determines what the price would be in three months' time, after the cost of borrowing the money is included. The next ingredient was the implied volatility, which is based on calculations involving daily price changes. This is known as standard deviation. Then he pressed 'enter', and the machine calculated the price: a one-year call option (to buy) would be $11.25, and a one-year put option (to sell) $10.97. The difference, he said, has to do with interest-rate calculations. I believed him.

The option price is like a stake on a horse race. The less likely the horse is to win (or the less likely an option is to be exercised), the less the stake will cost. The option price also reflects volatility: when markets are stable and prices are slow to change, options are less likely to be exercised, and so they become cheaper. When volatility is high, the option is more likely to finish up 'in the money', and consequently, the premium will cost more. Take the example of silver at $6.00 an ounce: if the buyer of the option believes the silver price is going to jump to $8.00, he will pay a lot more for an option to buy it.

If the client does exercise the option, an options-trader like Jarecki has to sell him the contracts. But the trader would have been re-hedging the option every day. He might eventually lose all of the premium he has received, but that constant hedging insures him against a major loss if silver does rise to $8.00. If he does not hedge, he might have made an expensive mistake.

With a quick grin, Geissler pointed out that these are now simple calculations for all traders. Fast computers using advanced software can quickly produce a variety of ever-more awesomely complicated combinations of options, with names like Iron Butterflies, Jellyrolls and Condors. This jargon makes derivatives even more alien to most people, whose closest point of contact with the world of finance is a quick conversation about the weather with the teller at the bank. As recent scandals in derivative markets prove, some financial directors of large companies, or local-government treasurers in places like Orange County, California, are little better informed.

Derivatives come in two varieties. 'Exchange-traded' means they are bought and sold on recognised futures exchanges, like the Chicago Mercantile Exchange (the Merc) or the London International Financial Futures Exchange (LIFFE). Customers for exchange-traded futures and options get a daily financial statement from the clearing-house, and can check prices in the newspaper the following day. But in the 'OTC' (over-the-counter) market, contracts are specially designed by traders for single customers or specialist groups, and prices are not published. In the jargon, the OTC market 'lacks transparency'. But that does not deter the clients: this is the fastest-growing sector of the derivatives business.

The traders who put together the most complex OTC options are often known as 'rocket scientists'. They have PhDs in mathematics rather than master's degrees in business administration, and they have a passion for the intricacies of computer software. The older bankers and accountants who are paid to manage these traders sometimes confess that they do not understand what they are up to. Roger Geissler is scathing about them. 'As far as I'm concerned, rocket scientists should stick to building rockets. What Wall Street has got is salesmen who produce a contract that is unique, that no one else can price, and the client doesn't understand.' No one, in effect, can check on the contracts, and this creates a flourishing environment for the three base motives that in Geissler's view drive financial markets. 'PIG,' he says fiercely. 'Panic, ignorance, greed.'

A recent example confirms how un-user-friendly the OTC market can be. Bankers Trust, the New York investment bank, sold an interest-rate swap to a card-manufacturer called Gibson Greetings Inc., and when interest rates moved in the wrong direction, Gibson began to lose large sums of money. Bankers Trust deliberately understated these losses. On a taped internal telephone call, an executive is heard discussing the way this ought to be presented to Gibson.

> I think that we should use this [downward market-price movement] as an opportunity. We should just call [Gibson], and maybe chip away at the differential a little more. I mean, we told him [the loss was] $8.1 million when the real number was 14. So now, if the real number is 16, we'll tell him that it is 11. You know, just slowly chip away at that differential between what it really is and what we're telling him.

Twenty-five years ago, Bankers Trust would not have been in any danger of being fined $10 million, as they were by the regulators in this case. Like other bankers and securities houses in New York, like Barings in London, and like Deutsche Bank or Daiwa in the rest of the world, it did not participate even in the futures markets which preceded the options and swaps business.

Dealing then was an obscure activity, though a profitable one. If Henry Jarecki is to be believed, the banks only became involved when they realised how much money people like he and Roger Geissler were making in the early 1980s.

This is not an entirely fanciful proposition. When gold and silver prices rose to record levels in 1979 and 1980, Jarecki and Geissler were leading players. Panic in Saudi Arabia where fundamentalists invaded Mecca caused a flight into gold. The price of silver was propelled upwards because Bunker and Herbert Hunt of Dallas, Texas and some members of the Saudi royal family tried to corner the silver market. Those were exhilarating and perilous times for every bullion-dealer. Record prices and heavy trading volumes left both Geissler and Jarecki to meet bigger margin calls than they had ever contemplated. Both faced the possibility of being wiped out. But both survived, partly because they were able to borrow unprecedented sums from their bankers. Since these loans were so large, the bankers began to insist on knowing more about their operation. When Jarecki and Geissler emerged on the right side of the market – making hundreds of millions of dollars in Jarecki's case, and tens of millions in Geissler's – their bankers (Chase Manhattan in New York and Standard Chartered in London) took a rosy view of the business. There seemed, they thought, to be no reason why they should not take part in it themselves.

Salomon Brothers, who were taken over by a bullion-dealer called Phillip Brothers, got into the business too. They were followed by investment banks like Morgan Stanley and Bankers Trust. When the bankers and the traders went to war, as they often did in New York investment banks during the 1980s, the traders usually won. They were the ones who were making the money.

Within a decade, and despite misgivings at the Bank of England, all Britain's high-street banks had subsidiaries dealing in derivatives markets. When the London International Financial Futures Exchange sought permission to begin trading in 1982, the deputy governor, Sir Kit MacMahon, expressed serious doubts. He feared that derivatives might increase risk rather than spreading it, which had been their original aim. But the Bank gave the go-ahead eventually, and, within a few years, this obscure corner of market trading had become the most glamorous activity in world finance.

Before the 1980s, brokers worked for clients, selling shares and bonds and taking commissions on the deals they did. They had a low profile ('he's something in the City'), and earned comfortable, but not spectacular, livings. No newspapers or novelists ever got excited about salesmen with their municipal bonds, or traders in the futures markets. Traders in derivatives were different. They could make trading mortgages seem chic. Newspaper photographs and television footage of them pirou-etting in the trading-pits in Chicago, New York, Tokyo and London became commonplace. The pictorial image of a soli-tary, disconsolate trader absorbing his losses became a cliché. Tom Wolfe wrote a wonderful novel, *Bonfire of the Vanities*, whose main character was a bond-trader; a knowing and witty book about Salomon Brothers' traders, *Liar's Poker*, was number 1 in the *New York Times*' bestsellers list. Television turned traders into a soap opera (*Capital City*); film-makers made movies (*Trading Places*) about futures markets.

A busy pit on one of the two sprawling floors of the Chicago Mercantile Exchange is a peculiarly late-twentieth-century composite of energy, sound and colour. When the market is moving, the pit heaves. Though derivatives markets do have an economic purpose, the viewer is instantly reminded of a casino – except that the stakes are higher and the rules are subtly different.

Roger Geissler showed me a training manual written by a friend of his called Mark Elardo. It is entitled *The Complete Trader's Bag of Tricks. MAKE MORE MONEY AND HAVE MORE FUN DOING IT! Kick Some Ass*. Elardo insists that fiercely competitive young traders must never forget the first lesson: 'There is no such thing as a sure bet.'

Rather, trading is like flipping a weighted coin. If you judge this weighted coin is 80 per cent likely to come up in your favour, you flip a lot. If only 51 per cent your way, you might not toss at all. By the way, winning this game doesn't mean you flip only when you're better than 50-per-cent favourite of a positive outcome. If your coin will cost you $1 [in] nine out of ten flips, but *pays* you $20 when you win, you'll toss that for ever! Moreover, you must consider how secure your estimate is; a coin that is definitely 51 per cent might be better than a very unsure 80 per cent.

If they go by the book, these traders will not be nice people. The manual advises:

> You spend as much time with the guys in the crowd around you than with probably any other people in your life. Watch them, and you'll soon get to know them. Know them, and you'll discern how big their orders are. Know their orders, and you've got a lean. Lean, and you'll make more money and have more fun doing it. One guy I know traded index options off D-mark and yen futures. Every rally in the dollar he's buying calls. No kidding. How did I know this? He told me. And he told me because I asked him. Whoever most believes I am his friend I can take best advantage of.

Elardo observes that reason rarely governs the behaviour of pit traders. 'Make up a pretend ego, a giant one at that, and throw it around indiscriminately. Even if the crowd believes you're hopelessly insane, they will tend to follow you if you are a large force in the market. This tendency of the crowd to do as you do can be used against the crowd with deadly results.' Elardo's key words are 'pretend ego'. Traders may behave like stage performers, but they do not speak make-believe lines. When they are winning, they must understand that it can't go on; and when they are losing, they must cut the loss as quickly as possible. 'A good trader has no ego,' says Leo Melamed, one of the architects of financial futures-trading in Chicago.

Melamed belongs to the old school. He trades on his own account (if he loses, it's his money), or on behalf of clients (if he loses, they will go somewhere else). But the big players in the derivatives markets are no longer local traders like Melamed: they are banks and securities houses. They have clients, and executing clients' orders is part of their business, but they also trade with their own money. This is called proprietary trading, and the volume varies. Gung-ho securities houses like Salomon Brothers do more of it than J. P. Morgan, because, prudent bankers do less. Daiwa did more of it than it thought it was doing. Barings tried to have its cake and eat it, by doing both. But the thing to remember is that proprietary trading has very little to do with modern commercial banking.

Proprietary trading is a throwback to the buccaneering days of Francis and Alexander Baring. Banks turned to it for various reasons, some because they were forbidden to offer a full range of banking services (the Glass–Steagal Act prevents US commercial banks from selling securities), others because they had forgotten how to make money out of banking (British high street banks became brilliant at backing losers, at home and abroad). Trading was one way commercial banks, investment banks and merchant banks could make big bucks, and traders could earn huge sums of money.

In *Liar's Poker*, Michael Lewis describes the trader's role vividly.

A trader places bets in the markets on behalf of Salomon Brothers. A salesman was the trader's mouthpiece to most of the outside world . . . [but] the difference between a trader and a salesman was more than a matter of function. The traders ruled the shop, and it wasn't hard to see why. A salesman's year-end bonus was determined by traders. A trader's bonus was determined by the profits in his trading books . . . That the tyranny of the trader was institutionalised shouldn't surprise anyone. Traders were the people closest to the money . . . Good bond-traders and fast brains and enormous stamina. They watched the markets twelve and sometimes sixteen hours a day – and not just the market in bonds; they watched dozens of financial and commodity markets – stocks, oil, natural gas, currencies, and anything else that might in some way influence the bond market . . . Few of them cared to talk about their jobs; they were as reticent as veterans of an unpopular war. They valued profits. And money. Especially money, and all the things that money could buy, and all the kudos that attached to the person with the most of it.

Hedge funds like George Soros's Quantum fund were quite open about proprietary trading: it was a much quicker way of increasing the value of client investments than boring old stockbroking. Previously, funds like Quantum had been investors in a portfolio of bonds and equities. Soros helped transform them into trading vehicles. Although they were called hedge funds, they took risks as well as spreading them. Hedge funds became famous and infamous on the same day in 1991, when Soros made close to a billion dollars by selling sterling. It was a decisive moment in the economic history of the century: a once-great nation proved incapable of protecting its still-influential currency against a phalanx of well-financed and ruthless currency speculators. It was not the first time that a speculative attack had occurred, but it was the first time one had received so much publicity. Soros became the best-known financier of his time.

Traders only worked for banks; they never embraced their culture. Their loyalty was to their income stream, and the two words guaranteed to turn them on were 'compensation package'. When another bank offered them a better package, they moved on. Sir Kit MacMahon, who left the Bank of England to become chairman of the Midland Bank, recalls the difficulty he had in persuading traders to stay put. 'They don't want a seat on the board. They want to sit at their screens and deal.' When one of them wanted more money to stay, MacMahon reluctantly agreed to let him have an extra £20,000. The trader let the chairman know he spent £20,000 in a weekend.

Trading profits in very good years could amount to hundreds of millions of dollars, or tens of millions of pounds, and the traders who made the money gave themselves a name which echoed the macho aggression of the business, and the sexual nature of their language. They were the big, swinging dicks.

Both Jarecki and Melamed began to worry when options-trading really took off in the early 1990s. Melamed did not feel at home, as he did in the bullion or base-metals markets. 'You can't touch or feel options. Being brought up as a futures-trader, you get to know what your loss is all the time. I could always feel the risk in futures.'

Jarecki's concern is that huge volumes of trade in derivative contracts will lead to wild gyrations in prices. His fear is that such upheavals will eventually bankrupt a major derivatives-dealer, and that if the contagion spreads to all the counter-parties, the crisis will become systemic. This would plunge the banking system itself into crisis. 'The disaster will come, and they will say: "You contributed to the destruction of Western civilisation."' Jarecki says this jokingly, but it is not a joke. He means it.

Such sensational consequences were far from the mind of Andrew Baylis in 1989. He bought for Baring Securities a 'put' (to sell) option to protect the firm's profits against a slump in business on the Tokyo stock exchange. But Nick Leeson was not the sort of person who thought in terms of protecting the firm's profits, nor of long-term cyclical movements in the markets. He wanted to become a derivatives-trader because that was the way to join the big, swinging dicks.

4

The Stabbath

There are many explanations for the fall in the Japanese stock market in January 1990. The simplest is that the bulls will always be overtaken by the bears at some stage of the business cycle. In Tokyo, this happened much later than the most enthusiastic booster of the stock market could have dared to hope. The long bull-market run had made Christopher Heath rich, and Baring Securities had added lustre to the reputation of the City's oldest merchant bank. Even as the market fell, Heath and his gang were squeezing one last gush of profit out of it.

When he placed it late in October 1989, Andrew Baylis's bet that the Tokyo stock market was about to crash looked daft. The options he had bought for £500,000 from Banque National de Paris when the Nikkei 225 stood at 35,000 were 'in the money' only when the Nikkei index fell well below 30,000. For two more months, the Nikkei moved steadily in the opposite direction. By the New Year of 1990 it had reached 38,915. 'Marked to market each day in 1989, the bet didn't look clever,' Christopher Heath recalls. However, a little more than three months later, the Nikkei had fallen below 30,000, and when Baylis exercised his option to sell the Nikkei 225 index, he made a profit of £20 million.

This brilliant coup, based on a shrewd forecast, was quite in keeping with Baring Securities in the 1980s. But the collapsing Tokyo market in general caused pain. Margins became increasingly competitive, and commission income slumped. The profit on Baylis's option had to pay ballooning overheads (there were now twenty-one Baring Securities offices in nineteen countries), and the bonuses for another year. Heath had to discover how to transform a phenomenon of the 1980s into a fixture of the 1990s. The Baylis millions bought him time; perhaps too much time.

Three years later, Baring Securities was no longer robust: it was vulnerable to jittery markets and perfunctory management. But the greatest hazard was Barings' savage office politics. No apology was made for this. Andrew Tuckey, who became chairman of both Baring Brothers & Co. and Baring Securities (Peter Baring was chairman of the holding company, Barings plc), told friends that investment banking and securities-broking were 'tension businesses' run by people who were moving and jockeying, and who were judged by their profits. That is the nature of the investment business, he would say. He spoke from experience.

Among the choices open to Baring Securities, only one was fairly modest. While profit had been spewing out of Japan, the firm had spread out into south-east Asia. As the economies of nations like Korea, the Philippines, Thailand and Indonesia began to burst open, there was money to be made there, too. Andrew Fraser argued that the Tokyo office ought to be downsized, at the expense of salesmen and researchers, and the savings invested in the emerging economies of Asia.

This perfectly sound proposal held no appeal for Heath. The reason why was no secret. Richard Greer, who ran the Tokyo office, had detected in Heath a reluctance to rely merely on conventional agency business, making commissions from buying and selling shares. It lacked the flash and dash of holding positions in the Japanese warrant market, and profits accumulated much more gradually. Besides, reducing the operation in Tokyo would mean Baring Securities surrendering any chance of playing in the premier league there with the big boys from New York.

An optimist by nature, Heath instinctively reacted against

proposals based on the assumption that things might get worse, especially when these came from Andrew Fraser. 'He and Christopher had fallen out over the crash in 1987, and although Andrew had a clearer sense of why the business was going wrong, he had much less of a voice than anyone else because Christopher hated hearing it,' says a Barings banker who kept an eye on the brokers. Further down the line, the brokers were also falling out with each other. Heath notes: 'Brokers are like turkeys. If there isn't enough corn around, they start picking at each other. When they saw we weren't making super-profits any more, a lot of infighting started. Asia against Japan.'

Heath had always had doubts about Barings' European operation. Andrew Tuckey at the bank had been keen to combine Baring Securities' excellent reputation for research with the bank's corporate financiers, but this had never been profitable. Heath says: 'There were a lot of prima donnas in Europe with high prices on their heads. It didn't gel, and it was expensive in terms of overheads, space and management time.'

Heath himself was now on a treadmill. By 1991 the staff, which then numbered 1,300, had grown used to a diet of fat bonuses. Profits derived from agency business in the falling stock market in 1991 were not enough to go on feeding the bonus pool. Yet the management of a broking business is driven by the fear that, if it does not pay the bonuses, its best staff will be poached by firms that can.

Desperately seeking a solution, Heath decided Baring Securities should start trading on its own account, concentrating on proprietary trading rather than agency broking. He thought he knew the right people to do it, too: he had heard about a disenchanted three-man dealing team at Salomon Brothers in London. 'There were money-makers,' says Heath, 'trading the D-mark one day, the yen the next, then the D-mark cross-rate with sterling, then some debt instruments. Backing trends. I spent a couple of months negotiating with these guys: dinners, lunches, getting to know them. I finally got their agreement to come; and only then did I think I ought to let Andrew Tuckey know.'

Tuckey and Michael Baring, who ran the bank's treasury and trading department, which had a dozy reputation within the bank, met the team from Salomon and were impressed. They agreed to hire them, but Tuckey imposed a condition: if they were going to work for Barings, it would have to be at the bank with Michael Baring, not in the securities business with Heath. His argument was that, since they would be trading in the same markets as the bank, other traders would pick up conflicting signals if one Barings arm was, say, going long on the yen as buyers, and the other arm was selling the yen short. This condition was unacceptable. Heath did not want the bank to get whatever profits his protégés made, and the team from Salomon did not want to work for the bank. So they didn't join either Baring Securities or the bank.

Heath was tempted to raise the matter at his first main board meeting, but Tuckey advised him against it. 'He told me, "I think it would be a great mistake for you make an issue out of this. I suggest you drop it,"' says Heath, who dropped it. The affair had one significant consequence. Michael Baring thought proprietary trading in the specialist debt market looked so promising that he hired a trader from Bankers Trust, a bearded Australian called Ron Baker, to run a team in the bank's treasury department.

Heath finally became a director of the holding company, Barings plc, in 1991. Tuckey had spent some time persuading him to join the main board, tempting him with the notion that, after Peter Baring's retirement, the Barings Group would be run by three people – Tuckey, John Bolsover of Baring Asset Management, and Heath himself. Miles Rivett-Carnac, one of the deputy chairmen of Barings plc, who went shooting with Heath and liked him, none the less worried that Baring Securities was going to blow up, simply because of its success. 'We thought the best thing was to bring Christopher right into the centre.' They wanted to be sure he was inside their tent pissing out, rather than outside pissing in. A stumbling-block was Heath's swollen earnings, which were much higher than those of any other board member. It cost Barings £6 million to buy

Heath out of his profit-sharing agreement before he agreed to join the board.

Heath remained chief executive of Baring Securities, but as a member of the board he was forced to wear other hats besides, and this made it more difficult for him to take partisan positions. Some of Heath's partners at Barings Securities felt they were battling to retain control of their firm, and that the opposition, led by Andrew Tuckey, was winning.

The issue was the firm's capital. Without more capital, Baring Securities could not deal with the consequences of the declining Tokyo market. The debate about the capitalisation of Baring Securities might sound faintly academic, but it aroused bitter passions. At one meeting held to discuss the subject, Tuckey walked out. 'I had simply stated, quite clearly, that we needed more capital in our group if we were going to take the business that was available to us, and Tuckey completely lost his cool,' says Heath.

Heath did need that capital. Some of his clients had expressed concern about the balance sheet: they were doing deals with Baring Securities involving hundreds of millions of dollars, and they wanted to know what would happen if Barings went 'puff in the night' as Heath put it. Prudence dictated that these big clients deal with big banks like Morgan Stanley, Goldman Sachs and Salomon Brothers. Heath hated being reminded that he was not in that league, and he never would be unless Baring Securities had more capital.

Since bonuses and dividends for the boys, and not the accumulation of capital for the business, was the way the City of London kept the score, bonuses always took priority in the golden years. The capital of Baring Securities grew more slowly than it ought to have done. It was topped up with short-term bank loans taken out by a subsidiary called Baring Securities International Holdings Ltd (BSIHL), which capitalised overseas subsidiaries in places like Korea. But by borrowing short (the bank loans were renewed annually) and lending long (the subsidiaries required permanent capital), Baring Securities was ignoring one of the fundamental rules of finance. The bank loans were a time-bomb.

Ian Martin, the finance director, thought that a capital injection by Barings plc of £50 to £60 million would do the trick. Unfortunately, Andrew Tuckey had other spending plans. Tuckey saw Barings as a three-legged stool. One leg was the asset-management business, which was making money. Another was Heath's securities operation, which had provided £50 million of the group's £65 million profit in 1989. The third was the bank – Tuckey's leg – which, of the three, was the least profitable by far.

The solution came as a pleasant surprise to Tuckey. The relationship between Barings and a New York investment bank called Dillon Read had always been close. Their managements felt they had more in common with each other than with the rest of the London and New York merchant banks. When Dillon Read's senior people came to London, they were always made welcome at Barings, and when they looked in during 1991 they had an interesting proposition to make.

Dillon Read was losing money in Europe, and Barings was losing money in corporate finance in New York. The sensible solution was for Barings to take over Dillon Read's business in Europe, and for Dillon Read to ally with Barings to make a success of the New York operation. The proposed method was not a merger, but Barings' purchase of a 40 per cent stake in Dillon Read, costing £75 million. Tuckey saw this as just the opportunity he needed to make his leg in the group as profitable as the other two. Peter Baring and Miles Rivett-Carnac agreed. Since they were respectively chairman and deputy-chairman, there was not much further discussion.

Rivett-Carnac remembers the excitement they all felt. 'Everyone was so overwhelmed at what a fantastic opportunity it was.' Except at Baring Securities, where everyone was distinctly underwhelmed. 'Every alarm bell rang there, and the bank was taken by surprise at the way Securities felt about it. It certainly wasn't a deliberately vicious thing,' Rivett-Carnac recalls.

Heath and his allies were very angry indeed: £75 million was just what they needed.

Andrew Baylis, always the severest critic of the bank among Heath's henchmen, completely lost his temper. Four years later, his voice still rose in anger and contempt when he remembered the Dillon Read purchase.

> That brought us up short. I saw a number of people at the bank, and I said: 'What on earth are you doing? We have in Baring Securities one of the most successful stories of the past decade. You're refusing to fund us, and you're spending millions on some second-rate investment bank in the hope that you can get into American corporate finance. For Christ's sake, get real.' As you can imagine, that went down brilliantly.

Baylis would have been even crosser if he had known that senior bank people like Rivett-Carnac thought tight controls on the capital of Baring Securities acted as a useful form of discipline.

But Baring Securities was finding it very hard to adjust to the 1990s. Apart from the week of the crash in 1987 and an odd week in 1991, it had never previously failed to make money, but by 1992 losses were being reported month after month. Within Baring Securities this was a cause for concern rather than panic. They reassured themselves by saying that the securities business was cyclical.

During the bullish 1980s it had been easy to forget that basic rule: most of the brokers who learned their business with Heath had never experienced a falling market. But the bankers at Baring Brothers were more interested in the short-term losses than in long-term patterns. Peter Norris later remarked:

> A combination of a declining market and management failings was coming home to roost. In investment banking, the sad truth is that in a bull market you can run a poorly organised business at a profit. Christopher's hope that Baring Securities would wipe the floor with Morgan Stanley meant that the engine was in top gear and the foot was on the floor. But the wheels were falling off.

Tuckey had recalled Peter Norris from Hong Kong, where he had managed to build a working relationship between the corporate financiers and the brokers, using Baring Brothers to arrange share issues and Baring Securities' distribution network to sell them. Tuckey proposed that he do the same thing in London. Even Heath thought it seemed like a good idea.

Peter Norris was a very clever young man. Dark-haired with eyes to match, lean and athletic, with a quick, nervous laugh, he had joined Barings straight from Oxford in 1976. Immediately, his intelligence came to be highly regarded. 'When Peter said something was simple, you'd take out your notebook so that you could work it all out after he had finished,' remarks one colleague. Norris had a banker's interest in plotting and planning and a broker's passion for making money. As a schoolboy, his grandparents had taken him racing, and he loved horses. He kept a betting book for seven seasons, making a profit in three of them. He had contemplated becoming a racehorse-trainer, but that cost more money than he had. Norris had other accomplishments. He had learned how to cook from his mother, who ran a cooking school, and could produce dinner for twenty-four, a skill which came in useful when his first wife, Louise, started a catering company providing lunches and dinners in clients' homes. But Norris treated that as a hobby. He wanted to make serious money, and the way to do that was to become a merchant banker.

Norris worked for Barings for eight years, enjoying learning his trade, and taking credit for a couple of clever innovations in the markets. But because he found Barings conservative and felt he was not very well paid, he moved to the London office of Goldman Sachs in 1985. Goldman Sachs was not at all conservative, paid very well, and was not a happy ship. 'There were a lot of politics in the firm that I didn't understand. While I never felt I had to question the motives of the people I'd worked with at Barings, I felt I had to do that some of the time at Goldman Sachs.' By 1988 Norris wanted to quit, and he asked Andrew Tuckey if he had any thoughts. At that moment, the man who ran Baring Brothers in Asia was leaving Hong

Kong, and Tuckey offered Norris his job. 'It all fitted together as if it were meant to happen,' Norris says.

Norris was celebrated for his remarkable grasp of detail. He often exhibited deeper knowledge of a department's business than the departmental head, which was more a way of influencing people than of winning friends. Colleagues were attracted by his mind ('He was the cleverest man I've met in the City,' says Richard Greer). But others found him arrogant, cold and sharp. A former colleague in Hong Kong reports that he had a fifty-fifty reputation when he was there – half the office liked him, the other half couldn't stand him. One of Heath's friends told him Norris played tennis and was a good egg. Another reported that he could be equivocal, particularly with the truth.

Norris was thirty-seven years old when he returned to London, where he spent some of his bonuses financing the expansion of his wife's business into upmarket delicatessens (the company's name, Duff and Trotter, would sound familiar to readers of P. G. Wodehouse). Baring Securities had now moved from its crowded, cheerful office in Portsoken Street to a new neo-Art-Deco skyscraper called America Square near Fenchurch Street. It was convenient for the Essex Men, but not for Heath, who lived in Hampshire, nor for Norris, who had bought a manor house in Bedfordshire. The move to America Square in 1992 was costly, and added to Baring Securities' losses. Its balance sheet was looking groggy.

In June 1992, Tuckey told Heath that if Baring Securities wanted new capital from the bank, it would have to slash £20 million from its overheads. Heath is a man who prefers hiring people to firing them, and this was not the kind of challenge he enjoyed. Together with Baylis and Ian Martin, he came up with a five-page report which met Tuckey's target by making big cuts in the European and Australian operations. But it didn't help the figures much. The re-structuring would cost another £7 million, and there were still the bonuses to pay, which amounted to at least £10 million. As bonuses were sacrosanct, Baylis felt no need to apologise for them. His best brokers and analysts in south-east Asia and Latin America, where

Barings' was the market leader, reported that they were getting job offers every hour on the hour. Good bonuses bound them to Barings with golden handcuffs.

Heath's re-structuring proposals met with no approval from Tuckey, nor from Peter Baring and Miles Rivett-Carnac. They wanted a more detailed scrutiny of the business. Baylis did not dissent. 'We had grown very rapidly, and it is an utterly fair criticism that our management control and structure had probably not evolved at the same rate as the business. We still behaved as though we were a small firm, and had fingers in too many pies. We'd grown fat in some places, and it was in need of a review.'

What Heath and Baylis chiefly objected to was the person chosen to conduct the review. Tuckey felt that a fresh pair of eyes would be useful, and selected those of Norris, a bank man who had infiltrated the securities operation. Heath and Baylis saw the Norris investigation as the pretext on which Tuckey planned to rob Baring Securities of its independence. Talking about it later, Heath used a Chinese expression to describe the relationship between Tuckey and Norris: they were as close as the teeth and the lips. That was genteel compared to Baylis's nickname for Norris, 'Blue Peter' (blue because the position of his head prevented him from breathing in enough oxygen).

To protect his interests, Heath insisted that Norris should be partnered by one of his own close colleagues, Richard Greer from Tokyo. Norris and Greer worked behind closed doors, probing into which parts of the business made money, which management functions worked well. It was already clear that some did not. The auditors Coopers & Lybrand reported in 1992 that there had been a breakdown in control procedures in the futures and options area, and the Securities and Futures Authority (SFA) found a number of breaches of its rules during an inspection in June 1992.

As Norris and Greer worked through the summer, Baring Securities' losses grew. The main proposal in their report was a 15 per cent cut in staff, backed by a disciplined determination to concentrate on what worked, and to get rid of the rest.

Tuckey approved, but offered Norris no help in selling the proposals to Heath and his colleagues. Norris had to do that by himself. 'I spent dreadful days locked in a room trying to explain what was required.' Heath hated it, too. 'It was a ghastly feeling of doom and gloom. We'd never cut back before, and it was a matter of defending various areas and people: "No, you can't get rid of Fred because he's close to Harry."'

Heath and Baylis knew that, once they agreed to the report, they would have surrendered their independence to Baring Brothers. What made this a particularly bitter pill was that each of them believed this had been Andrew Tuckey's hidden agenda for some time. 'You'd never get him to admit it under 30,000 volts, but Andrew Tuckey, while enjoying the returns from Baring Securities, always found it difficult to accept the contribution and the status we had,' says Baylis.

If they were going to fight for their independence, this was the time to do it. The hard core of the original management of Baring Securities met twice to discuss their strategy. They had a choice. They could quit, and set up on their own; or they could stay and sharpen up the business, and hope to arrange a sale to a more compatible owner. The bold thing to do was to quit, but Andrew Fraser and Diarmaid Kelly did not favour that. And because the team was split, the revolt petered out. They decided to stay, and to let Tuckey know that they wanted to retain the option to look for another purchaser.

The day of the mass blood-letting at Baring Securities, 26 September 1992, was macabre. A security man at the front desk had a list of Baring Securities' employees: if your name was on it, you were asked to proceed directly to the third floor, where you were fired. The third floor quickly became known as the gas chamber. In return for accepting these redundancies, Baring Brothers granted Baring Securities a $75 million loan facility to boost its capital.

Under the management re-organisation, Heath became executive chairman. The five managing directors were all allies of his, although Fraser and Kelly were doubtful disciples. Peter Norris became chief operating officer; and his relations with

Heath were rocky from the start. Because Norris insisted that bonuses should be more evenly distributed, the old profit-sharing scheme was dumped. Heath's cronies didn't like it. The personal relationship between Heath and Norris deteriorated.

Soon after Norris became chief operating officer, Heath went to Hong Kong, where he was dragged into a wrangle over salaries. He recommended to Norris that a rule should be bent to resolve the difficulty. Norris replied that if Heath felt strongly about it, he should join the management-committee discussion on a conference call that evening. Heath said he and the head of the office were going to the races that evening. 'Well, if you've got nothing better to do than go to the races . . .' said Norris. Each insists the other slammed down the telephone.

As a former Hong Kong hand, Norris knew that going to the races in the Hong Kong and Shanghai Bank box, as Heath was, was a productive way of doing business; and he rang Heath the following day to apologise. But the exchange deepened Heath's dislike of his chief operating officer. He objected to Norris's habit of taking the head of the table when they were both at a meeting. 'He very much took control,' recalls Heath.

Although none of them knew it then, the fortunes of Baring Securities changed course, quite by chance, in September 1992, the same month as the re-organisation. The only available evidence shows an operating loss for the twelve months to 30 September 1992 of £39,437,000, which converted into a loss on ordinary activities, after tax, of £11,266,000. And that was expected to get worse, not better. Indeed, Baring Brothers, the bankers, had told the Bank of England that autumn that the closure of Baring Securities was a possibility if the losses continued to grow. The SFA, was 'very concerned' about the Barings Group.

Since this closure option was never discussed with Heath, knowledge of it must have been confined to the tight circle around Tuckey and Peter Baring. Between Tuckey and Heath, only two options were discussed. One was an injection of more capital from an outside investor, which would be used to build a vigorous proprietary-trading operation. A trader called Jerome Waxman was hired from Salomon Brothers, apparently for that purpose. But Tuckey opposed bringing in outside capital. He observed that if you sell a 25 per cent stake in the business, you end up with 75 per cent of the profits and 100 per cent of the responsibilities.

Since that option was closed, Heath's preference was for Barings to sell Baring Securities to someone who would inject more capital, but the in-house corporate financiers told the brokers that you couldn't sell a business from a position of weakness, and dismissed the idea as fanciful. Indeed, Tuckey went further than that. Baylis recalls: 'We were formally warned that any attempt to find a buyer for the business would be deemed a breach of our fiduciary duties as directors, and would be treated accordingly.'

Only one feasible option remained, and it was the kind of proposal Heath and Baylis would have expected from the conservative bankers at Baring Brothers. They wanted nothing to do with proprietary trading – 'We don't understand the business in the same way we do others, and we're risk-averse.' That left the agency business in emerging markets, and the developing corporate financier–broker partnership in equity capital markets. Andrew Baylis responded curtly that while this might satisfy bankers, there was no way such a business could generate the bonuses his colleagues expected. But Baylis could not wage the war to its conclusion. He was diagnosed as having cancer in November 1992, and he was *hors de combat* for the duration.

The debate over proprietary trading dragged on through the winter. Heath was travelling extensively and growing progressively more disenchanted. And he had other things on his mind. He was having an affair – and with a Baring who was half his age. Samantha Baring, a tall blonde with a toothy smile, was a distant cousin of Peter and Nicholas. 'She didn't know Peter from a bar of soap,' says Heath, but an association with another Baring, however distant her relationship with Peter, caused a rather bigger buzz than if Heath had forged an alliance with a Samantha Smith. Heath was serious about the affair, and left his wife, Maggie. But Samantha called it off in December 1992.

The Bank of England was still concerned about Baring Securities that winter. In February 1993, Peter Norris led a Barings delegation to the bank to meet Christopher Thompson, the supervisor who looked after the group. The minutes of the meeting, taken by the Barings team, record a bloodcurdling episode.

Thompson alarmed Norris by revealing that the Bank of England thought the parlous state of Baring Securities might topple the 231-year-old merchant bank. The fear, Thompson said, was that the speed of Baring Securities' earnings collapse might threaten the existence of Baring Brothers & Co. Norris bravely insisted that things were not that bad, and that Baring Securities' business really had improved. The atmosphere at work did not lighten Heath's mood, however, and the fears of the Bank of England weakened his position in relation to that of the new men such as Norris.

Heath had brushes with Tuckey on the management committee. Some of his old colleagues had turned against him – Andrew Fraser had become an ally of Peter Norris – and Heath thought the bankers who were infiltrating the securities business did not know how to run it. When he talked vaguely about quitting, John Bolsover, from Asset Management, tried to reassure him. (Peter Baring's advice might have been more influential: he reminded Heath that if he left he would have to repay some of the £6 million they had paid him as his profit share.) Heath says he was told that the board of the plc was behind him. 'What I didn't realise was that they were right behind me with their knives.' The only thing holding Tuckey back was the fear that if Heath left, 100 loyalists would follow him, crippling the company.

Heath had asked Tuckey to have a word with Andrew Fraser, who, he felt, was wounding him by his outspoken opposition. But if a word was had, it merely led to a coup against Heath, for his own colleagues told Tuckey that there would be hardly any deserters in the event of Heath's departure. Afterwards Tuckey and his allies said they had had no alternative to firing Christopher Heath because his own people wanted him out, but once they knew the business was safe, the bankers did not hesitate to plunge in the knife themselves.

Norris was surprised that the decision to confront Heath was eventually taken by Peter Baring. It taught him something about his patron. 'Andrew didn't like delivering bad news. He could shy away from the final cut, in my experience.'

Like all the best salesmen, Heath tells a good anecdote, and one of his best is the story of his dismissal from Barings. On Saturday 22 March 1993, Heath says he had a temperature and spent most of the day in bed. His recuperation was interrupted by a telephone call.

'Christopher, this is Peter Baring.'

'How are you, Peter?'

'Ten o'clock tomorrow morning. Number 8, Bishopsgate. See you then.'

'Can I ask what this is about?'

'I don't talk about these matters on the telephone.'

Later in the day, Heath received more news by a roundabout route. Richard Greer, now in Chile, had heard from London that there was going to be a coup in Baring Securities that weekend.

Heath says that for their meeting the following morning, Peter Baring deliberately angled his glasses so that Heath could not see his eyes.

'This is a very sad day for Barings, and I think it is a sad day for you. Basically, Christopher, we'd like you to resign.'

'May I ask why?'

'We really want to give the new management a chance, a free rein. They feel that your presence is an inhibiting factor in changing the direction of the business.'

Heath said that Baring was not being fair: he, Heath, had been on the road for the last three months, marketing the new business. Baring replied that he had heard that Heath was doing a very good job, and suggested he might consider a consultancy.

To Heath's relief, no further mention was made of his repaying part of his £6 million super-bonus. 'You are not alone,' said Baring, handing him a copy of a press release which stated that, of his former associates, Andrew Baylis and Ian Martin were also sacked, and Andrew Fraser and Diarmaid Kelly became deputy chairmen of Baring Securities under Miles Rivett-Carnac, who was recalled from a brief retirement to assume its chairmanship. Peter Norris became chief executive officer.

'It was a total surprise,' Heath said two years later. He refers to the day it happened as the 'Stabbath'.

Among the letters Heath received was one from Andrew Tuckey, who wrote:

> As the dust begins to settle, I wanted to write you a personal note to say how deeply sorry I am that events have turned out as they have. I always greatly enjoyed working with you and have felt stimulated by your vision and energy, and benefited from the charm and humour of your company. These past years have really been good fun, and working with people you like and respect is what it is all about. Whatever happens from here on, history will recall the remarkable impact you made personally on securities markets in general and Barings in particular. I know we will remain friends and I very much hope to see plenty of you at number 8.

Tuckey did not see Heath at Bishopsgate, and they did not remain friends. Heath regarded Tuckey and his lieutenant Norris as the architects of his downfall, and no senior figure in Barings' management would disagree with him. Miles Rivett-Carnac comments: 'Peter [Baring] would have been aware that he was about to depart himself. The future was Andrew's, so the make-up of the management had to be Andrew's call.' As a political battle, this was, in the end, no contest.

When Heath talked to his fellow victims about what had gone wrong, Ian Martin suggested that the difference between Heath and Tuckey had automatically placed Heath in the weaker position. While Heath valued money, Tuckey wanted power. Heath liked making money so that he could buy race-horses, sail his yacht in the Mediterranean, shoot with his cronies and entertain at Annabel's. Tuckey liked power because it gave him patronage, and led to a seat on the board of the Royal Opera House. Playing his cards right would probably result in his being asked to join the court of the Bank of England. Instead of Annabel's, Tuckey was a member of White's. It would never be 'Sir Christopher', whereas 'Sir Andrew' seemed inevitable.

Having won a great battle, Andrew Tuckey planned to absorb Baring Securities into Baring Brothers & Co. to form a new business called Baring Investment Bank. The merger would doubtless create internal difficulties, but Tuckey considered that the bankers would provide an orderly and stable environment for the brokers. There would be no more nonsense about proprietary trading. Internal-audit and risk-management systems would be put in; they would even have a personnel department.

Not everyone was as certain as Tuckey that the brokers needed the bankers. On the day after the Stabbath, Heath ran into Leonard Ingrams, who commiserated with him. He knew what it was like to lose a battle with Tuckey.

'Who's taken over your job?' asked Ingrams.

'Norris.'

'That fellow. He used to run Duff and Trotter. That went bust. Wouldn't be surprised if he doesn't do the same to Barings.'

It was a casual remark, meant to be flippant. Not true, of course. It made Heath laugh, and cheered him up.

Although it was to fade a little as the years went by, Heath left an indelible mark on Barings. Plenty of evidence of the crusty conservative past was still to be found, but in nine years Baring Securities had altered the traditional culture of Baring Brothers. Members of the family who became directors of the bank had always managed to live comfortably, but by the time Heath arrived narrowly held shareholdings had been replaced by bonuses. Baring Securities made so much money that the bonuses became a bonanza. Although the biggest bonuses were reserved for the bosses of Baring Securities, everyone got one, from the latest Baring to become chairman of the board to the most junior settlements clerk. This may appear admirably democratic, but it was, in fact, divisive, setting brokers and salesmen against bankers and corporate financiers, newly hired hands against veterans, and energetic young men against the experienced old guard. Money had become the main, perhaps the sole, standard of judgement of a person's value, and, by that standard, Heath had done astonishingly well. The culture clash almost tore Barings apart.

In the early days of Baring Securities, the management style was based on nothing more than an instinctive feel for the business. Christopher Heath was the prince of salesmen; Andrew Baylis had a firm grip on risk management; Ian Martin looked after the books, and kept the staff on their toes. But, as Baring Securities grew, instinct was no longer a sufficient alternative to methodical management.

Any aspect of Baring Securities that did not make money was labelled as an 'overhead'. Since one way to maximise profits and bonuses was to minimise overheads, a number of departments acquired the status of second-class citizens. The latest information technology and sound credit controls were 'overheads'; so was a well-trained and staffed settlements department, the back office where the traders' tickets were checked, contracts issued and margin payments made to various exchanges.

Settlements had never had a high priority in Baring Securities. Resources were not committed to developing global computer systems which would enable management in London to know the firm's position anywhere in the world; nor was information technology applied to risk management. 'It was all done on the back of an envelope,' says John Guy, who ran the settlements department until the early 1990s.

Working in the back office requires a different kind of temperament from a job on the trading-floor. It is painstaking work which demands patience and resignation, for good settlements clerks are like the enemy, always on the look-out for traders who make mistakes, whether by accident or design. One of Baring Securities' problems was that promising youngsters lacking such a temperament were recruited into the settlements department. All they wanted was a chance to switch to the trading-floor, for the glamour and the bigger bonuses.

When Heath announced the expansion into futures and options in 1989, John Guy was told to hire clerks who knew about derivatives, and who would settle down in the settlements department. Guy was impressed by the confidence and specialist experience of a twenty-two-year-old working in futures and options at Morgan Stanley. His name was Nick Leeson, and he joined Baring Securities as a clerk in 1989.

Christopher Heath made a deep impression on Baring Securities. His people worked tremendously hard and expected to make pots of money. When stationed abroad, they were cocky and contemptuous, treating head office as an obstacle to be overcome. Nick Leeson was too junior to have been hired personally by Heath, but he was definitely one of Heath's people.

5

The Education of Nicholas Leeson

Nicholas William Leeson was born on 25 February 1967 in the King Street Maternity Hospital in Watford. His second name was his father's, though his father was never known as William. Harry Leeson, as he was known, was a plasterer. His wife, Anne, was a nurse at a mental hospital not far from where they lived in Orbital Crescent in the suburb of Leavesden in north Watford. Nicholas was the first of four children: Richard was two years younger than him, and Victoria and Sarah were seven and ten years younger respectively.

In the 1960s, Watford was already a dormitory for London. The fast train to Euston takes only fifteen minutes, and the journey on the M1 can be done in an hour. But it still had a life of its own: it was a large printing centre at a time when the unions still dominated the industry. 'The print' provided a good living for thousands of local people, and Watford was part of the prosperous south-east, like the new town of Milton Keynes to the north and Basildon in Essex, where traditional working-class voters discovered the Conservative Party. This sprawling region around London was the birthplace of the acquisitive working class, or 'Essex Man'.

Harry Leeson shared at least some of the virtues of this liberated working class. Self-employed, he started work at dawn and continued till dusk, when he would often have a few pints with his neighbours at the Hare, round the corner from Haines Way, where the Leesons moved in 1973. Number 144 is a plain, two-storey council house in a well-kept terrace, decorated with a band of red tiles.

Despite his occupation, there is no evidence that Harry Leeson lavished much attention on his own house. But when, after their son's arrest, photographs taken furtively from over the garden fence appeared, showing a cooker dumped in the back garden, the Leesons were extremely cross. The photograph suggested that they lived in a slum: the cooker was there only because Harry had recently fitted a new kitchen. Their pride was hurt.

Stephen Pollard, Leeson's lawyer, gained the impression that Anne Leeson was an organised, intelligent, middle-class woman. She would have been at home in the house in Haines Way, which stands opposite a primary school with green, open space beyond it. It might have been a bit drab, but it was certainly not underprivileged.

The education of Nicholas Leeson began at Kingsway Junior Mixed School, and continued at Parmiter's in the neighbouring suburb of Garston. Parmiter's, once a grammar school in Bethnal Green in east London, had moved to the country and become a comprehensive school. But its grammar-school roots were still in evidence: the pupils were expected to wear uniform and were encouraged to develop expectations. A former governor of the Bank of Canada was an Old Parmitarian.

As a boy he was Nicky, doing his 'dyb, dyb, dybs' in the Cubs, and moving on to the Boy Scouts, where he became a Sixer, or patrol leader. The scoutmaster remembers a neat, responsible boy, kind to those he led. He was the sort of quiet, respectful child who might have expected to become a clerk in a high-street bank, or to work for the council. Indeed, he was considered a suitable representative to meet the Queen when she visited his school to celebrate its 300th anniversary in 1981.

Leeson's O-Level results were the work of a steady, if unspectacular student: an A in maths, Bs in English language, English literature and history, a couple of Cs, and a Grade 1 in French. He clearly showed some aptitude for mathematics, though when he took the additional maths O-Level exam, he failed it completely. His teachers found him hard-working, and expected him to do well in his A-Levels two years later.

At Parmiter's he showed promise as a footballer, and was a key player in the school team. He was a sweeper, in a defensive role at the back of the team; not big – about five feet ten – but fairly skilful (he used both right and left feet), and committed. He also became a prefect.

But this picture is misleading. In fact, Leeson's late adolescence and early manhood were a bitterly exacting time for him. In the classroom he proved a disappointment. His A-Level results were dismal: a C in English literature and a D in history. Maths was a disaster. When he became an international celebrity who had traded and lost a fortune in futures and options, this failure to pass A-Level maths was trumpeted throughout the world as an example of his employers' shortsightedness. Hardly anyone took any notice when his sister Victoria pointed out that he had re-taken that maths A-Level and passed it.

Anne Leeson died of cancer when she was still in her forties and Nicholas was twenty. Lindsay Eastwood, a reporter on the *Watford Observer* who established a close relationship with the family after Leeson's arrest, noticed that, whenever the subject of Nick's mother came up, the family became mute. 'That's all in the past. We don't want to talk about it,' was all they said. It was as if the grief had never left them. Pollard believes that Leeson was traumatised by his mother's death. At twenty, he was still at the tail end of his adolescence, and the person who had provided him with standards of right and wrong had gone. He had lost the person whom he most wanted to please.

While he was still at school, Leeson moved on from his friends in the Boy Scouts and took up with a group of streetwise boys who liked playing football and drinking beer. Out of school, and with money in their pockets, they went on playing football and drank a lot more beer.

Leeson did go to work in a bank, but not in the high street. Parmiter's had not lost its link with the City of London when it moved to Watford. Since Leeson's exam results were not good enough for him to consider university, he looked for a City job. He was hired by Coutts & Co., one of the prestigious names of British banking, although by 1985, when Leeson joined the staff, its independence was a thing of the past, and Coutts had become a subsidiary of the National Westminster Bank.

Working for Coutts set Leeson slightly apart from his hard-drinking, football-playing friends. Celebrating rather too well the twenty-first birthday of one of the gang in Harlow, they found themselves put in the police cells for a while to sober up. On their release, Leeson noticed that he was treated differently from the rest by the policeman behind the desk. With his Coutts & Co chequebook and cashcard, he did not seem to quite belong in that company. They were lager louts; he already had the trappings of a yuppie.

In the 1980s, there was no better place for a school-leaver to find work than the City of London. The financial-services industry was growing at an average rate of 12 per cent a year. New jobs were being created all the time, and there was a persistent and chronic shortage of labour. The wages were good, and the bonuses great. The City's major banks began to entice the cream of the graduates from Oxford and Cambridge, but, as the volume of business grew, so did the demand for clerical workers. Such clerks had once sat on high stools and written neatly in leather-bound registers. Now they used advanced software in powerful computerised information systems. In the old days, the necessary reading, writing and arithmetic had been taught at school, but in the new City, recruits had to learn the business on the job. Nicholas Leeson's further education took place in the City of London.

Coutts & Co. was stoutly representative of the old banking fraternity in the City, so no excitement there. After a couple of years, Leeson moved on to Morgan Stanley, the New York investment bank. American banks were not only leading the City's expansion, they were changing the tone of the place. Many English bankers still thought it was in bad taste to talk about making lots of money, but the Americans assumed that banking had no other purpose. The aspiring working-class children from Essex, Kent and Hertfordshire who now came to work in the City were like the Americans. Being a yuppie meant never apologising for wanting to spend, spend, spend.

The Americans understood the importance of a sound infrastructure. Branches of securities houses like Merrill Lynch did not become fully operational until risk-management and settlements systems had been bedded down. Compared to the babble of the trading floor, these back-office jobs lacked glamour, but they were taken deadly seriously at Morgan Stanley.

In Watford Leeson was one of the lads, behaving exuberantly, like a bun-throwing derivatives-trader. In the City, he was quieter, anxious to learn and to please. 'A very pleasant personality, not at all flash,' says one of his bosses from those days. These were the attributes required of a settlements clerk.

In the late 1980s, Morgan Stanley was making a lot of money in Japan in the new markets for futures and options when they were just becoming known as derivatives markets. In a global marketplace, of course, trading on the Tokyo and Osaka exchanges can be done from all over the world. Without ever leaving London, Leeson learned about settling futures-and-options trades in Japan. It was his experience in these Japanese markets that clinched his job at Baring Securities when he applied for it in 1989. Baring Securities had started to trade in Japanese futures and options in 1989, and the only man in settlements who knew anything about those markets had been headhunted by a competitor. So John Guy got together a dozen or so candidates for interviews. Leeson's experience impressed Guy and Ian Martin, the finance director, and they gave him the job. Guy cannot now recall what the salary was, but thinks it must have been over £20,000. It sounds like a lot of money and responsibility for a twenty-two-year-old. Guy says it was 'not unusual'.

Some years later, Leeson told Stephen Pollard that, at about this time, he began to feel 'schizophrenic'. He spent his weekdays in the City performing complicated tasks, and the weekend with his pals, who had no idea what it was he did. At the weekend, it was the usual round of beer and football (birds seem to have come a distant third). The gang he belonged to had a reputation locally. Arriving late and drunk at a football-club dinner, they turned disruption into chaos before being thrown out. He never behaved like that in the City.

Colleagues from the early 1990s remember a young man who tended to keep himself to himself. He did not make close friends at work, and when he did join colleagues for a drink, his consumption was fairly modest: 'they'd have a couple of pints and a few gin and tonics. Nick got quite giggly after a couple of pints,' says Guy. What impressed Guy about Leeson was his self-assurance: 'He'd come to me and say, "Look John, we've got a problem, but it's my problem; I'll deal with it."' When people at Baring Securities asked Guy how Leeson was doing, he replied that Nick was a star.

At Morgan Stanley, the environment had been highly disciplined; at Baring Securities, it was organised chaos. Problem-solving took a high priority. In 1990 a serious difficulty arose in Jakarta. Indonesia was typical of the emerging markets in which Baring Securities revelled. By the early 1990s, all were expanding so fast that none of their settlements departments was able to cope. Kuala Lumpur, Bangkok and Singapore all experienced trouble, but Jakarta was a disaster. Unless it was sorted out quickly, losses would run into millions of pounds. A team of four was required to deal with the problem. Two were to come from Hong Kong, and two from London. Guy thought Leeson was the right man for the job, but the choice of the second person from London was less obvious. Guy took a risk. Despite the fact that she had only just joined Barings, he asked a lively young woman called Lisa Sims to join Leeson in Indonesia. She was the daughter of a newspaper printer, pretty and bright. They would be gone for some months.

Jakarta was a totally fresh experience for Leeson and Lisa. The team swam in the pool at their hotel and ate out together each night. Though Leeson sat in a bank all day sorting through piles of share certificates from the stock exchange, which was tedious work, this seemed like the good life. Better still, Lisa was a good companion.

The Barings team did a conspicuously good job in Jakarta. The Hong Kong and Shanghai bank was sufficiently impressed to ask Barings to show them how to run their back office. Leeson was not the leader of the team, but he had made his mark. William Daniel, who ran Baring Securities' office in Jakarta at the time, remembers him well. 'He was someone with a bit more energy and ambition than the usual back-office clerk. He was clearly going to be frustrated if all Barings had to offer him was a job shuffling share certificates.'

When they got back from Indonesia, Guy noticed that Leeson was solicitous about Lisa, blushing on her behalf when she was allowed to overhear dirty jokes. 'She was one of the lads, but he always treated her like a lady,' says Guy. Leeson and Lisa announced their engagement shortly afterwards.

On his return to London, Leeson was assigned by Ian Martin to one of the teams in the business development group, which was a euphemism for a team which sorted out areas of chaos. His first job was an internal inquiry in settlements. This had been triggered by a telephone call from a client, who asked why he had not been asked to cough up some margin payments on contracts he had purchased through Baring Securities. The answer to that question revealed a problem with another client by the name of PCFC – and also some curious behaviour on the derivatives-settlements desk.

PCFC was a financial adviser which invested funds on behalf of clients, and it had seemed legitimate: it was a member of FIMBRA, the industry's regulatory body, and its references checked out. But Leeson's investigation showed that the man who ran the company was using, against all the rules, his clients' funds to do some proprietary trading on his own behalf. Since he was trading heavily, the margin calls ran into hundreds of thousands of pounds, yet his margin payments were in tens of thousands. This shortfall normally appears in a statement called a margin-critical report, but in this case that document had been suppressed. No criminal charges were brought, but two settlements clerks and their boss were sacked.

The episode showed how an unscrupulous investor could manipulate his clients' funds to finance his own trading activities, and how the company's reporting system could be bypassed. Martin was sufficiently impressed by the part Leeson played in the investigation to put him in charge of the derivatives-settlements desk for a while.

The whole PCFC experience was a crucial stage in Leeson's further education: working for the business development group was like an intensive course in finance. By the time he left, he was adept at much more than settlements: he understood the computer software systems and he could read a balance sheet.

Leeson then went back to Japanese futures-and-options settlements, which was now a vital area for Baring Securities – it was one of the few that was making money. Helping to put it right the breakdown in control procedures had taught him more about the intricacies of funding trading in Tokyo and Osaka. But an internal memo written by one of the managers in Tokyo to the deputy chairman of Baring Securities in London in December 1991 shows that Leeson's ambitions lay elsewhere: 'I greatly appreciate Nick Leeson's help (even though he has been dying to get out of the area for two years).'

Leeson had confessed to John Guy that he felt like a change. 'He said to me, "John, I have a low boredom threshold. I don't want to be a settlements clerk for ever."' He got his chance to move early in 1992, when Baring Securities decided to open a subsidiary in Singapore that would be dedicated to trading futures and options. Besides running the back office, the person who ran it would also execute clients' orders on the floor of the exchange. Leeson put his hand up, and Ian Martin had no hesitation in giving him the job. Martin thought he had excelled within his peer group: 'Excellence is a matter of putting in hours, and he worked hard; he also had intellectual ability and good lateral thinking. He was a cut above the rest. He had no experience as a trader, but it was a matter of learning on the job.'

The intelligence Martin referred to was not the academic kind. When Pollard asked Leeson what reading matter he wanted him to bring from London to the prison in Frankfurt, it was football magazines, *Viz*, *Private Eye*, plus an occasional *Time* or *Newsweek*. But his brain was quick, disciplined and well organised.

Lisa was pleased – and so would his mother have been – to see Leeson get on well. He and Lisa were to be married on 21 March 1992, and Barings wanted him to begin work in Singapore at the beginning of April. The ceremony took place in the parish church of St Edmund the King and Martyr, in Kingsdown in Kent, where Lisa's parents lived. They went to Venice briefly, and spent a few further days in Scotland before flying out to Singapore.

Later, Lisa would complain that Nick did not share his feelings with her, that he bottled things up. There were still two distinct sides to his character. As if to prove it, the responsible, hard-working City executive had run up a debt of £639 with Hitachi, and judgment had been given against him in Watford County Court in February 1991. When Leeson married, he was about to be taken to court again, by the National Westminster Bank, for a larger sum – £2,426.

One part of him was still the Boy Scout, anxious to please and to be liked. This was the Nick Leeson they knew and trusted at Baring Securities. The other side of him appeared only in Watford: wilder, more lawless, a rule-breaker. His City friends might not have recognised him there.

Leeson said goodbye to his Watford friends in March. One of them asked if he would be making any money in Singapore. Leeson laughed, 'Shagloads of it,' he said.

6

The Game Begins

By the time Leeson arrived in Singapore, there was not much you could tell him about the turbulent management style of Baring Securities. Indeed, he was already an example of it himself. Two days after he arrived to reconnoitre the scene, Baring Securities in London received a request from the Securities and Futures Authority for more information about the two outstanding County Court judgments against him for unpaid debt.

All traders in London are licensed by the SFA, which conducts its own inquiries into the fitness of the candidates. Leeson, who had applied for a London licence before learning of the opportunity in Singapore, had not admitted these offences in his form. Had he done so, he would not have been permitted to trade. There would have been ways of dealing with this problem. The SFA had a category – 'conditional acceptance' – that would have suited Leeson's case. But both Barings and Leeson were in a hurry. This was a niggle that could wait until Leeson's return to London.

Any powerful compliance department in the City's securities business would insist that a trader who was not eligible for a licence should be banned from trading anywhere. At Baring Securities, however, the environment was permissive. Veterans of the office can imagine the response: 'He's been a bit of a lad, but how many of us are squeaky clean?'

*   *   *

79

Baring Securities had been operating in Singapore since 1987, with its activities centred on the stock exchange, both there and in Kuala Lumpur. The local subsidiary was called Baring Securities (Singapore) Ltd, and it did not conduct business on SIMEX, the Singapore International Monetary Exchange. Instead Barings' futures-and-options trades were executed and cleared by Chase Manhattan. By 1992, the volume of futures-and-options business was growing fast, and it seemed profligate to pay commission to a competitor. Barings therefore applied in February for clearing membership of SIMEX, and bought three seats on the exchange in May. A new company was established to operate this business. Its name was Baring Futures (Singapore) Ltd.

Most of the staff were recruited locally, but Mike Killian, Barings' senior salesman in Tokyo, who would be putting a good deal of business through Singapore, wanted someone there who was fluent in the English idiom as well as the language. The job to which Leeson was appointed was unusual in the securities industry. Because of his experience, his role was to head the settlement operations, but, besides that, he was asked to be the Baring Futures' floor manager on SIMEX as well. This was extraordinary because it is one of the basic rules of the securities business that settlements and trading responsibilities are strictly segregated. The task of the settlements clerk is to keep the trader on the straight and narrow, making sure that no errors occur, and fixing them quickly if they do. The trader's job is to make money. These two disciplines do not sit easily with each other. When the inspectors appointed by Singapore's minister for finance reported on the collapse of Barings, their view was that giving Leeson a dual role was 'an ill-judged decision'. But judgement hardly came into it.

The newly married Leesons moved into a plain, six-storey apartment building at 29 Anguilla Park, a tree-lined street within earshot of the buzz of heavy traffic on Orchard Boulevard and Paterson Road. Situated on a small hill a couple of miles from the financial district, this urban suburb is where expatriate merchant families once lived in houses with spacious gardens, close to the Tanglin Club and the British high commission. The club and high commission are still to be found there, but most of the houses have been demolished, the land subdivided and apartment blocks built on it. Twenty-nine Anguilla Park is modest compared to the newer twenty-five- and thirty-storey blocks that surround it.

Not far away are the hotels and shops of Orchard Road. This area of Singapore is dedicated to shopping, a gaudy commercial for the 'little economic miracle' which transformed Singapore from a colonial outpost to an east Asian 'tiger economy'. Leeson has said that when he arrived in Singapore his salary was less than he had been earning in London, in which case Lisa would have had to window-shop: retail prices in Singapore are generally higher than those in London.

J. G. Farrell's fine novel *The Singapore Grip* begins with an intriguing notion: 'The city of Singapore was not built up gradually in the way most cities are, by a natural deposit of commerce or at a traditional confluence of trade routes. It was simply invented one morning by a man looking at a map.' That was in 1819, and the man was Sir Stanford Raffles. About 160 years later, Singapore was re-invented by a man who was impatient with the past. He was Lee Kwan Yew, the first prime minister of the independent republic of Singapore. Nick Leeson had a role to play in the modern city-state that was Lee's re-invention of his country.

Raffles' idea had been to create a port halfway between India and China to extend the reach of the British empire. Singapore became all Raffles dreamed it might be, exporting to Europe and America tin and rubber from Malaya and pepper and spice from Sumatra and Sarawak. Expatriates from Britain prospered; the Chinese did the heavy labour. Lee Kwan Yew, a Straits-Chinese Cambridge-educated lawyer, was determined to re-distribute the wealth among the Chinese, and, incidentally, the Malays and Indians, who complete the population of 3 million crowded on to a small island measuring twenty-six miles by fourteen, just north of the equator at the extremity of the Malay peninsula.

After Singapore became independent in 1965, having been expelled from the Malaysian Confederation, the port grew steadily, and thirty years later it was the biggest in the world after Rotterdam. But shipping alone was not sufficient to create the wealth that Lee Kwan Yew wanted to be able to spread. Local manufacturing industries shrewdly concentrated on making obscure electronic parts, but there was not enough land or labour for them to prosper to the extent Lee required. He wanted Singapore to become the Switzerland of south-east Asia, and to achieve that the country needed to attract international businesses built on money and banking, investment and financial markets. Lee declared: 'Singapore has the attributes to be the Chicago or Zurich of east Asia.' Go there, and it does not sound daft. All you need do is look around you.

Standing in Raffles Place, at the heart of the financial centre, you are penned in by soaring towers of shiny steel, of grey and bronze marble, and of bleached concrete, rising between fifty and sixty-five storeys. These skyscrapers, which would dwarf anything in London, would not look out of place in New York or Chicago. Like the Victorian City bankers who understood that a magnificent display of wealth in the banking hall reassures the customers that their money is safe, their contemporary Singaporean counterparts have lavished space and money on high banking halls for all to gaze at.

From high up in one of the bank towers, the evidence of Singapore's economic miracle stretches out in front of you: the clutter of cargo ships anchored offshore waiting for a mooring in the port, tall buildings bearing the name of every famous hotel chain in Asia (though the nicest of them is still called after Sir Stanford); the substantial department stores along Orchard Road; the apartment blocks that look out to sea and back on to the commercial centre, Anguilla Park among them. The city is a monument not only to Lee Kwan Yew, but to the materialism and material wealth of the last phase of the twentieth century.

There is a price to pay for all this, of course. Although power never corrupted Lee Kwan Yew and his colleagues absolutely, it certainly went to their heads. After some years in charge, they felt their economic success was proof that they knew best. Lee saw no room for conflict in the Switzerland of south-east Asia, and political opposition has been swept aside. Although enemies of the regime are more likely to find work hard to come by than to be thrown in jail, the apparatus of the state is deployed without mercy against anyone who actively opposes Lee Kwan Yew's philosophy.

A Faustian bargain has been made between Lee's ruling party and the people. The people concede power to the PAP (People's Action Party) in return for a guarantee of prosperity. Originality of thought and independence of action are bred out of most children at school, although they can never be entirely suppressed. (The place to find them, today, is in a Singapore restaurant or food hall.) The labour force is well educated, bilingual, well mannered and docile. The free market is allowed to operate; the rule of law is regarded as a valuable asset. As is not the case with most of its neighbours, corruption is rare in Singapore, and, when exposed, is harshly dealt with. As a place to do business, it meets exactly the specifications of bankers and financiers from overseas. In 1995 *Fortune* magazine declared it the second-best place in the world to do business, after the San Francisco Bay area.

Civil liberties, then, do not come high on the list of state priorities. Some rules seem merely ridiculous (the prohibition on the import and sale of chewing gum), while others are harsh (hanging drug-smugglers and caning hooligans). The press is a loyal mouthpiece for the government, and foreign newspapers and magazines which carry intemperate criticism of Singapore are banned, or their circulation is limited. Censure from civil libertarians abroad, who see Singapore in Western terms and seek to impose the West's values upon the country, is met with incredulity and contempt. It can prove expensive too; the *International Herald Tribune* was forced to pay heavy damages when it was found guilty of libelling two senior members of the government. Although Singapore has a parliament and a judiciary based on Western models, it is run mostly by Chinese. Overseas criticism feeds Singapore's latent paranoia, and so reinforces social cohesion.

This paranoia infects foreigners, too, because the rules do not apply only to Singaporeans. The Monetary Authority of Singapore (MAS), which regulates banks and markets, is part of the same state apparatus that controls social behaviour. The MAS refuses foreign regulators permission to inspect the Singapore subsidiaries of banks that fall within their jurisdiction: they like doing it themselves. This does not prevent rules being broken, but it makes expatriate managers conscious of the perils of being caught. Leeson was a slow learner.

Baring Securities' top man in Singapore was a Scotsman called James Bax. Well regarded by the local financial establishment, Bax looked after a business that traded equities on the Singapore stock exchange and provided research for clients in Singapore and Malaysia. Unlike many of his colleagues, who hardly had time to unpack before moving on to another assignment, Bax was something of a fixture in Singapore; he liked being a big fish in a small pond, and lived better than he would have done in London in one of the black and white mock-Tudor houses in the status-conscious suburb of Mount Pleasant. Before moving to Barings in 1986, Bax had been a local analyst with the London stockbrokers Hoare Govett, but he had successfully made the transition from research to sales, and by 1992 was in charge of sales throughout east Asia.

Colleagues, who remarked on his physical similarity to John Major, thought him a decent, unassuming family man. His Scottish wife worked shifts at the *Straits Times* and wrote occasionally for the *Economist*. In a tension business like Baring Securities, where animosity was common, Bax had enemies. Some were people he had fired. Others who still worked for Barings did not like his fierce defence of his own patch. There had been an embarrassing dust-up with the stock exchange in Kuala Lumpur in 1992, but he had survived that.

On the whole, Bax was regarded as a thoroughly competent manager.

Bax's lieutenant was Simon Jones, the finance director of Baring Securities (Singapore). Jones is a fluent linguist who speaks eight languages. The fluency of his Chinese enabled him to run a tight ship. The locally recruited staff were afraid of him, but they also joined him for a drink after work. Jones's temper was legendary; anyone who had visited Singapore had a story about Jones screaming at a waiter or a car-park attendant. Seniority was no defence against Jones's wrath, either – visitors from head office found themselves relegated to windowless rooms, and conversation with local members of staff was not encouraged. A Tokyo colleague commented: 'There wasn't anyone on the planet Jones hadn't had a fight with.' Jones got away with this because he dealt efficiently with the crucial business of settling trades on the stock exchange.

Bax and Jones were among Barings' best-regarded teams, and they complemented each other admirably. Bax travelled so extensively that junior staff like Leeson rarely set eyes on him. Jones, who spent most of his time in Singapore, kept the back office under control. But the relationship was not simple. Bax was the boss, but he had no experience of settlements. Bax needed Jones, and Jones knew it. Whenever Jones gave offence, he would appeal to Bax for protection. Bax, fearful of losing such an able colleague, would deal with the office politics. As long as they operated efficiently, Bax and Jones appeared safe. In London, the office became known as 'Fortress Singapore'.

When Baring Futures (Singapore), Leeson's outfit, was established, Simon Jones and James Bax were both on the board of directors (the chairman was Christopher Heath), and Jones confidently expected to be in charge of whoever was selected to run the new SIMEX operation.

In September 1995, when Leeson was interviewed for television by Sir David Frost, parts of the long recording ended up on the cutting-room floor. Much of the material that was not transmitted is crucial evidence to the full Leeson story. And

Leeson refers to the confusion that surrounded his arrival in Singapore.

> [My title] was a subject of some discussion and argument between both Simon Jones and the guy that was moving me out there, Tony Dickel. Everybody was fighting for their pound of flesh, and there was a lot of confrontation over reporting lines, titles, salaries. It wasn't something I got involved in myself. I was quite keen on the move, and I left Tony Dickel to negotiate.

The dispute was never satisfactorily resolved. On 24 March 1992, Ian Martin, the finance director in London, faxed Simon Jones in Singapore and Mike Killian in Tokyo, stating that Leeson would be in charge of Baring Futures' SIMEX operation and would act as floor manager. 'He will report to Simon Jones and Gordon Bowser,' wrote Martin. Bowser was responsible for futures-and-options settlements in London. Martin explained later that the decision to have Leeson report to London was deliberate: much of the business done in Singapore would be on behalf of the Tokyo office, and the reporting of Japanese trading worldwide, which included London and New York, was being consolidated in London.

Jones was not pleased. He complained to Bax, who wrote a prescient memorandum to Andrew Fraser, the head of equity-broking and trading in London. It was quoted in the Board of Banking Supervision report.

> My concern is that once again we are in danger of setting up a structure which will subsequently prove disastrous, and with which we will succeed either in losing a lot of money or client goodwill or probably both ... In my view it is critical that we should keep clear reporting lines, and if this office is involved in SIMEX at all then Nick should report to Simon [Jones] and then be ultimately responsible for the operation side.

Three years later, Andrew Fraser was at a loss to recall what the ominous words 'once again' referred to. Others were sure that Bax must have been alluding to the chaos in Jakarta that Leeson had helped to put in order. But, as published in the

Baring Securities (Singapore) Pte Ltd
10 Collyer Quay, #06-01 Ocean Building, Singapore 0104

FAX TRANSMISSION

2 of 4

25 March 1992

To : Andrew Fraser
Fm : James Bax

SIMEX

The following fax was received from Ian Martin this morning.
(Note that he has not included me on the fax distribution).

My concern is that once again we are in danger of setting up a
structure which will subsequently prove disastrous and with which
we will succeed in losing either a lot of money or client
goodwill or probably both.

As I understand it from Tony Dickel the object of activating our
SIMEX seat is to provide an execution service for the options and
futures people in London and Osaka. Subsequently, if successful,
we could build up a sales team in Singapore but this is not
currently a priority. Orders would be sent directly from (a)
Mike Killian's team in Osaka (b) London desk via telex (c) direct
client orders to the floor.

Tony Dickel has recommended (and Simon Jones and I agree) that
Nick Leeson should be the manager of futures and options
settlement in Singapore reporting to Simon Jones. This office
will therefore be responsible for the efficient running of the
operation in the same way that we currently settle our Thai
business.

Having agreed this structure (we thought) with Tony Dickel, Ian
is now talking in terms of Nick as "head of our SIMEX operation
...." and "report(ing) to both Simon Jones and Gordon Bowser".

In my view it is critical that we should keep clear reporting
lines and if this office is involved in SIMEX at all then Nick
should report to Simon, and then be ultimately responsible for
the operations side. If this is not the case then involvement
of both Simon and myself (as current Directors of Baring Futures
(S)) is inappropriate, and needs review.

As a final point (and probably not to be repeated) I gather from
Tony Dickel that Nick Leeson is more likely to be motivated in
the new role by reporting directly to Simon, without any other
"fingers in the pie." Perhaps as Tony Dickel will be seeing you
in Taiwan you can have a word with him to see how he feels.

Regards

Line of responsibility: James Bax tries to strengthen 'Fortress Singapore' supervisor's report, the fax is incomplete. In the full text, Bax, after complaining that Martin's fax had not been sent to him, rehearses his interpretation of Baring Futures' Singapore operation.

> As I understand it from Tony Dickel, the object of activating our SIMEX seat is to provide an execution service for the options and futures people in London and Osaka. Subsequently, if successful, we could build up a sales team in Singapore, but this is not currently a priority . . .
>
> Tony Dickel recommended (and Simon Jones and I agree) that Nick Leeson should be manager of the futures and options settlement in Singapore, reporting to Simon Jones. This office will then be responsible for the efficient running of the operation, in the same way that we currently settle our Thai business.
>
> Having agreed this structure (we thought) with Tony Dickel, Ian [Martin] is now talking in terms of Nick as 'head of our SIMEX operation . . .' and 'reporting to both Simon Jones and Gordon Bowser'.

The second sentence in the supervisors' report came next. The whole paragraph reads:

> In my view it is critical that we should keep clear reporting lines, and if this office is involved in SIMEX at all then Nick should report to Simon, and then be ultimately responsible for the operations side. If this is not the case, then involvement of both Simon and myself (as current directors of Baring Futures [Singapore]) is inappropriate and needs review.
>
> As a final point (and probably not to be repeated) I gather from Tony Dickel that Nick Leeson is more likely to be motivated in the new role by reporting directly to Simon, without any other 'fingers in the pie'. Perhaps as Tony Dickel will be seeing you in Taiwan, you can have a word with him to see how he feels.

After the catastrophe, Christopher Heath and his inner circle were anxious to distance themselves from Leeson's appointment. They insisted that the job they had given him was of no importance: he was just a clerk. The implication was that, if they had remained in charge, Leeson would not have been capable of playing his own secret game. 'He was just a tele-phone clerk, executing orders in Singapore,' says Ian Martin, describing a mechanical clerical operation involving nothing more complicated than the transmission of orders received by phone or fax to the trader on the SIMEX floor. Leeson, how-ever, had more ambitious plans, and being an execution clerk gave him the access to the trading-floor he needed to realise them. Had he been ordered to concentrate on settlements only, he could not have traded as well.

There was a complete misunderstanding of his role from the start. Bax believed that Leeson was in charge only of settle-ments. He understood that if Baring Futures was successful, a sales team working directly with clients might be built up in Singapore, although there was no suggestion that Leeson would run it. Bax felt strongly that, if Leeson was in charge only of settlements, and if he was reporting to Bowser in London, then the involvement of Jones and himself was 'inappropriate'.

The outcome of this skirmish was that Baring Securities' directors in Singapore not only misunderstood the breadth of Leeson's job specification, but they were also very reluctant to supervise him. Had Jones been given complete authority over Leeson, he would probably have done a proper supervision job. But he was not a man to share, and the quarrel about lines of responsibility had offended him, so he took no more than a passing interest in Baring Futures. Leeson was able to start as he meant to go on: not only in charge of settlements, but as an execution clerk as well, who might later be permitted to build a sales team.

Barings in London had identified the areas that required particular attention in Singapore. Gordon Bowser, the risk manager in London, had written a memorandum on his return from Singapore in April 1992 in which he emphasised the need for tight control by the accounts people of reconciliation of the money paid by Barings to SIMEX on behalf of clients, and the money received from the clients. Bowser recommended that reconciliation be separated from Leeson's settlements depart-ment. This procedure, he wrote, should be agreed between

Jones and Dickel. But no agreement was reached. Leeson, as the man in charge of settlements, was able to decide unilaterally that reconciliation would not be part of the routine.

A good many of the orders Leeson would execute for Barings on SIMEX came from Mike Killian in Tokyo, who, as the man in charge of the product Leeson was trading, was another of the people to whom he was responsible. Killian, who is from Chicago, talked a lot. He was known as the 'great schmoozer' in Tokyo, and sometimes when he had finished talking, his colleagues could not make sense of what he had said. But he was a good salesman, earned a big bonus and knew the Singapore market, having worked there for a while with Chase Manhattan. Killian was happy to take credit for the Singapore operation when it was going well. Responsibility was a different matter: Killian was later quite clear about that. Leeson was someone else's responsibility. One person who disagreed with Killian about this was Leeson himself. In the unedited transcript of the Frost interview, Leeson names Killian as one of the people to whom he was reporting in 1992.

So, far from being clear, as Bax had wished, Leeson's reporting lines were either blurred or broken right from the start. And there was one more factor which made it difficult to keep an eye on him. The Baring Securities office, where Bax and Jones worked, was on the twenty-fourth floor of a new building called Ocean Tower, a showpiece on Raffles Place, built for the Hong Kong and Shanghai Bank. Baring Futures was in the same building, but on the fourteenth floor. Out of sight, out of mind. Leeson's isolation happened partly by accident, and the splitting of his reporting line between Jones, Bowser and Killian was not intended to give him a free rein, but that is exactly what he had.

Meanwhile, Leeson himself was taking the steps required to become more than just an execution clerk. Had he been merely that, he would have relayed orders to the floor traders, and there would have been no need for him to have become a registered trader on SIMEX himself. But he sat, and passed, the futures-trading test set by the Institute of Banking and

Finance. On 21 July he submitted his application for registration as an associated person to SIMEX, and on 12 August his application was approved. As in London, his application contained no mention of the civil judgments against him for unpaid debts in the County Court.

SIMEX, the market which Barings joined in July 1992, looked like any other international financial futures exchange. All these markets are imitations, some paler than others, of the Mercantile Exchange in Chicago, though none is as big. The Merc is on two floors, each almost the size of a football pitch. SIMEX had gone so far as to establish an alliance with the Mercantile Exchange, known as a mutual offset system, which enabled traders to buy and sell contracts in each other's markets, and created a genuine global market, open almost twenty-four hours a day. Before SIMEX opened for business in 1984, there had been extensive consultations between Singapore and Chicago. Leo Melamed was a particular hero in Singapore, and he was delighted that the exchange he had helped to found a little over ten years earlier had become a model for others. The SIMEX rulebook is a copy of Chicago's, and, although there are fewer people to make it, the din of dealers in open outcry has the same frenzied quality. The colour-clashes are the same: red, ochre and stripes of red and white and black and white, like football jerseys re-styled as blazers. Barings' colours were suitable for the Queen's bankers: navy and gold.

There is, however, one oasis of calm in the exchange, interrupted only occasionally by short, disciplined flurries of activity. The sale of options requires keyboards, screens and calculators, operated by impassive members of the exchange staff. The traders stand and wait patiently for a client to come along, reading the paper and doing the crossword. In the rowdy pits nearby, nine out of ten traders are Chinese, but among the options-traders there are more white faces.

At SIMEX, the most vigorous pits trade Eurodollars, which held no interest for Barings in Singapore, and a trio of peculiarly Asian contracts – in Japanese Government Bonds, Euroyen, and the Nikkei 225 – which did. The Nikkei contract had been a coup for SIMEX. They had obtained a licence from Nihon Keizai Shimbun to use their index, and offered a contract on the Japanese stock-market index in 1986 before any Japanese exchange did. The Japanese authorities had been suspicious that this kind of index trading could distort equity prices on the Tokyo stock exchange, and it was only later that they permitted a similar contract in Osaka. This opened up the chance for a profit to be seized when the price of the Nikkei 225 in Osaka differed from the price in Singapore. This is the business known as arbitrage.

Naturally, a rivalry grew between Osaka and Singapore. Despite stern words from the Monetary Authority of Singapore about strict application of the rules, SIMEX members established good relations with the exchange officials. When members made formal requests that particular rules might be waived, as they were entitled to do, the officials were usually obliging. One rule that was waived for Barings, for example, concerned position limits. It was a rule designed to prevent members from building up large holdings in any one contract.

One other major difference between Singapore and Osaka is that Osaka is a computer-based market in which trading is done electronically. SIMEX, like Chicago, prefers open outcry. Trades done in the pit are faster and easier to follow. Besides, the pit is more exciting than a silent, paperless market. Watching the pit and seeing tickets being flipped flamboyantly by traders to the desks alongside the pit where the deals are recorded, it seems miraculous that they are tracked correctly, or even at all. A remarkable proportion is recorded accurately, but open outcry does lead to mistakes being made. Companies understand this, and open special accounts called 'error accounts'. Disputed trades are placed in the error account until the disagreement is resolved. This usually happens within twenty-four hours, and well-run exchanges do not like disputed deals to lie in error accounts for more than a few days at the most. Nor do efficient traders.

Baring Futures (Singapore) Ltd opened an error account on

SIMEX on 3 July 1992. This was routine, but the five-number identification, 88888, was curious. Eight is well known to be a lucky number for the Chinese, and Eric Wolf, who works in the Chicago Mercantile Exchange's tough surveillance department, remarks that its use would have aroused his suspicions immediately. Leeson recalls the account being opened, but says he cannot remember whether it was he, or one of the Chinese computer operators, who gave it that number. 'I didn't have much to do with the computer system myself. There was a young lady working for me who would enter everything on to the machine, but I informed her to open an error account and it was given the number double eight, triple eight,' Leeson told David Frost. He suggested in that interview that, while he formally reported to London, the reason the error account was opened in Singapore was that the London office was concerned that too many errors might attract the attention of regulators from the Securities and Futures Authority. That reasoning is odd: if the errors were of a kind likely to arouse the suspicions of the SFA, they would surely have interested SIMEX as well.

A few days after the error account was opened, Leeson instructed Dr Edmund Wong, the computer-systems consultant retained by Barings in Singapore, to change the software programme. Wong's CONTAC system automatically reported daily to London four separate items on each account: a trade file, recording the day's trading activity; a price file noting closing prices; a margin file listing all margin balances; and the 'London gross', which detailed the firm's positions. Dr Wong was instructed to exclude three of these items on the 88888 account from the daily electronic report to London. All that was reported was the margin file. Because he understood London's office procedures, Leeson knew which of the daily files had to be deleted. He ignored the margin file because he had observed himself that it was not used, or even looked at. This was not the action of a dedicated settlements clerk. It could only have been designed to deceive the office in London.

What it meant was that when the daily margin file arrived in London, the automatic sorting system did not recognise the account number. No information was therefore transferred into Barings' internal reporting system, called First Futures. The information held in London was displayed on two screens. One showed the margin balances on the CONTAC system in Singapore, and included the margin file from 88888. The second showed the balances which had been transferred to the First Futures screen, and had no record of 88888. The only screen that was scrutinised in London was First Futures.

Leeson states that this instruction to Dr Wong was in response to a message from Gordon Bowser in London.

> At that stage, we were doing business for London accounts, for the Tokyo accounts, and also for the bona fide Singapore error account, and so all trades were sent to Gordon Bowser or somebody in the settlements area. After two or three days, when they were receiving this mass of trades they didn't recognise, because they didn't have the correct account numbers for the London system, they were going through a pretty arduous procedure every day after we'd gone home, trying to work out whether they needed those trades or not. So the phone call came from London saying, 'Please don't send us the trades in these accounts any more.'

Leeson notes that 'probably two months later' Gordon Bowser in London changed his mind, and that Singapore, Tokyo and Osaka were each given error accounts beginning with the number 9 (at SIMEX it was 99002). Although it was never re-numbered to begin with a 9, Leeson claimed that the 88888 account was also intended to be an error account, that it was originally employed as one, and that it was only used for other purposes in 1994, when the scale of his trading mushroomed out of control. This suggests that he slid carelessly into an extraordinary adventure in the futures-and-options markets. The truth of that claim rests in the use he made of the 88888 account. It was either his late alibi, or it was from the start the hub and pivot of his deception.

Leeson gave a detailed, intricate explanation for the reason he first used the 88888 account, dating it back to 'probably about September 1992'. In one of the lengthy excerpts edited out of the Frost interview, he described the problems he'd had in setting up his operation.

> Simon Jones had his own settlement area that was directly responsible to him, and he was very concerned that things in the office for Baring Futures Singapore were run on a very similar line to the way he was doing it on the securities side ... he didn't want salaries out of line ... So there would be numerous people I wanted to employ, and the person giving the OK on the final employment was usually Simon Jones. He would be the person signing their employment letters and talking to them after I'd spoken to them, and he was typically very concerned about the size of the salary. We probably went through a process whereby twenty people that I would have liked to recruit, both for the back office and the trading-floor, weren't accepted because he wasn't prepared to pay the salary ... He's a very aggressive person, always wants to be the person on top, and so when he's employing somebody he never wants to pay them any more money than they're currently getting. Now, to me, if you're looking for a new job, you're usually looking for more money ... a certain amount of premium needs to be paid. Simon Jones would over-emphasise the bonus payments, and would try and attract people for usually the same amount of money; if he could, he'd try to get them for even less. It was a difficult process, we weren't getting the people that we needed.
>
> Mike Killian ... was also concerned about increasing his cost base too quickly. So we were in a process where the business was ballooning, and staff recruitment just wasn't happening. Added to that, we joined SIMEX at the same stage as Morgan Stanley, who poached a lot of staff from Chase Manhattan, and the exchange imposed a three-month notice period on all members of staff. If we were going to recruit anybody now, they had to serve the three-month period as well.

In September there was a sudden spurt of business on SIMEX. The volume that month was 1.4 million contracts, and of those, 452,000 were on the Nikkei 225, compared to 1.1 million and 339,000 the following month. Barings were operating with a skeleton staff, and Leeson and his new colleagues were often required to work late to settle the trades done during the day.

> We were really struggling. There were twelve telephones ringing and there were only six pairs of hands, and we couldn't answer them all . . . One of the locals had a young lady working for him and she was standing up a lot of the day and he said, 'Look, she can't carry on doing this work. The doctor said she's got a bad back. She needs to do something where she can sit down. Can you use her?' It was a godsend to me . . . Somebody who could work straight away and help us out. So I employed the young lady; no problem with Simon Jones, because the salary was next to nothing.

Leeson's story is that this young woman, who had no experience in a trading-house like Baring Futures, one Friday picked up a phone and executed a customer order. Everyone else was too busy to keep an eye on her, and later that evening Leeson discovered that, instead of buying twenty lots of Nikkei 225 futures, she had sold twenty lots. He estimated the cost of the error at £20,000.

What happened next is described in a cut from the Frost interview.

> I spoke to Simon Jones about it. Wasn't too happy. Although he was talking more about hitting her bonus or sacking her, [he] suggested that I report the error to Andrew Baylis in London. By the time I had finished the discussion with Simon Jones . . . it was approaching midnight on the Friday, which is five or six o'clock UK time, and so Andrew Baylis isn't going to be around. I thought, as far as doing this now or on Monday, there isn't a lot of difference. He's not going to see whatever I write until Monday morning. Lisa was at home. I'd been working until midnight every night and I needed to get back. We were also supposed to be going out with a group of brokers who were doing some business for us at the time.

Nick and Lisa went to the Hard Rock Café on Orchard Road, where they met the young woman who had made the mistake. She had heard about the error, and was crying and worried about the consequences. Leeson picks up the story in another passage from his interview which was not transmitted.

To me, it wasn't her fault. It was a combination of Simon Jones's, Mike Killian's and my fault. There was too much work and we needed people desperately ... and we weren't able to get them, either through petty-mindedness of people at Barings or because of conditions that had been imposed on us by the Exchange. It's not like I shouted at her. I felt sorry for her and I didn't really blame her ... On Monday, when I'd gone back to work, I've probably had good intentions of writing the report up to Andrew Baylis, [but] the market's been crazy again, the settlements systems all fell down, and, by the end of the day ... I'm trying to solve today's problems without going back to anything that happened on Friday. It's been forgotten ... the girls in the back office were having a lot of trouble reconciling reports that were coming from Singapore. About the time that the error reared its ugly head again was Thursday, when the girls had actually managed to do some reconciliations because the reports had been incomplete from both sides, and there had been many errors. By that stage, the problem of the error has resurfaced, because now it's given us a reconciliation problem, it's compounded itself in my own mind in that, OK, I haven't told Andrew Baylis straight away. I've got no excuse for not telling him for four days. I mean, I'd known about it for four or five days.

In the interview as it was broadcast, Leeson's story was cut to a sentence. 'I also feel very sorry for the girl in that I don't want her to lose her job. I mean, she did subsequently resign very soon afterwards, and so, to answer your question, that is the first trade that made its way into the five-eights account.'

A touching story, plausible even, but simply not true.

The Singapore inspectors, who had access to all the files on the 88888 account at SIMEX and at Baring Futures, say that Leeson began to use the account on the day it was opened, 3 July 1992, some ten weeks or so before he claims he used it to help out the poor girl who had made a mistake. During July, before his SIMEX registration was confirmed, Leeson bought and sold 2,051 Nikkei futures, and made a loss right away. In terms of his eventual losses, it was a modest one (about £40,000). By the end of August, the loss had built up to £320,000. Once again, in the context of his eventual losses, it is a negligible sum, but one that was already big enough to disturb an experienced floor trader. Late in August Leeson had bought 189 long Nikkei futures. Long futures with no short futures meant that his position was unhedged. It is clear that, from the start, Leeson was intent on a substantial gamble with the firm's money.

By August 1992 the volume of business in the 88888 account was sufficient for it to be reportable under SIMEX rules. On 26 August, Leeson faxed to SIMEX a BC4 form, used to identify the owner of an account for which more than 100 contracts had been traded. On the form, the owner of the 88888 account was given as 'Baring Securities London – Error Account', and it was described as a related house account. A little later that same day, SIMEX received an amended BC4 form. It was identical in every respect, except that the words 'Error Account' had been removed. Leeson must have known that, if anyone inspected the account, they would realise that it was being used for trading, not for fixing errors.

Without intending to do so, Bowser in London was making this possible. A rigorous reconciliation would have shown that Barings was actually providing the funds to support losses in the 88888 account. But since Bowser believed Singapore was reconciling the accounts, he saw no point in duplication. On a couple of occasions, Bowser's staff had roughly reconciled the two sides of the ledger, and found a deficit of between £2 and £3 million. Although we can now see that Leeson's losses on the 88888 account probably accounted for most of this deficit, Bowser told colleagues later that he saw no reason to question it; London's reconciliation was only an estimate, after all.

Leeson had also obtained a vital concession from Bowser, who agreed to advance funds to Singapore to meet clients' margin calls in Singapore before the exchange had asked for the money. Leeson's argument was technical, based on the way SIMEX raised margins and the difficulty of borrowing money quickly from Japanese banks. Bowser acquiesced. From now on, Leeson could call on London to provide funds without providing any details. It meant he had money to play with.

By October Leeson had started to sell options. The positions he took in Nikkei 225 options were also unhedged. Henry Jarecki, whose concept of options-trading was founded on a judicious system of hedging, would have been appalled, but Leeson ignored all the rules from the start. Selling options was the most complex of the games Leeson was playing; even so, it was the only market in which he was not, so far, losing serious money. An estimated loss in his options portfolio of £70,000 in October was offset by a profit of £75,000 in November.

Leeson's trading in futures, on the other hand, was getting him into deep trouble. During September, when he says SIMEX was so busy, his losses rose from £300,000 to over £3 million. In October they were £4.5 million. There was an improvement in November: the cumulative deficit fell to just under £2 million and stayed around that level for the next four months.

The Bank of England's report later estimated Leeson's trading loss in 1992 at £2 million. Questioned about this by David Frost, Leeson first said that he didn't agree with the Bank of England's figure, then added: 'Whether it's 2 million or 1 million is not really the point.' He claimed that the fault lay in SIMEX's settlement system, which was still incapable of coping with the new volume of business: reconciliation often went on well into the night in Singapore, when both Tokyo and London had gone home. Some large positions could not be reconciled, and Leeson described the consequences. 'When the market's opening up 400 points higher and you had a position where you were short 200 contracts from the night before, that's pretty big figures. You're talking about something like £160,000 . . . and, you know, these trades also found themselves into the five-eights account, and the concealment continued.'

But it was not simply a question of concealment. A serious case of deception and forgery was under way. At the end of September, Leeson had a little job for the settlements staff. He instructed them to make a debit on the terminal that was directly linked to Citibank in Singapore of £4 million from the firm's 'bank funds received/receivable', and to credit 'client account (88888)' with the same sum. This was, of course, very nearly the same amount as the deficit in the 88888 account. The paper transfer of funds meant that the 88888 account would now show a small positive balance, or a zero balance, at the end of each month, and would not, therefore, attract attention in either London or Singapore. These entries would be reversed at the beginning of the following month so that the bank funds received/receivable account was back to normal. The settlements clerks acquiesced in Leeson's deception, but none of them blew the whistle. 'I can only describe it as blind loyalty,' Leeson told Frost.

But the hefty loss in the 88888 account after only three months of trading created a tricky problem which could not be entrusted to the good will of the settlements staff. Baring Securities' financial year ended on 30 September, and accounts were prepared by a reputable international firm, Deloitte and Touche, at their office in Singapore. The Singapore inspectors' report tells us that the auditors knew about the 88888 account. But they believed that it was an error account, and did not 'review or test the transactions recorded therein up to that date because, inter alia, the account had an insignificant year-end balance'.

The real balance on 30 September 1992 was far from insignificant – the 88888 account was more than £3 million in the red. If the accountants had discovered that, Leeson's game would have been up within three months. He had to stop Deloittes investigating the account.

What happened next was that Deloittes received a confirmation that the account need not be investigated. Barings in London said that there was only 'an insignificant balance in the account', which is what accountants would expect in an error account. The confirmation came in the form of a fax, or a photocopy of a fax (the inspectors are not certain) from Gordon Bowser, the derivatives manager in London. The standard procedure requires auditors to obtain confirmations directly from third parties, but the Singapore inspectors say that in this case it was not followed. Gordon Bowser believes he may have sent a confirmation referring to an account numbered 99002 on 2 October 1994. He does not, however, recall anything about an 88888 account. Moreover, when Bowser was later shown a copy of the confirmation for that account, he noticed that the figure 2 in the date used in the confirmation of the 99002 account had been replaced with a 7. 'Bowser says he has usually written 7 in the continental style, and so he believes the date was not written by him,' reports the Board of Banking Supervision.

If it was not written by Bowser, the only person who could have written it was Leeson. He had falsified the confirmation, and let Deloittes have it some time in October or November. He would have copied the confirmation for account 99002 and changed it so that it appeared to refer to the 88888 account. Bowser himself could hardly have written it: had he been the author of the fax in its final form, he would have had to have been aware of the existence of the 88888 account. And he wasn't.

Leeson told David Frost that, from September 1992, he had a lot of sleepless nights. That bit I can believe entirely.

7

Why It All Happened

Panic broke out at Barings in London in September 1992. As we saw in Chapter 4, later that month overheads would be slashed by 25 per cent, and 200 people would be sacked; and when that happened, the parlous state of Baring Securities would become public knowledge. Senior executives like Andrew Tuckey were gripped by the fear that other banks would decide Baring Securities was a poor risk. This was a serious matter, since a large part of Baring Securities' core capital – the cash that backed its business – took the form of loans from a consortium of banks. Some were British, like Barclays and Lloyds, others were from abroad, such as Dresdener Bank and the Hong Kong and Shanghai. So, just in case the banks decided to pull the plug, Barings looked for something, someone else – anything – to substitute for the bank loans.

Shortly before the announcement of the crisis measures, a quick deal was done with one of Baring Asset Management's best clients. Prince Khalid Abdullah, a senior royal in Saudi Arabia, who had huge cash deposits in London, was persuaded to lend the company $75 million, a sum that could be transferred immediately to Baring Securities' capital reserves in case of need. That done, Barings approached Barclays and the other banks in a more confident frame of mind. They would like to roll over the loans, they said, but if the banks chose to call them in, they would be repaid in full. The banks didn't call the loans in. Panic over.

But the bankers at Baring Brothers & Co. felt they had learned about the impending crisis in Baring Securities rather too late in the day. Led by Andrew Tuckey, they decided to pay closer attention to the capital position of the bank's securities subsidiary. Not long afterwards, one of the deputies in the treasury and trading department, Tony Hawes, a veteran who had been at Barings since he was a boy, was deputed to find out how the capital of the bank and the securities business might be merged to prevent such a panic recurring. Hawes' instructions were not to disturb the natives. 'Christopher Heath wouldn't have liked it, because the merger would give the Barings bankers too much control over Barings brokers, and the last impression we wanted to give was that this was a takeover by "another bloody banker",' Hawes said later.

Nobody at Barings was at all happy: not the bankers, not the securities-brokers and traders. Even after the blood-letting of September 1992, which pruned the securities business and stabilised the costs, the bankers still mistrusted the brokers – particularly while Christopher Heath remained chairman. And the brokers still thought the bankers were wilfully obstructing the growth of their trading business.

But six months later, after the Stabbath, when Heath and his close lieutenants were sacked, the bank felt free to impose the policies that they hoped might eventually heal these divisions. One principal objective was a radical shift in the way Barings capitalised its activities. After all, there had been internal disagreements between bankers and brokers about the division of Barings' capital between them. How much simpler life would be if they both had access to the same store of capital. Tony Hawes' covert operation of late 1992 was transformed into a committee in April 1993 to study a process with the forbidding name of 'solo-consolidation'. Hawes, who had been threatened with early retirement, became Baring Securities' treasurer instead.

Solo-consolidation, and its part in a more general re-organisation of Barings, is a complicated but vital part of the story of the collapse of the company, as two of the leading characters later made plain. Peter Norris, chief executive officer of Baring Securities: 'Solo-consolidation was the engine room that created the collapse.' George Maclean, a director of Baring Brothers & Co.: '[Solo-consolidation] was the weak link that we will never forgive ourselves for. The collapse couldn't have happened without solo-consolidation. That is the starting point, as far as I am concerned.'

As we have seen, Leeson had already begun his unauthorised trading and his fraud, and had established his means of evading detection. In London in 1993, Barings was constructing a rickety structure that would allow Leeson to continue getting away with his crime until the bank's capital was exhausted and Barings was bust.

Miles Rivett-Carnac had been drafted in as chairman of Baring Securities when Christopher Heath was sacked. 'I knew it would be a difficult people-type time for the bank,' he said later. He had retired as vice-chairman of Barings plc at the end of 1992, but his retirement lasted less than three months. An obvious candidate – avuncular, and trusted by both bankers and brokers – he was only just recovering from the exhausting round of farewell parties; he would come back, he said, on the condition that he did not have to retire again.

Rivett-Carnac was chairman of the management committee, and he set out to pacify those within the firm who thought the distribution of the bonus pool was inequitable. (They thought too much had gone to Heath and his close colleagues, at their expense.) He visited fourteen of the overseas offices, his object being, he says, to pat everyone on the head. One of these trips was to Singapore. Rivett-Carnac had always thought highly of James Bax, and he knew of Simon Jones's reputation as the strongest administrator in the region. 'When you talked to [Jones], he made out that he was on top of it. One would have thought of Singapore as one of our strongest offices at the time,' Rivett-Carnac recalled. He did not remember meeting

Leeson. But why should he? Bax's equities-broking did 90 per cent of the business in Singapore at the time.

Rivett-Carnac's appointment added weight to the conservative faction in the debate about the future between those who favoured a relatively safe agency business, and those who favoured the greater risk of own-account trading, profiting from the wins and taking the losses – or proprietary trading. The cause of the proprietary traders had been led by Christopher Heath and Andrew Baylis, and once they had gone the argument seemed to be over. Rivett-Carnac, Andrew Tuckey and Peter Norris all believed that agency business was best. Proprietary trading was risk-taking, and the culture of the bank was risk-averse. Norris was confident that enough money could be made from the commission on share-trading in emerging markets. Tuckey liked the idea of 'added value' – using the securities operation to sell capital issues arranged by Barings' corporate financiers.

But the debate was not over. A small group of Barings traders in Tokyo were still engaged in proprietary trading. Their reasoning was like Heath's: they saw many good clients among institutional investors executing their own trades instead of leaving them to Barings. Since agency business was in decline, they turned to proprietary trading. They insisted that the form it took was risk-averse, but it provided a platform for more extravagant forms of proprietary trading that were practised later.

After the collapse of the stock market in Tokyo in 1990, the only way of making big money there was by trading, and the Barings people became good at it. There was a brilliant options-trader named Su Khoo, an English-educated, Malaysian-born Chinese. Fernando Gueler, a Californian whose intense dedication led friends to describe him as a techno-peasant, loved tweaking the software in the trading-room to improve the quality and the flow of information from the market, and to speed the execution of their orders. Another American, Benjamin Fuchs, used Gueler's computer programs to take advantage of anomalies between two markets for shares on the Tokyo stock exchange. One was the cash price of a basket of shares in the Nikkei 225 index, quoted in Tokyo. The second was a futures contract on the Nikkei 225 index in Osaka. Both contracts were based on the same product, but occasionally the prices quoted in Tokyo and Osaka would diverge. These moments were not easy to spot, but a smart trader with a computer program could work out when there was profit to be had from arbitrage between the two markets. This was called 'cash futures arbitrage'. That arbitrage was not done for clients: it was done for Barings.

In 1993, it became clear to traders in Tokyo that this futures leg of arbitrage could be executed more cheaply in Singapore than in Osaka. Margin requirements on SIMEX were 15 per cent of a contract's face value, compared with 30 per cent on the Osaka stock exchange. Profits would, therefore, be increased by trading through Singapore. Tokyo began asking the Singapore office to execute Nikkei 225 trades on SIMEX early in 1993, and the trader who assumed the role as Tokyo's man on SIMEX was Nick Leeson. Through the spring and summer, when he was still primarily executing trades for clients of Mike Killian in Tokyo, the volume of business he conducted on behalf of the proprietary traders in Tokyo began to take up more of his time, and he did it well.

By October 1993 Leeson was considered competent enough to be given discretion about when and at what price he would trade on behalf of Barings. The volume of his proprietary trading grew gradually, but by the end of 1993 he was established in the SIMEX pits as a proprietary trader with his own speciality – arbitrage on Nikkei 225 futures between Singapore and Osaka. For a settlements clerk whose ambition had always been to become a trader, it was a momentous change. This was the climax of a good year for Leeson. In June, after a little more than a year in Singapore, he had been promoted to the post of assistant director and general manager. Killian thought it would help him make friends among senior managers in the securities business, but the title gave him power that embraced the whole operation. On the floor, he was a trader; in the back office, he was in charge of settlements; and now, among the managers at Citibank, he was a general manager with *carte blanche* to discuss operational issues. He had cards printed: 'Nicholas Leeson, General Manager'. Not bad for a twenty-six-year-old.

Leeson's own trading in his 88888 account was relatively quiet for most of 1993, and that summer his losses dwindled almost to zero. They fell for four consecutive months until July, when the cumulative loss for the month was £34,147. Profitable options-trading was the reason for the improvement in his position: two good months in March and April are recorded in the Singapore inspectors' table of cumulative monthly losses in the 88888 account. Leeson spoke about these in his Frost interview, though his comments were dropped from the broadcast version: 'During the early part of 1993, I sold a number of option positions, and basically it was the expiry of these . . . that resulted in the profits coming back into the account and the account coming back into a credit position.' Leeson told Frost that the weekend after this happened, he and Lisa had friends round for a barbecue, and he talked about the problem of the losses quite openly. He did not, however, explain how they had been accumulated.

He could not quit then, while he was almost ahead. He told Frost that he regretted not having done so. 'I'd missed my opportunity in May. That was my fault. I should have just wiped my hands clean and gone back home to England. It had got out of hand. All I wanted to do was just to get back to a situation where everything was back in order and be on the next plane out of there. I'd had enough.'

But if he had wiped his hands, Leeson would not have been able to emulate the slick SIMEX floor traders he had come to admire. Skilful, well-capitalised American proprietary-trading companies like First Continental Trading (FCT) from Chicago, and Spear, Leeds & Kellogg from New York cleared their trades through Barings. Leeson got to know their elite traders, the market-makers, who dominated the pits. These traders were paid a share of the company's profits; they could earn more than $1 million in a year. One of them, an FCT trader named Danny Argyropoulous, became a particular pal: on SIMEX, Leeson did him favours; when trading was over for the day, they drank beer together. Argyropoulous was the kind of trader Leeson wanted to become.

The difficulty was that Leeson knew no way of becoming an elite trader himself without exploiting his secret 88888 account. He was using it in a canny way to build his reputation among Barings' traders in Tokyo. They would ask Leeson to execute, on their behalf, a sell order at the prevailing price, say $99.20. Leeson would report the sale to Tokyo at $99.50, giving Tokyo an unexpected profit of 30 cents. Leeson had sold at the prevailing price ($99.20), and the subsequent 30-cent loss was absorbed by the 88888 account. Naturally, Leeson's 'skill' at executing Tokyo's orders was admired by established traders like Gueler. As a mark of their confidence, Leeson, was permitted to start trading options for clients in October 1993.

That was a boon to him. By October 1993, the loss on the 88888 account was up again – to £5.7 million. In November and December, the losses rose sharply, and by the end of the year they were £24.39 million. The Bank of England calculated that if Leeson's losses had been deducted from Barings' profits that year, the profits would have fallen from £68.3 million to £57.8 million.

But the loss never showed up in the accounts because Leeson had written options which had sold for £30 million. This was the most hazardous transaction he had entered into so far because, if the market had moved against him, the potential loss was unlimited. But, if his deception was to continue, Leeson had no choice. Although he never received the option premiums in cash – the premium is automatically remitted to the exchange as margin for the deal – the £30 million appeared as a credit in Leeson's profit-and-loss account, balancing his real loss in the 88888 account, and hiding his trail.

Leeson admitted to Frost that he used his covert account to trade options. Despite this, he also went on telling Frost that, throughout 1993 and well into 1994, the sole purpose of the account was to cope with errors. These were being made by his colleagues as well, he said, and he was covering up for them. Leeson claimed that part of the problem was his gift for friendship, and the difficulty he found in saying no. 'I'm very easy to get along with . . . and I think one of my biggest failings is that I allow people to get away with too much. And, you know, I'm always trying to please.'

Leeson added that he had not felt able to confess his losses to James Bax, who ran Baring Securities in Singapore. 'I don't like letting people down. That's the hardest thing I find to do, and not being able to have that conversation was no fault of James Bax's. It was just something internal, inside of me, that was the hardest thing to face.'

If Leeson had confessed to the loss of £25 million at the end of 1993, he would have wiped out almost a quarter of Baring Securities' profits for the year, but he would not have wiped out the firm. To everyone's surprise, Barings as a whole was having a very good year. It had moved from loss to profit in September 1992, which was the month of the sackings, the promotion of Peter Norris and the shouldering upstairs of Christopher Heath. The markets changed direction that month, and throughout 1993 revenues from emerging markets in Asia were bounding ahead. Norris was able to boast that Baring Securities had not made a loss in any month since he took over as chief operating officer.

The mood of the autumn of 1993 is captured in a very unusual way. Peter Baring visited Brian Quinn, the head of banking supervision at the Bank of England, to reassure him that there was nothing to worry about at Barings. The meeting between the blue-blooded banker and the canny Scotsman in Quinn's room overlooking the Garden Court is described in a memorable paragraph in the Board of Banking Supervision's report.

On 13 September Peter Baring called on Quinn. The note of the meeting records Peter Baring as saying, with respect to the Baring

Securities Limited sub-group, that: 'the recovery in profitability had been amazing, leaving Barings to conclude that it was not actually very difficult to make money in the securities business'. He told Quinn that the BSL sub-group 'would be the biggest contributor to the [group's] profits in what was likely to be a record first half'.

You feel that the autumn sun must have been slanting in through the elegant window, with all being for the best in the best of all possible worlds.

Barings' relationship with the Bank of England was influenced by tradition and reputation. The supervision of Barings was described by the supervisors themselves as 'informal but effective'. Quinn justified the informality by referring to the 'continuity' of Barings' management – in other words, it was run by bankers called Baring. Sir John Baring had been a member of the court of the Bank for years, and the nature of the relationship is well illustrated by the comfortable, confiding conversation between Quinn and Peter Baring.

The supervisor who looked after Barings was Christopher Thompson, a supervisor of the old school who was less keen on spreadsheet analysis than on the personal touch. As recounted in Chapter 5, he had startled a Barings delegation, led by Peter Norris, which had visited him in February 1993 by discussing the possibility that Baring Securities' parlous state might actually break Barings Bank. Later in that conversation, Thompson did not inspire confidence in the effectiveness of the Bank's supervision when he admitted that the Bank did not really understand Baring Securities' business. Long afterwards, when this was reported by the Board of Banking Supervision, Eddie George scoffed at the implication of such incompetence: confessing to ignorance, he claimed, was a clever way of getting people to explain their business. But Barings' relationship with the Bank's Supervision Department during the ensuing months suggests that Thompson's admission was entirely accurate: there is no convincing evidence that the Bank ever did learn about the securities business.

The regulations that supervisors impose on banks are designed to keep them stable and solvent. They are based on complicated formulas worked out by accountants, but the principle is a simple one: no bank should risk more money than it can afford to lose. A bank's business is backed by its core capital, and no more than the sum of that capital should ever be at risk. What also concerns regulators is large exposures to individual clients or markets, a large exposure being anything more than 10 per cent of the bank's capital. The Bank of England, consequently, wants to know, in a written report, about any large exposures. Exposing more than 25 per cent of a bank's capital without the specific approval of the Bank (known as a treasury concession) is just not on.

In 1992, Barings was finding these rules awkward. While Baring Securities was losing money, its capital was being depleted, and when the crisis was at its worst, the capital had fallen to about £50 million. This was not enough to fund any revival in its fortunes. Because Baring Brothers needed to lend Baring Securities more than 25 per cent of its capital, it obtained the necessary treasury concession, allowing loans of up to £150 million. None the less, Barings found it a nuisance having to get the permission of the Bank of England every time it wanted to move capital from one part of the Barings Group to another.

There was also an annoying problem in Osaka. Barings was now doing so much business there that the Osaka stock exchange insisted on a large deposit for margin payments. This deposit was so large, in fact, that it came to more than the permissible limit of 25 per cent of Barings' capital.

Regular meetings on both these matters took place during 1993 between the Bank of England's supervisors and Barings' managers, and these meetings were later extensively reported in the Board of Banking Supervision's report. Anyone ploughing through this is struck by the absence of clarity and the potential for misunderstanding.

By the summer of 1993, Tony Hawes' solo-consolidation committee was committed to the principle of bringing together the capital of the group – bankers and brokers – and was doing battle with a heap of details. Many aspects of solo-consolidation would make the eyes of the most zealous company lawyers glaze over, but they have a bearing on this story, and there is no evading them. The main one involves agency and proprietary trading.

Before solo-consolidation, all trades eventually appeared on the books of Baring Securities London Ltd (BSLL). After solo-consolidation, agency trades would be booked by Baring Securities Ltd (BSL); proprietary trades would be booked by BSLL. This was done to keep BSLL free of the scrutiny of the Bank of England supervisors. Before solo-consolidation, BSLL had a treasury concession of £85 million. Excluding BSLL from solo-consolidation meant that the treasury concession no longer applied. Outside the net, BSLL could finance proprietary trading by borrowing from outside banks as well as from Barings, and since the £85 million loan limit no longer applied, Barings found it easier to meet unusually large calls for more margin from its overseas offices. From Singapore, for instance.

The solo-consolidation of Barings was the first of its kind in the City, and it raised many questions within the Bank of England. A note written in September 1993 by one of the Barings negotiators, reported: '[Carol] Sergeant and [Christopher] Thompson acknowledged that they are in a state of disarray on the subject.' Carol Sergeant, as head of major UK banks supervision, was Thompson's boss, and her concern was that solo-consolidation was taking place for the wrong reasons. She warned that the Bank would be ignorant about overseas subsidiaries; about risk limits; and about Barings' ability to manage the change. Sergeant used the term 'regulatory arbitrage', by which she meant playing off one supervisor (the Bank) against another (the Securities and Futures Authority – the SFA – which regulated securities firms like Baring Securities).

But Thompson was more sanguine. He thought the Bank's criteria for solo-consolidation had probably been met. He wrote to Barings on 4 November to say that the Bank would treat it as solo-consolidated, 'pending further consideration at the Bank'. There appears to have been no further consideration. To all intents and purposes, provisional meant permanent.

Thompson also helped in the matter of Barings' large exposure on the Osaka stock exchange, which broke the 25 per cent limit. This was another complex business, involving fine distinctions between clients' funds and Barings' funds, but the fact was that Barings had been told by the Osaka authorities to put up £90 million in the first six months of 1993 if it wanted to go on trading there, and this was 31.6 per cent of its consolidated capital base: 6 per cent more than the permitted level. By the end of 1993, this had risen to 44.6 per cent. Both these figures required Barings to submit LE (large-exposure) returns to the Bank of England, but they never did so. Quite when this happened is uncertain, but Christopher Thompson granted Barings an 'informal concession', allowing it to exceed the 25 per cent rule in Osaka.

In 1995 the Board of Banking Supervision reported stoically: 'Because the granting of this concession is not documented, it is not possible to state with certainty when it took effect.' However, Thompson thought it was granted in 1993. He had not explicitly waived the requirement, because there were still questions to be resolved, but Barings behaved as though he had. No LE returns for Osaka were submitted by Barings to the Bank of England after 1993, which meant the Bank's supervisors had no way of monitoring the sharp rise in the Barings exposure to Osaka in 1994. Thompson's 'informal concession' was staggering. It was more in keeping with the way the Bank of England was run more than a generation ago, when there were no written rules and assent was given on a nod and a wink. It's a pity that the nod and wink Thompson gave Barings could not have been captured on video and preserved in the Bank of England Museum.

While preparing for solo-consolidation, Hawes had come across an intriguing anomaly which he was at a loss to explain. Baring Securities functioned like a bank in a way. It took deposits in the form of money from clients to meet the margin calls demanded by the exchanges in which they had positions. These deposits were then transferred to the exchanges. Since what came in went straight out again, there should have been no credit or debit balances in the account. But a debit of £15 million turned up, quite unaccountably. Baring Securities was paying out on behalf of clients more than was coming in from them. This unreconciled amount was described in the balance sheet as 'loans to clients'.

Hawes asked Lynn Henderson from Baring Securities' financial control department to investigate. In April 1993, she produced a page-long memo outlining a reasonable explanation, which Hawes describes as 'broad-brush', but which had to do for the time being. 'We wanted to meet the solo-consolidation deadline and this wasn't a top priority,' he says. However, Hawes was still unsatisfied, and he asked Henderson to find out which clients were behind the unreconciled account, and to check their credit. There was only one big 'client', of course: Leeson in Singapore. But, as was the way at Barings, months went by, and a potent mixture of personalities and office politics prevented the inquiry that might have uncovered this fact.

Lynn Henderson had been the senior financial controller at Baring Securities until Geoff Broadhurst, from Baring Brothers, became the new finance director in February 1992. Henderson, who had been accustomed to having her own way, did not relish Broadhurst's appointment. When a new financial controller was appointed in August, she suffered a second demotion. In October, she was made redundant. Hawes remonstrated with Broadhurst, asking that Henderson's study into the loans to clients should be completed. But she had already had six months to finish the task, and Hawes was overruled. Would she have discovered that the 'loans' were to Leeson? 'Hard to say. She might have found him,' says Hawes.

But profits were good, so there was no urgency about investigating the £15 million debit. Tony Hawes was not a man to crack the whip, and no one took up the investigation where Lynn Henderson had left off.

In Singapore in 1993, Leeson was in trouble with SIMEX.

Exchange officials were entitled to inspect members' trading records in their offices, and in April 1993 those inspecting Leeson's found a number of violations. These were not serious, and the fine was only S$23,000, but a formal letter was sent to Simon Jones listing them. One item referred to a trade ticket dated 18 February 1993, for the account numbered 88888. The ticket was attached to the letter, but Jones either did not read the letter, or did not understand it. Leeson was not asked to explain what the 88888 account was for. Another chance had been missed.

In London, solo-consolidation had created a momentum towards the eventual merger of the two cultures in Barings. In the spring of 1993, only six months after having been told he was about to take early retirement, Tony Hawes, from the old culture, was asked to stay on as treasurer of Baring Securities. He was soon joined there by other former colleagues from the bank. One of Peter Norris's first decisions when he became chief executive officer in March 1993 was to merge Baring Securities' equity-derivatives business – run by Leeson in Singapore and Fernando Gueler in Tokyo – with the Baring Brothers financial products group. This had two crucial consequences. The first was that good and experienced traders quit. Bruce Johnson, who had the clearest understanding of risk management in the options market, and Su Khoo, who had performed brilliantly in Tokyo before transferring to London, each found the new regime uncongenial. The second consequence was that proprietary trading became the responsibility of Ron Baker, who ran the bank's financial products group.

Baker was incompatible with aspects of both Barings' cultures. He was a brash Australian who wore coloured shirts, which did not please the bankers; and he was bearded, which was a mark against him with Christopher Heath ('Never trust a man with a beard,' he used to say). Baker had been hired from Bankers Trust in 1992 to run a specialist debt-trading operation. This was proprietary trading, but it took a less risky form than futures and options. Basically, Baker, trading in London, bought bonds from Japan which had fallen from their original value, and made money by selling them on in Europe at a higher price. He was enthusiastic and he knew a bit about derivatives, though not about the market-traded kind with which Gueler and Leeson were involved: his was mainly an OTC (over-the-counter) business. Later, Baker confessed that he lacked experience in the area, though he had successfully mastered inexperience in the past. But he added: 'If you ally lack of experience . . . to other failures in the organisation . . . the failure to give me information [meant] I was learning off absolute crap information, [and] that meant getting up a learning curve was impossible.'

One area in which Baker felt under-informed was that of risk management. A risk committee was established in October 1993, to meet daily and discuss trading positions and credit risks. Two old-fashioned Barings bankers were recruited to lend weight to it: George Maclean, the head of the banking group, and Ian Hopkins, the head of treasury and trading at the bank. Risk was always on the daily agenda of their treasury committee at Baring Brothers, but no one on the committee had hands-on experience of the area they were discussing, and there was no one who could explain its intricacies to them. They still believed, for instance, that there were no proprietary positions, and that therefore there was no risk. The outcome was not surprising. Sajeed Sacranie, who was Peter Norris's personal assistant, observed: 'These risk committees started off, and there was a lack of financial information for them to use at that time. They somehow just petered away.' Sacranie was the man responsible for monitoring risk. He reported to Broadhurst. And, by his own admission, Broadhurst, at the time, had no experience of risk management, either.

These personnel moves were the prelude to the formation of the new investment bank, eventually known as Baring Investment Bank, or BIB. It had not yet been named, but Andrew Tuckey, orchestrating the move in the background, was staffing the organisation with men he knew, people from Baring Brothers who would not hanker after the days of Christopher Heath. In December, for example, he asked Tony Gamby to become head of settlements. Gamby is an amiable north Londoner, conscientious and hard-working; once appointed, he was committed to the idea of the merged business. But Gamby's appointment confirmed that the dominant culture would be that of Baring Brothers: his skill was in settling equities, not futures and options. The operational people who had been with Christopher Heath's Baring Securities traders hardly got a look-in, and only one of the four constituent parts of BIB had a collective memory of Baring Securities stretching back more than fifteen months. That was the agency business run by Andrew Fraser and Diarmaid Kelly.

But the predominantly banking culture did not create cohesion in the new investment bank. Quite the reverse. Miles Rivett-Carnac was chairman of the management committee, but there were so many disagreements that his role became that of referee rather than chairman. 'I used to shut people up a bit,' he says. 'It's a securities-industry tendency. It's all about establishing and holding turf – people talk in terms of "my team", "my desk", "my profit sharing".'

Under Norris's active management, a number of Heath's old teams had their turf taken away from under their feet. The seats of Baring Securities' empire in New York, Hong Kong and Tokyo all underwent drastic re-organisation. The only centre that was left to its own devices was Fortress Singapore. Norris's view was that 'if it ain't broke, don't fix it'. Doubts about the temperament of Simon Jones were spreading, but questions about his future were given no priority.

One facet of Baring Securities that did not alter as much as Tuckey had forecast was its operational style. Profits were flowing again, partly because Heath's buccaneering tradition had not been killed off. Far from being risk-averse, like Barings' bankers, Norris's Baring Securities was still heavily engaged in proprietary trading in Tokyo and Singapore, and in some hair-raising broking business in New York.

The bonuses for 1993 reflected a very good year in these markets and others. Peter Baring's bonus rose from £150,000 to £1,000,000; Andrew Tuckey did even better – his was up from £420,000 to £1,400,000. But while they were enjoying their nights at the opera, the atmosphere in the officers' quarters was becoming rancid. Ian Hopkins and Geoff Broadhurst did not speak to each other. Ron Baker did not like Hawes, and called him Forrest Gump, after the simpleton in the eponymous movie. Norris was respected, but his intense concentration, his intelligence and his energy frightened the old bank men. He was not the sort of person you would talk to about your anxieties over a glass at the end of the day. And Norris was indeed rather contemptuous of bank veterans who had been used to starting work at about half-past nine and leaving shortly after five. Though they got in earlier now, at around nine, the traders had by then already been at their screens for an hour and a half.

Norris's allies were Broadhurst, Baker and Gamby, who shared his energy and commitment. By comparison, the older bankers – Maclean, Hopkins and Geoffrey Barnett, the chief operating officer of Baring Brothers and Co. – showed noticeably less enthusiasm and drive. Activists like Broadhurst and Gamby were acutely conscious of the differences between them. They performed heroic deeds of modern travel, touching down in New York, Hong Kong, Tokyo, and getting back, through Singapore (where they had to put up with the hostility of Simon Jones, who hated everyone from London indiscriminately) to London, in the space of a week. The old bankers, on the other hand, rarely left the office.

The merger on the two sides of Barings was fuelled by solo-consolidation. And now that the two companies were viewed as a whole, controls on the credit lines to the traders in the Far East were applied less stringently. Barings no longer had to look over its shoulder at the Bank of England supervisors, never mind report its large exposures in Osaka.

Leeson's losses were rising sharply: they almost doubled in January 1994. Because of solo-consolidation, these large sums were harder to spot on the balance sheet (because the new system was more complicated and more difficult to understand), and easier for Leeson to obtain (because there was more capital available). Solo-consolidation did not lead to heightened suspicion; rather the reverse. Tony Hawes can see it now: 'Without solo-consolidation, Leeson would have been spotted sooner, because the strain on Baring Securities' finances would have been spotted sooner. Maybe by the second quarter in 1994 the pain would have been acute,' he says. As it was, by the time the pain became acute, Leeson had lost Barings' entire capital.

8

Miracle-Worker

Tony Hawes' title at Baring Investment Bank was group treasurer. I asked him where he had trained as an accountant, but it turned out that he hadn't. Hawes had joined Barings straight from school in 1961, starting in the mail-room. When he had served his apprenticeship there, his place was taken by a member of the family who did not share Sir John Baring's belief in the virtue of tedious work, and who quit after a couple of days. So it was back to the mail-room for Tony Hawes.

However, Hawes was patient and loyal, and made his way step by step through the various grades in the treasury and trading department. As Leonard Ingrams' assistant in Saudi Arabia, Hawes helped to re-cycle oil money through Western capital markets. He spent eighteen months in Riyadh, nine of them on his own because his wife could not stand the heat, before returning home. Hawes was an obliging man.

Back in London, he rejoined treasury and trading. The treasury department was not highly regarded in the 1980s: the traders there were not much good at making money. Hawes himself appreciated what it was like to lose money as a trader. He understood the dealing-room, and shared the pleasure the good traders experienced when they made big money.

Hawes is a burly man with a mop of grey hair; his smile is tentative, his expression quizzical. He admired the Barings, and was never critical of the old guard or the bank. He could be relied on not to make a fuss, or to push for a better place in the queue, or to force an argument on reluctant colleagues. His colleagues recognised in him a good but sometimes muddled mind. For example, Hawes once drew a diagram charting financial responsibility within Barings. It took up a number of foolscap pages, and to use it he had to shuffle the pages, turning some at right-angles to others in order to make a point. The information was there, but its presentation was so complicated that hardly anyone understood it. The presentation of the solo-consolidation project similarly almost defied comprehension.

By 1990, Ian Hopkins, the finance director of Baring Brothers, had become head of treasury and trading, leapfrogging Hawes. Hawes found the situation awkward, and his boss difficult to get to know, although he tried his best. For his part, Hopkins decided that, after thirty-nine years with the firm, it was time for Hawes to take early retirement. A date was fixed. Before he left, however, Hawes was seconded to Baring Securities. Within a year, he had become the architect of solo-consolidation, and in May 1993 he became group treasurer.

There were two ways of handling the tension that arose from the merger between Baring Brothers and Baring Securities, which would create the Baring Investment Bank, BIB, later in 1994. Hawes' way was to keep his head down. Ron Baker, on the other hand, was a go-getter who fought to keep the turf he held and plunged in to colonise other trading areas that lacked a leader. Baker, the Australian, and his assistant, Mary Walz, who called herself a farm girl from Michigan but who had an MBA from the prestigious Wharton School in Philadelphia, were still viewed as outsiders – and not only within Baring Securities: the bankers at Baring Brothers also regarded them as vaguely alien figures. None the less, they both had a firm hold on the executive pole, and were climbing steadily up it.

Late in 1993, Baker's financial products group took over derivatives-trading, and this brought Nick Leeson into his orbit. Leeson had executed orders for the proprietary traders in Tokyo, and had begun to branch out on his own, spotting anomalies between the prices quoted on SIMEX and those of the Osaka stock exchange. There were a couple of reasons why these prices diverged. First, since the Osaka market was a paperless, electronic exchange, it was – like most organisations competing with computer-driven operations – sometimes slower to record price changes than the manic, manual SIMEX in Singapore. Second, Osaka and Singapore attracted different kinds of trader, whose different priorities often led to brief discrepancies appearing between the two. This was arbitrage, though it was known at Barings as the switching business. Done properly, it was perfectly legitimate, the bread and butter of derivatives-trading.

The switching business officially turned Leeson into a proprietary trader. His position was formally recognised in March 1994. The Baring Securities risk committee in London set out his position limits, telling him how much switching he was permitted in his Japanese Government Bond (or JGB) arbitrage-trading book. In June, these position limits were extended: he was allowed to take unhedged positions of up to 200 Nikkei 225 futures contracts, 100 JGB futures, and 500 Euroyen futures. There seemed nothing dramatic about this at the time: these unhedged positions were allowed to be maintained only during the day; none could be carried overnight. Trading options was not mentioned. There was no fuss; no one outside Barings was told about it. But giving Leeson recognition as a proprietary trader for Barings was significant, because it lent authenticity to the profits he was declaring. Barings in London thought it knew where those profits were coming from.

What Barings was permitting Leeson to do, and what he was actually doing on the floor of SIMEX, were, of course, two quite different matters. In January 1994, before he was authorised to trade 200 Nikkei 225 contracts, Leeson booked no fewer than 50,000 futures and options in the Nikkei 225 through his 88888 account. The losses on his covert dealings already amounted to more than £50 million. Most, though not all, of this was because of his incompetent trading. Another reason why Leeson's losses were as large as they were was that he raided his 88888 account so that he could remit profits to Barings in London and Tokyo.

In the first six months of 1994, Baring Futures (Singapore) swelled the profits of Baring Securities in London by £6.7 million, and those of Baring Securities in Japan by £5.8 million. Good managers in the securities business ought to be as suspicious of startling profits as they are of heavy losses. Leeson's £12.5 million should have qualified him for a sceptical audit.

Although Ron Baker had met Leeson in Tokyo late in 1993, he did not visit Singapore until the spring of 1994, when he was accompanied by Ash Lewis, who ran Baring Brothers' internal-audit department. She had audited Baker's own department, and he admired her work. He hoped she would do the internal audit that was planned for Baring Futures in Singapore, and during his trip he identified the areas that needed investigation. After the crash, he told Bank of England investigators:

> I spent a day with [Leeson] in the SIMEX pit, and I spent another day discussing the business . . . It was clear to me from the minute I walked into the SIMEX pit that it was going to be very hard for anyone, let alone me, to make much of a value judgement about what was happening . . . or what the flow of information was. You are reliant on the people who are in it and doing it.
>
> It also seemed to me, talking the thing through . . . with Ash Lewis, that the key thing to do was to get the control part of it sorted out. If you had that sorted out, and if you had proper cash-flow reconciliation and proper dissection of responsibilities, the thing was pretty simple.

But on their return to London, Ron Baker discovered that the Singapore Futures audit had already been allocated to James Baker, one of the team going to Singapore from Baring Securities, rather than to Ash Lewis's department in Baring Brothers. It was office politics again. When James Baker had learned that Ash Lewis had been appointed to head up a combined Baring Investment Bank audit department, he had declared that he would not work under her, and left the department shortly afterwards. The internal audit began badly. It would not be carried out by the senior auditor in the firm, but it would be the last to be done by James Baker. The audit was originally scheduled to start early in 1994. Predictably, Simon Jones successfully delayed it: he sought to delay inquiries by London as a matter of practice. A crisis in the New York office created even more delays. But these hold-ups should have given James Baker plenty of time to acquaint himself with the problem.

Before he arrived in Singapore, Baker was briefed by Tony Hawes, who not only harboured doubts about Leeson, but appreciated how difficult it might prove to expose him. Baker wrote: 'If something was amiss in Singapore (e.g. fraud, error, backlog) Tony is not confident that any of the senior clerks would speak up.' On Leeson's twin role in trading and settlements: '[Hawes] believes that [Simon Jones] basically leaves [Nick Leeson] to his own devices. While he has no evidence to suggest that Nick Leeson has indeed abused his position, the potential for doing so needs examining.'

Hawes' particular concern, however, was the amount of cash being sent to Singapore at short notice. Baker noted: 'One specific concern in the futures area is the level of margin calls paid by BSL London without knowing precisely on whose behalf the cash is being paid.' A second warning came from Sajeed Sacranie, Peter Norris's assistant, who thought that, by mixing agency and proprietary trading, Leeson was probably breaking SIMEX rules. That went on the agenda too. All the right questions were drafted. Proper answers to them would have exposed Leeson. So what happened?

James Baker spent two weeks in Singapore in July and August 1994. After the collapse, his internal-audit report was leaked in Singapore, and it perfectly reflects the permissive style of management that was cultivated at Barings bank: business first, control second.

Baker's report began in the way it should have done. Disclosing that Leeson's proprietary trading had made profits of $30 million in the first seven months of 1994, he wrote: 'One focus of our audit was to seek answers to some questions raised by such exceptional results.' He noted that the profits arose from Barings' sizeable client base, and its ability to conduct arbitrage between Singapore and Osaka. But he declared Leeson innocent of any breach of SIMEX rules in mixing the two. Baker was more concerned about two threats to the continued flow of profits. The first of these was a decline in market volumes and volatility. The second was personal: 'The loss [to the company] of Baring Futures (Singapore)'s general manager' – Nick Leeson.

Baker had become an admirer of Leeson's. He wrote: 'Without him BF(S) would lack a trader with the right combination of experience of trading sizeable lots, and a detailed appreciation of the trading strategies, familiarity with the local traders' limits and practices, and contacts among traders and officials.' Baker was more critical of what he considered Leeson's control of both front and back offices: this was 'an excessive concentration of power,' he said. But the report then noted that the back office had functioned efficiently under the arrangement: 'The general manager likes to be involved in the back office, and does not regard it as an undue burden.' (On my copy of Baker's report, this rates two exclamation marks in the margin.) Baker was also insouciant about the issue that had worried Tony Hawes: the fact that Leeson was in charge of reconciling the accounts with the margin funds sent from London. 'Transactions between these offices and BF(S) are subject to reconciliation controls,' he wrote.

Nevertheless, James Baker recommended that Leeson should not continue reviewing SIMEX deposit, variation and collateral reconciliations. In particular, he should no longer be solely responsible for supervising the back office. Yet Baker recommended that Leeson should remain involved in two areas: he should 'be available to assist with reconciliation problems'; and he would 'of course' continue to arrange funding in conjunction with group treasury. This meant Leeson, in fact, retained the back-office powers that were important to him.

Baker recommended a comprehensive review of Leeson's funding requirements. He also paid attention to Leeson's position limits, noting that, while his futures trading was under control, he was permitted to do as much arbitrage business as he chose. '[These positions] can carry considerable funding costs, and eventually must be unwound with an element of market risk.'

Baker did not foresee any serious crisis, because he believed that Hawes in London would call a halt if the cost escalated dangerously. But he did propose that the risk committees should consider introducing position limits on Leeson's arbitrage trading. In fact, he went further: Baker thought that Leeson's Singapore operation should come under the scrutiny of a risk-and-compliance officer who was not a member of the trading team, and who reported to a different departmental head.

But the principal recommendation of James Baker's report concerned Leeson himself. As we have seen, his stated object had been to probe Leeson's exceptional profits. His conclusion was merely that the reason for these profits was Leeson's exceptional ability. In the executive summary of his report, Baker stated that retaining the level of profits depended on retaining Leeson for 'as long as possible'. His conclusion was: 'Although there is some strength in depth in the trading team, the loss of [Leeson's] services to a competitor would spread the erosion of BF(S)'s profitability greatly.' Leeson couldn't have got a better review if he had written it himself.

If the report caused pleasure and relief in Singapore, there was no hint of it. After a few weeks of silence, Leeson and Simon Jones, the chief operations officer in Singapore, said that the recommendation about separating trading and settlements would be implemented immediately, and Jones added his personal assurance that settlements were adequately supervised. But, in fact, Jones did nothing to end Leeson's control of the back office. He rejected the idea of employing a full-time risk-and-compliance officer. Instead, he appointed one of his subordinates to do the job part-time.

James Baker was wrong in assuming that reconciliation controls were a routine part of the settlements process. Barings' executives in London must have shared this assumption, because none of those who read this in his report drew attention to it.

Tony Hawes agreed that there should be a comprehensive review of funding requirements. He said it would be done 'over the coming year'. By the time of the collapse, it had not been done.

Ian Hopkins said the suggestion that Leeson be given position limits for his arbitrage trades was on the risk committee's agenda, and a final decision would be taken shortly. There is no record of any such decision having been taken.

All Barings' senior managers in London appreciated that there was some kind of problem in Singapore, but none of them thought it was Leeson. And the main obstacle to their taking a hard look at the operation was the legendary figure of Simon Jones. In September 1993, Neil Andrews, then head of settlements in London, had had some tough questions to ask about controls in Leeson's area, but he had been sent away with a flea in his ear. No one from London relished a trip to Singapore. Before James Baker did his audit there, he was warned by Geoff Broadhurst that Jones was 'a very parochial individual'. Broadhurst slipped into Singapore for a couple of days while Baker was doing the audit at Baring Futures; he knew that Jones had a habit of giving auditors short shrift, and wanted to try to prevent it from happening again. Broadhurst had been nagging Norris about Jones for some months. When an adequate replacement could be found, he wanted Jones sacked. Baker himself was under no illusions about Jones: he admitted to the Singapore inspectors that he doubted whether Jones would implement his recommendations.

Jones got away with his obstinacy because he was protected by James Bax, the head of Baring Securities' Singapore office. Bax was well regarded in the firm, but, like Jones, he was stubbornly protective of his patch. Bax listened to London, but he sprang instinctively to Jones's defence. The Singapore inspectors' report gives a flavour of the competitive relationship between London and Singapore in a brisk footnote. 'Mr

Broadhurst stated [that] ... he convinced Mr Bax that Mr Jones should be replaced. Mr Broadhurst claimed that Mr Bax requested that Mr Broadhurst should liaise directly with Mr Bax until Mr Jones was dismissed. Mr Bax did not accept that he had agreed to dismiss Mr Jones. According to him Mr Jones's fate depended on his performance.'

Simon Jones had problems of his own. He was going through difficult divorce proceedings, and was reluctant to travel in case his estranged wife used his absence to show that he was unfit to look after their children. His weekly visiting rights on Wednesday afternoons made that a bad day for him. Because Leeson's profits seemed so dazzling, Leeson was becoming less vulnerable to criticism, and, sensing this, Jones became his advocate. Tony Gamby, the global settlements director in London, thought Jones did not fully understand the complexities of futures-trading, and relied on Leeson to explain it to him. 'He could have understood it if he'd wanted to, but he had no desire to. If Nick had said black was white, Jones would have believed him,' Gamby said later. Anyone who was going to take on Leeson would also have to take on Jones. That made it a forbidding prospect.

It was hard enough to unravel the acceptable side of Leeson's operation. To find out what he was really up to required a much tougher attitude than James Baker brought to his audit. To his credit, he had not ignored the message of Tony Hawes briefing: he had tried to identify precisely which accounts in Singapore were calling for money to be sent from London. Baker saw that the way to do this was to match margin calls made on London with individual accounts in Singapore – the process known as reconciliation. Though it is time-consuming, reconciliation is not difficult.

In the first draft of his report, Baker admitted that doing a daily reconciliation would be intolerably onerous. He said he would be happy with weekly reconciliation, but he wanted it begun 'as soon as possible'.

Reconciliation, Baker declared, would be useful in more ways than one. As well as finding out where the margin money was going, it would enable all trades in Singapore to be checked to make sure they were genuine. 'At present it is theoretically possible for fictitious house trades to be booked to BFS's system, and extra margin called,' he wrote, with unwitting accuracy. Interviewed by the Bank of England's investigators later, he explained: 'I thought that reconciliation would primarily stop any danger of margin being diverted by Singapore.'

But Baker's recommendation that Leeson's trades be subjected to reconciliation every week did not appear in any further drafts of the internal-audit report. Leeson argued Baker out of it. The Board of Banking Supervision appreciated the significance of the conversations between the two of them, and reported Baker's account of them in full.

> I raised the point [about reconciliation], say, about halfway through the audit with Nick Leeson, and discussed its merits. He was very much against completing the control, and implementing that point. He was of the view that the control was unnecessary, and that it would involve too much work, and would be unduly burdensome.
>
> I did not back down immediately, but I did back down after a couple of days. Geoff Broadhurst joined the audit for a day or so . . . and he joined me in my argument against Nick Leeson, essentially supporting the need for this control, whereas Nick Leeson was saying it would be too much work and we do not really need it.
>
> I think I suggested it did not have to be daily, that it could be done on a monthly basis, and even a control that takes a clerk two days to produce would not be unduly burdensome if it was completed just once a month. But still he argued against the point.
>
> I can only say that I took the point out of the report because I could not out-argue Nick on this point . . . Eventually I was out-argued, and I believe Geoff Broadhurst, who was joining the fray, if you like, concurred with me that we should take it out of the report . . . That was one point where Nick Leeson did argue his own corner pretty strongly . . . It never got to the stage of involving Simon Jones, because it had been removed towards the end of the two weeks when we brought Simon Jones in.

Broadhurst told the Bank of England that he recalled a brief discussion about reconciliation, and believed it had ended with Singapore meeting Baker halfway. 'I left Singapore on the understanding that there had been a compromise on the timing, but not in the substance of reconciliation itself,' he said. Broadhurst thought it was to happen on either a weekly or a monthly basis – he could not recall which – and he denies ever having 'concurred' with Baker's decision to omit reconciliation. 'I do not accept that I was out-argued by Nick Leeson,' he says emphatically. But, when he saw James Baker's finished report, Broadhurst, like Hawes, failed to query the omission of any reference to reconciliation in Singapore.

Broadhurst is an energetic, combative South African account-ant, intent on securing a good position for himself in his adopted country. He joined Baring Brothers in 1986, and by 1992 had become one of the first people from the bank to join the traders at Baring Securities. To him, the move seemed like a good one because it got him away from Ian Hopkins. Like Hawes, Broadhurst found Hopkins hard to get to know; he preferred working for Peter Norris. Under the Norris regime, Broadhurst was identified as one of the young Turks, working long hours in London and travelling abroad extensively. (Accumulating tens of thousands of air miles is one way in which young bankers demonstrate their manhood.) One of the rare criticisms made of Broadhurst in his annual staff assess-ment was that he travelled too much.

In Singapore, Broadhurst fell out with Simon Jones, and later, when Jones and Bax were grilled by the Singapore inspectors, both took the opportunity to protect their position at Broad-hurst's expense. Bax reported a conversation in which Broad-hurst had assured him that Baring Futures in Singapore had 'watertight' controls. 'This may have contributed to the decision to omit what was presented by Mr Leeson as a cumber-some and unnecessary reconciliation,' says a footnote to the inspectors' report, presumably quoting Bax.

Broadhurst's recollection of the conversation differs from Bax's. Having spent only seven days in Singapore, he lacked the experience, he says, to make a judgement about Baring Futures' controls.

Simon Jones told the inspectors that Broadhurst was keen to play down the section of the audit report that dwelled on Leeson's dual role in trading and settlements. 'Mr Jones suggested Mr Broadhurst was anxious not to upset Mr Leeson,' the inspectors reported. Broadhurst's reply to this is emphatic: 'Total bullshit. What else can I say?'

Barings' responses to James Baker's internal audit are those of a management that seemed to be wading through treacle. There was no consensus, even about non-controversial ideas, and there was a staggering lack of urgency in the execution of their actions. Tony Hawes had identified the problem of unreconciled trades in Singapore: he knew that there were tens of millions of pounds – the sum involved fluctuated as the months went by – that were not properly accounted for. But though the audit report provided no answers, Hawes took comfort from it. 'We thought there couldn't have been anything too wrong, or they'd have spotted it.' Looking back, Hawes remarked: 'There was no excuse for not making reconciliation the highest priority. But there always seemed to be something else more pressing.'

So the problem was not a failure to identify the problem: Hawes had been particularly good at that. It was the failure to act. They had a precedent from which to learn: in April 1994, a Wall Street trader named Joseph Jett, who had declared a wholly false profit of $350 million, was exposed by his employer, Kidder Peabody. Barings' reaction was to order an immediate review of its own risk controls, and the conclusion it reached was that the controls left something to be desired. The board was told that a system was required that would enable Barings' management in London to know what was happening everywhere else in the world. 'Such a system is in the process of being developed,' the board was told.

Gamby was anxious to develop a new set of risk-management controls. The primitive system operated by his

BARING FUTURES (SINGAPORE) PTE LIMITED

3 BACK OFFICE CONTROLS

3.1 Concentration of Responsibilities in the role of General Manager

Despite the significant turnover of BF(S) it is a relatively small company with straightforward systems. Perhaps as a consequence of this both the front and back office operations are managed and controlled by the General Manager, Nick Leeson.

This represents an excessive concentration of powers; companies commonly divide responsibility for initiating, settling and recording transactions among different areas to reduce the possibility of error and fraud.

The back office has functioned efficiently under the current arrangements. The General Manager likes to be involved in the back office and does not regard it as an undue burden. There are also mitigating factors which serve to reduce the concentration of power in the General Manager's role:

- With a single exception, BF(S) do not settle with clients directly but with other Baring Securities offices, primarily London. Transactions between these offices and BF(S) are subject to reconciliation controls.

- BF(S)'s management and statutory accounts are produced by the accounts department of Baring Securities (Singapore) who receive a monthly trial balance from BF(S).

- BF(S)'s systems and records are subject to detailed regulatory audits.

In normal circumstances it would not be desirable for one individual to combine the roles of dealing and trading manager with those of settlements and accounting manager. Given the lack of experienced and senior staff in the back office, we recognise that the General Manager must continue to take an active role in the detailed operations of both the front and the back office.

Recommendation

BF(S)'s back office should be reorganised so that the General Manager is no longer directly responsible for the back office. Specifically the General Manager should not:

Retain sole responsibility for the supervision of BF(S)'s back office team;
Retain cheque-signing or journal-passing powers;
Review and sign off SIMEX deposit, variation margin and collateral reconciliations; and
Review and sign off bank reconciliations.

Management Response; Nick Leeson, Simon Jones

As agreed with Internal Audit these are not normal circumstances for BF(S) considering the current absence of third party customers. Should these emerge, the role of the General Manager will obviously change. However, with immediate effect the General Manager will cease to perform the functions itemised. Bank reconciliations will be transferred to the combined BF(S), BS(S) and BIF accounts department. A Financial Manager will sign off all journals, new account openings, and perform the reviews recommended. The Director of Finance (BS(S) / BS(F)) will ensure the adequate supervision of all settlement and recording processes.

Dual responsibility: James Baker attacks Leeson's back office function settlements department in London relied on reports from Barings' own traders about prices and the volume of their business. As a prudent settlements man, Gamby had no wish to rely on intermediaries for information: when the facts do not suit them, traders can be tempted to be economical with the truth. Gamby wanted to acquire an advanced system of information technology that would give him direct access to market information all over the world.

Nothing more was heard of this plan until January 1995. During 1994, some risk-controllers were appointed, in London, Tokyo and Hong Kong. But Jones said it wasn't necessary, and Fortress Singapore remained inviolate.

While Leeson's bosses were mesmerised by his profits, his fellow traders were intrigued by his strategy. They wanted to know more about the mechanics of it. Most curious of all were the Barings traders in Tokyo who were operating in the same market.

The Tokyo traders never ceased to be startled by the strides Leeson had made in a mere two years, and by the profits he had made. 'At the time I was surprised to learn he even knew what an option delta was,' says Fernando Gueler, by then head of proprietary derivatives-trading in Tokyo. But when the general manager of SIMEX, Ang Swee Tian, visited Tokyo, he sought out the top brass to tell him how enthusiastic they were at SIMEX about Nick Leeson. They hoped, the SIMEX man said, that Barings would encourage Leeson to do even more business on their exchange. The Tokyo office finally decided that Leeson was a very good broker-salesman, though they often entertained a nagging suspicion that things were happening in Singapore which they were not meant to understand.

Something odd, for instance, happened in the autumn of 1994. One night a Tokyo trader noticed a discrepancy in the trading volume on the SIMEX Japanese Government Bond market. He knew that Leeson had been active in the market that day, but the screen did not reflect that level of business. It showed only a small volume. Talking into the squawk box, the Tokyo man pointed this out. Leeson told him that he had done some cross-trades after the market closed, which had not yet been recorded. About twenty minutes later, a new figure for the volume of JGB trading that day, which was more consistent with what Tokyo knew, popped up on the screen.

The Tokyo trader mentioned this discrepancy to Mary Walz in London. He could not understand why the SIMEX officials were not complaining, since these trades seemed to bend the rules. In London and Tokyo, it was assumed that the officials must be turning a blind eye to them: they had a motive for doing so, because SIMEX benefited from heavy trading volumes that made its market look more active than that of its competitors in Osaka.

But SIMEX officials would have been accustomed to the sight of Leeson on the trading-floor after the close of business on the exchange. His appearance in the SIMEX pit a few minutes after the official close of business had become almost a ritual. Just as Leeson masked his secret 88888 account by calling it an error account, so he fabricated some of his phoney profits by cross-trading.

Normally, cross-trading is a technical activity intended to transfer through the exchange buy-and-sell orders between two clients belonging to the same firm. It is permitted as a convenience, and neither buyer nor seller profits. What Leeson did was to cross trades between the 88888 account and various Barings accounts in London and Tokyo at higher prices than those he had paid on the exchange. By pretending that he had sold contracts for more than the actual sale price, he could declare the artificial difference as profit to Barings. But a profit on one side of the transaction created a loss on the other. These losses were always put into the 88888 account.

He could not have got away with this deception without the collaboration of senior clerks in the Singapore office – the same people Hawes had said he did not think would speak up if something was amiss. Although they chose not to emphasise it, the evidence of collaboration is to be found in the Singapore inspectors' report. This describes how Leeson in Singapore prevented Baring Securities in Tokyo or London from finding out the real purpose of all those cross-trades after the market had closed.

Leeson ordered two price lists to be drawn up. One showed the prices of his trades on SIMEX – let's call it the A list; the other showed the altered prices he used to bolster Barings' profit – the B list. Should Barings in Tokyo ask for a copy of Singapore's transactions that day, they were to be shown the B list. The inspectors' report explains: 'The line traders prepared a revised list showing the adjusted prices and faxed the erroneous list to Baring Securities (Japan). After this had been done, they re-wrote the daily list of transactions to show the original details applicable to the trades.' This was the A list. Once it was completed, the booth staff on the trading-floor keyed the A list into the SIMEX computer system. It is inconceivable that the line traders or the booth staff could have regarded this as normal practice, but no one breathed a word about it, either to Simon Jones or to SIMEX.

By means of this deception, Leeson had remitted 'profits' of £8 million to Tokyo in 1993. And the biggest part of this gratifying sum came in the last three months of the year, the months in which it was becoming clear to the traders in Tokyo that Leeson was a pretty good trader, quite capable of undertaking proprietary trading on his own in Singapore. This was also the period when Ron Baker, who had taken responsibility for proprietary trading in the autumn of 1993, was visiting Tokyo regularly to find out how it worked. Baker was surprised to find out about the arbitrage, or switching, business between Osaka and Singapore. No one had told him about it. But since it was so profitable, he was happy to contribute to Leeson's costs from his budget.

When the bonuses for 1993 were being discussed in January. 1994, Ron Baker spoke out strongly in favour of a generous bonus for Leeson. He was awarded £130,000, compared with £35,746 in 1992. The decision to give Leeson his own position limits in March 1994 seemed unremarkable, in the circumstances. 'At that point in time,' Ron Baker said later, 'I never thought much about why it was so profitable. I can only guess as to what might have been going on during 1994, but I do not think in retrospect Nick took much notice or cared much about what I said . . . I thought Nick was a lone star and did his own thing.'

What Baker liked was the way Leeson 'worked the information curve' (though he cannot have known just how Leeson exploited it). When he received a large client order from Killian in Tokyo for execution on SIMEX, he would immediately buy a similar number of contracts on the Osaka exchange. If the price rose, he would sell at a profit – to Barings. If the price did not rise, he would fill the client's order in Singapore, and cancel the deal in Osaka.

When a trader on a futures exchange buys for his own account before filling a client's order, it is known as front-running. It is against the rules. James Baker's audit report had concluded that Leeson was not breaking SIMEX rules, and had argued that, because his order was placed on a different exchange, it was arbitrage. But there cannot be any argument about it: Leeson was front-running.

Dodges like 'working the information curve' convinced Ron Baker and other managers in London that Singapore was a special case. In Tokyo, Fernando Gueler was not so sanguine. As he watched Leeson's profits rising, he became concerned about his own role. In July 1994, Gueler told Mary Walz how stupid it seemed that Leeson's reported positions should merely be monitored by him over the telephone. He felt he did not have enough information to do the job properly.

Before the summer, Leeson's arbitrage trading profits had been lumped together with Baring Securities' profit and loss on trading activities in Japan or Hong Kong. At that time, it was hard to know how much he was making, or which profit was coming from Tokyo's proprietary trading in Osaka and which from options-trading in Hong Kong. But in midsummer Leeson was given a separate trading-book for his Nikkei arbitrage. From then on, it was possible for Barings to calculate exactly how much profit Leeson himself was making.

*   *   *

He was cocky now; in the midsummer of 1994, he changed his computer password to Superman. The market-makers at FCT and SLK had admitted him to their 'club', introducing him to high-powered visitors from the US, and the impression he made on them was not encouraging ('He was the most ordinary soul,' says an executive of the Chicago exchange who met Leeson that summer). But in Singapore judgements were different: Leeson was a star. And he was beginning to behave as if there was nothing he could not get away with. He had been banned from the Singapore Cricket Club for a year in 1993, for hitting a fellow member who had questioned his right to use the snooker table. He was in fact emulating the trader referred to in Mark Elardo's training manual, quoted in Chapter 3, which he could not have read: 'Make up a pretend ego, a giant one at that, and throw it around indiscriminately.'

This arrogance could have put an end to his brilliant career in Singapore before the final denouement. Leeson was a regular customer at the bars on Boat Quay, a terrace bordering the Singapore River where it swells out just before entering the sea. Boat Quay evokes a distant memory of colonial times, when ships bringing rubber from Malaya and spices from Sumatra unloaded their cargo at the go-downs, or warehouses, along the quayside. In a city that does not show much respect for its architectural heritage, Boat Quay was likely to survive only by radically altering its function. Now it is a booming tourist attraction where bars and restaurants, with tables and umbrellas, line the quay. It is ersatz, but there is a buzz about the place, and it is conveniently situated for the financial district.

After work, Leeson would drink beer in Harry's Bar (the only thing this has in common with its Venetian namesake is a waterfront location), and the Off Quay pub. This is a narrow bar with windows down the side, which gives out on to tall tables at which people stand and drink in the open air. At the Off Quay pub one night in June, he and a friend did something so daft that it was reported in the *Straits Times*, Singapore's English-speaking newspaper. The report read:

A twenty-one-year-old woman who had been in the pub with a few friends earlier on told police that she saw Leeson, a married man, staring at her through the pub's glass doors while she was standing outside. When she ignored him, the pair pulled down their trousers and exposed their buttocks to her.

The woman, whose identity was withheld, called the police and both men were detained. On 23 August, they pleaded guilty in court and were each fined S$200. The fine was paid.

Mooning like this might just pass at, say, a Watford football match, but the Singapore police do not tolerate laddish behaviour. Leeson and his friend, who both spent a night in jail, got off very lightly, especially as the Singaporean authorities were acutely conscious of misdemeanours at the time. An American schoolboy named Michael Fay (no relation of the author) had been convicted of vandalism and punished with four lashes of the cane. This created an international uproar, but the Singaporean government, in its faintly warped way, seems to draw strength from such reactions. Leeson's offence could have been prosecuted under the same Vandalism Act, which makes it an offence to outrage a woman's modesty.

That he did not make a dash for the airport or suffer the same fate as Fay may well have been because Bax made sure he had a good lawyer, and possibly because Ang Swee Tian, SIMEX's general manager, who had spoken so well of Leeson in Tokyo, intervened on his behalf. He was certainly understood to have done so by Tony Hawes and other Barings managers. Leeson was already too valuable to the exchange to be allowed to become the victim of police or immigration officials.

Barings in London knew all about the incident, and put it down to a heady mixture of booze and the expatriate life. But they had to work hard to persuade the *International Financial Review* to drop a gossip item about Leeson's conviction. Barings had a double interest: protecting both their good name and their single most profitable trader. Only later did anyone make a judgement about Leeson's own lack of judgement.

While he seemed talkative and hail-fellow-well-met, Leeson was not easy to know. The Tokyo traders spoke to him each morning on the squawk box that linked Tokyo and Singapore, to clear the lines for the day's trading between Tokyo, Osaka and Singapore. Since Leeson was scrupulous about entertaining visiting Barings' traders after work when they were in Singapore, several of them had spent some time with him. Leeson, the protégé, gravitated naturally towards his patron, Mike Killian, when he visited Tokyo, but he and the Tokyo traders had talked after hours too. Nevertheless Leeson remained a mystery to them. 'We were the air force and he was the marines,' says Gueler.

In October, Leeson's profits were so good that Gueler decided there was no way he could be abiding by the exchange's rules. There was not much activity in the Nikkei 225 index, so volatility was down, and that would normally depress profits. But Leeson's profits were up. It made no sense to Gueler. He suspected Leeson was front-running as a matter of course. Once more he complained to Mary Walz, warning her that Barings ought to be careful.

'Mary took it as a compliance issue,' says Gueler. Yet she did alert Ron Baker, who reassured Gueler that James Baker's audit report had concluded that Leeson was not obtaining an unfair advantage. Once Gueler, who admired Ron Baker, learned that the auditors had crawled over the Singapore office for a couple of weeks, he decided there was not much more he could do or say. But this exchange illustrates well the conditions that complicate this story. The Board of Banking Supervision reported the episode as follows: 'Gueler told us that Ron Baker then called him and said: "Look, Fernando, we hear what you say. Everything is OK in Singapore." We asked Ron Baker if Walz or Gueler expressed concern about Leeson's profitability. His response was: "No one ever expressed it to me as a problem."' Gueler, as we have seen, says he had done exactly that.

Ron Baker was on a high. During the annual round of budget proposals for the coming year, most departments submitted pages of detailed forecasts for income and expenditure. A participant in one of the budget meetings in the autumn of 1994 remembers Baker's submission for the financial products group: it was faxed from abroad on a single sheet of paper. Baker simply listed the income projections for each of the four sections in the group. The total came to a profit forecast of £100 million for 1995. With a figure like that, his colleagues were disinclined to question Baker's methods.

Baker's adversary, Tony Hawes, kept on nagging. Early in October he visited Singapore intending to talk to Leeson personally about the margin requirements for his futures business. But as Hawes arrived in Singapore, Leeson did a last-minute bunk to London. Instead, Hawes met one of the settlements assistants, Norhaslinda Hassan, more simply known as Linda, and was appalled by her ignorance of futures and options. There was, for instance, a single entry of $100 million in the books that she was incapable of explaining. Hawes caught up with Leeson in London soon afterwards, but, lacking the office records, was unable to pin him down. Whatever explanation Leeson gave for the $100 million, it was accepted. Once more, Hawes' attempts to get to the bottom of the situation had had no effect.

The suspicions of Gueler and Hawes were entirely justified, but there was no evidence to support them. Leeson was taking unhedged, and therefore highly risky, positions in Nikkei 225 futures, positions that mocked the limits he had been given. In September 1994, his trading alone amounted to 7.2 per cent of all SIMEX's volume in the Nikkei, and was the main reason Barings received SIMEX's award for Trader of the Year. Mike Killian flew in from Tokyo to watch James Bax receive the award on Barings' behalf at SIMEX's tenth-anniversary banquet. No one there was inclined to listen to criticism of their record-busting young trader.

On the SIMEX floor, most of Leeson's trades were originally booked to Baring Securities, either in London or Tokyo. That gave them the appearance of legitimacy. But they could not possibly stay on those books. To avoid detection, Leeson ordered two of his floor traders to execute large orders thirty seconds before the close of the two daily trading sessions, at

2.15 p.m. and 7.10 p.m. Large positions were then transferred out of Baring Securities' accounts to the safe anonymity of the 88888 account. As with his after-hours cross-trading, Leeson would then adjust the prices of these trades to make the profits look even better. And when the profits were still not big enough, he would simply manufacture off-market cross-trades between the 88888 account and authentic Baring Securities accounts. The fact that off-market cross-trades are against the rules did not deter him at all.

But the real mystery was his options-trading. This was the key to Leeson's reputation inside Barings. In Tokyo the American traders called Leeson 'the Michael Jordan of trading' in a flattering comparison with the splendid basketball player. Gueler recalls: 'He was regarded almost as a miracle-worker.' Since his colleagues in London and Tokyo believed that Leeson abided by the rules, they assumed that when he was trading options he must be doing so on behalf of a client, or clients. He had never been permitted by Barings to sell or to trade options for the bank. It is, as we saw in Chapter 4, a complex business, best left to the experts in Tokyo, where Su Khoo had established Barings' reputation as a hothouse for options-trading in the early 1980s.

Leeson, who never obeyed rules, had sold an unprecedented – almost miraculous – volume of options. As the scale of his losses in Nikkei futures grew through the summer of 1994, Leeson had a prodigious debit in his profit-and-loss account, which had to be reduced before it attracted attention – from the auditors, for example, who began work each October. So Leeson wrote an astonishing number of options. The object was not to raise cash, but to have entries on the profit side of his ledger that would offset the losses in the 88888 account. Another advantage of options was that he could balance his book without calling for more funds from London to meet SIMEX's margin calls. The premium from the options he sold went straight to the exchange to meet its margin requirements. The disadvantage of selling so many options was that if Leeson ended up 'out of money', the potential losses might be counted in hundreds of millions of pounds.

As an options-trader, Leeson actually seemed to have a strategy. It was based on the assumption that the price of the underlying contract – in this case, Nikkei 225 futures – would not vary greatly in the coming months: in other words, that its volatility would be low. Just to recap: volatility is a major influence on the price of options. When volatility is high, there is a greater chance that the option will be exercised. Consequently, the price of the option will be high, measured at, say, 40 per cent of the price of the underlying contract. As volatility falls, so does the price of the option – to as low as, say, 10 per cent.

The technical term for what Leeson did is selling short-straddle futures. This doubled up the bet, because the buyer purchased the right to exercise the option to buy (call) or to sell (put) when the option expired. If volatility was low, as he assumed, the option would remain 'out of the money', and the buyers would not exercise their option. Leeson would then keep the option premium. On the other hand, if the market became volatile in either direction, up or down, his losses could be unlimited.

To grasp what happened next, it helps to remember Roger Geissler's guide to the jargon of options-trading (see Chapter 4). As a seller of short straddles, Leeson took the view that the Nikkei 225 would become less volatile. To the professional traders, he was 'short-volatility'. The traders who bought those short straddles were 'long-volatility'. For a variety of reasons that autumn, the professional traders working for firms like Goldman Sachs and Crédit Suisse First Boston were 'long-volatility'. Leeson sold so many short straddles, however, that, single-handed, he reduced volatility in the Nikkei 225. Even at Barings in Tokyo, the traders, watching in fascination, did not know exactly how many options Leeson had sold. They knew it was a substantial number, but, had they known the exact figure, they would have been flabbergasted. In September, he sold 13,700 options; the peak came in November with 22,000, and in December he sold 12,400. That put the professional traders on the wrong side of the market, and they began to get a bit nervous. If volatility went on falling, they were in danger of losing pots of money. This made them even more anxious to know who it was who was apparently selling such large quantities of options through Leeson.

Because Leeson did not – as far as Gueler knew – deal in options for Barings, Gueler believed that he must be executing trades on behalf of one of Barings' confidential clients whose identity was a secret to all but a handful of senior directors. But this client was trading on a scale unheard of. Gueler began to think of him as 'Client X'.

Leeson provided Barings with an identity for the mysterious client. He was called 'Philippe', and he was a real person: his full name was Philippe Bonnefoy, and he worked for a trading company called European Bank and Trust Ltd. He had had a perfectly respectable introduction to Barings through Ron Baker's representative in New York, Heather Nicol. The real existence of Philippe as a confidential client lent an air of legitimacy to Leeson's dealings.

Even so, Gueler could not believe that Philippe was a big enough client to be acting alone on such a scale. He decided that Philippe must be acting on behalf of the biggest traders in the business: the hedge funds in New York run by people like George Soros. Gueler speculated that two or three hedge funds might be acting together to squeeze the professional volatility traders, who were consequently being forced to buy more contracts to hedge their positions. If that was the right answer, Leeson was merely a conduit for a market manoeuvre that seemed, quite frankly, to be working brilliantly.

The strategy was so admired because of the relentless way Leeson went on selling options. Even his own colleagues did not believe he could continue to depress volatility in Nikkei 225 futures. At Barings in Osaka, one trader went long-volatility, taking the contrary position to Leeson's. But Leeson went on selling short straddles; volatility continued to fall; and when Barings' Osaka trader finally cut his losses, he had cost the firm $2 million. Only Leeson knew the real reason for this embarrassing loss by Barings in the derivatives market, but it caused him no remorse. Shortly afterwards, he and Lisa turned up as guests at the trader's wedding.

Philippe's existence reassured Gueler, as it did Baker, Norris and Mary Walz. 'We were not talking about him every day. He faded in and out of relevance,' she says. Ron Baker knew about Philippe, too; and Walz mentioned his name to Peter Norris when he asked questions about Leeson's positions in December 1994. Walz remembers Leeson telling her, around Christmas, that Philippe was going to sell more volatility.

But the truth was that the real Philippe's last trade with Barings had been on 27 June 1994, before Leeson began his options-selling spree. The only person selling volatility in December was Nick Leeson himself. The only person who could have explained the strategy was Nick Leeson, and he did not do so until after his arrest, when he was interviewed by David Frost. He gave his explanation, and it was then edited out of the interview. But this is what he said:

> At the time when I started selling [those] options, in September or maybe October, one of the fundamental ways of pricing an option is the volatility, and at that time volatility was maybe 40, 45 per cent. Because I'd be going through the process where I'd been selling options every month – it's just a supply-and-demand thing – I had to keep continually selling options to bring my account back to zero. So the volatility of options had also decreased drastically through to the end of '94, from 45 per cent to 10 per cent. So now you were having to sell more options to obtain the same amount of premium; while the volatility was high, I'd only had to sell a small amount. While the volatility was low, I'm having to sell thousands to receive the same amount of premium, and therefore I was increasing my risk more drastically.

Leeson makes his 'strategy' clear. He was not involved in a relentless attack on the market professionals at prestigious firms like Goldman Sachs. The real reason he was selling options was so that he could make a book-keeping entry that would balance his secret account. Because the scale of his purchases kept driving down the options premium, he had to sell more and more to bring in the same money. His strategy was difficult to fathom, because it wasn't a strategy that any professional dealer would contemplate.

Although these options did not expire until March 1995 and beyond, Leeson's 'anti-strategy' had been, in a way, remarkably successful. Had he sold off his option position on 31 December 1994, Leeson would actually have made a real profit of $114 million. This would have reduced his accumulated loss, but not by enough to make it any easier to live with. Depending on which figure you take, this deficit was by then either £163 million (Singapore inspectors), or £208 million (Board of Banking Supervision).

Though Tony Hawes' suspicions were being re-kindled by the end of 1994, only one person at Barings regarded the profits being made in Singapore with serious apprehension. Though his comment was not broadcast in the Frost interview, Leeson told Frost what his feelings had been at the end of December, when he went to a conference organised by Ron Baker's financial products group.

There was a party arranged in New York, which something like 250 people attended, of the futures-and-options department, based purely on the purported profits of Nick Leeson, really. And, you know, many slides were shown of the profit that was supposed to be made in Singapore. And this just added to the pressure; the people worked for me, you know, they were very good friends. I spent a lot of time with them, and we would go back to Singapore and all they would be talking about from that stage onward was their bonuses and their increased salaries, because up to that day, [although] they'd known that I'd been trading through the five-eights account, they had no idea of what purported profits were in Singapore. Swiss Bank, as an example, actually released a piece of literature about Barings, giving five possible reasons for the Barings position, one of those was suggesting that we were working on behalf of the government in stabilising and supporting the market. So there was lots being written about and, like I said, the world was watching me.

The world might have been watching, but it wasn't seeing.

9

Scissors and Paste

Nick Leeson, who had intended to become a Master of the Universe, had become a master of duplicity. By January 1995, the stress was showing. He was drinking heavily. Some nights, he drank to the point of stupefaction – in New York in December, and it was to happen again in February. He was putting on weight round his jowls, losing his boyish looks.

Famous spies like Philby, Burgess and Maclean drank heavily to ease the strain of a double life. For a spy, the danger of this is that drink can lead to loose talk. Normally, Leeson controlled the impulse to blurt or boast, but late one night in Singapore, drinking with an amiable young trainee, he did brag about his SIMEX positions. They were larger, he said, than Barings' entire capital. Those who subsequently heard about this amazing statement didn't grasp the implications; it was assumed that the drink had been doing the talking.

Even when he was sober, his behaviour was becoming unpredictable. During a routine conversation one morning in January, Leeson began to shout abuse at Fernando Gueler. Gueler was unnerved. He mentioned it later to Mary Walz in London, who told him that Leeson had probably got out of bed on the wrong side. But Gueler felt he had begun talking to Dr Jekyll and had then glimpsed Mr Hyde. It was the first evidence Leeson had given to a colleague that his Boy Scout character might have a darker side.

The month of January 1995 began and ended with two

breathtaking examples of Leeson's boldness. At the end of 1994, there was a £50 million hole in his 88888 account; that had to be filled before it was spotted by SIMEX, or by the accountants from Coopers & Lybrand, who were doing the annual audit. And, since the options market was saturated, Leeson had to come up with a different way of boosting his credit balance.

As with most fraud, it was the simplicity of his subterfuge that deceived his bosses. Only the language of the prosecution case brought against Leeson in December 1995 jerks us back from what sounds like crime fiction to the real world. 'On or about 30 December 1994, at about 7.45 a.m., the accused, who was at that time in London (where it was 11.45 p.m. the previous night) made a long-distance call to Linda at the Baring Futures office in Singapore.' Leeson wanted Linda (Norhaslinda Hassan) in the settlements office in Singapore to check the year-end cash, or equity, balance in his 88888 account.

The prosecution continued: 'When the accused learned from Linda that the balance was a deficit of minus 7.778 billion yen, he immediately instructed her over the phone to key into the CONTAC system an entry representing a sale from the account of 2,000 lots of Nikkei 225 December '95 put options, strike price of 21,500 and at a premium of 7,778. The accused had concocted these figures, as there was no such trade.' Expressed in US dollars, the deficit was $78,560,000, or a little under £50 million.

CONTAC, as we know, was the computerised system used by Barings to maintain records of customers' trading positions. When Linda keyed in this fictional trade, the premium would have erased the deficit in the 88888 account so that it showed 'final zero balance'.

But this was not all. Entering a fictitious trade on the CONTAC system set off a chain reaction which Leeson found hard to control. Once on CONTAC, Leeson's phoney option sale was routinely entered on the SIMEX accounting system, where it appeared as a premium due to be paid to Baring Futures (Singapore). Consequently, the sum was added to the balance in Barings' general trading ledger at the market. That happened to be in the red at the time, to the tune of 175,110,100 yen. So when the 7.778 billion yen had been credited to the account, the new SIMEX customer-account statement showed Barings nicely in credit with 7.602 billion yen.

Leeson was taking a break in England until 10 January. His problem was that when the settlements clerks returned from holiday on 3 January and conducted a routine reconciliation, they would base it on the new balance in the SIMEX account. Since any auditor worth his salt would trace the movement of money through the cash balances, Leeson issued another order: 'Over the telephone, the accused therefore instructed Linda to direct Nisa [one of her settlements colleagues] to ignore the new credit, and base the reconciliation on the earlier minus 175,110,100 yen balance.'

The instruction to the settlements clerks had the elegance of the most dashing sort of fraud. They were told to treat the false trade as though it had never existed. Leeson added that Linda should refer to him any subsequent queries from the auditors. The obliging Nisa, who took instructions from the indulgent Linda, was a senior settlements assistant.

By the time Leeson returned to Singapore on 10 January 1995, Coopers & Lybrand's annual audit of Barings' books in Singapore was well advanced. (Coopers had taken over from Deloittes in 1994.) The audit had begun in October, and the deadline for the provisional clearance to be sent to London was 3 February. Coopers' accountants were Chinese Singaporeans, Khoo Kun Wing, Seet Wee Teong and Pang Mui Mui. It was Pang, the youngest of the three, who spotted the discrepancy between the broker's small deficit balance and the billions of yen in the SIMEX customer account. Two days after Leeson's return from London, Pang asked him for an explanation.

Leeson blamed his tools: it was a system error; it had happened several times in the past; he would get on to the people who sold CONTAC systems to rectify the error and would provide her with a fresh reconciliation. The prosecution reported: 'However, despite Pang's persistent requests for the fresh reconciliation which he promised, the accused did not provide [one]. After several futile approaches to the accused, during which the accused continued to stonewall her, Pang raised the matter with her audit manager, Seet.'

The 3 February deadline was approaching quickly, but Leeson had other things on his mind besides the auditors' troublesome questions. On 28 December, while he was still on holiday, a routine inspection by SIMEX had uncovered a shortfall in the margin payments on the 88888 account. Since the back-office staff could not explain this, Soo Yu Chuan, SIMEX's senior vice-president in charge of audit and compliance, wrote to Simon Jones. His letter, dated 11 January 1995, is crucial to the story. After the collapse, a samizdat trade in Barings' internal documents soon sprang up, and Soo's letter would be a prized possession in any collection of leaked Barings material – especially after the Board of Banking Supervision report appeared containing only a heavily edited version of it.

Soo's compliance department had been checking on Barings on 28 December 1994, and had found that one of its biggest accounts appeared not to have met the exchange's initial margin requirement. 'We understand from your staff that the IM [initial margin] requirement was the margin requirement of the positions held by the sub-account, a/c no. 88888 of BSL–CSA.' BSL–CSA was an abbreviation of Baring Securities Ltd customer account number 99001. Here, at last, was a clear reference to the account Leeson had kept hidden from the Barings management.

Soo pointed out that the margin required for the 88888 account was $342,180,500, and yet the sum deposited with SIMEX stood at only $242,180,500. He wanted to know why the margin account was $100 million short. The settlement staff had suggested that the money missing from Barings' dollar account would be found in its yen account, but Soo had had found only 20.026 billion yen there. Since that came to $22 million, there was a deficit of $78 million. Without realising it, SIMEX had uncovered the reason for Leeson's desperate

1 and 2. Newsbreak: on 27 February 1995, the day when Nicholas Leeson, pictured right in his Baring trader's navy and gold jacket, became a household name as 'the man who broke the Queen's bank'. Leeson was still regarded as a fugitive

3. Bailing out: Eddie George, Governor of the Bank of England (right), and his deputy, Rupert Pennant-Rea, leave the Bank having failed to find a commercial bank to take over Barings and assume the risk of liquidating its losses

4. Arrest: Leeson is detained by German border police on 3 March 1995 when his flight from the far East touched down in Frankfurt. His wife, Lisa, had already called a London lawyer, and he expected to be put on the next flight to London

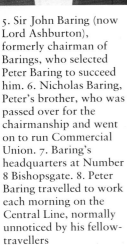

5. Sir John Baring (now Lord Ashburton), formerly chairman of Barings, who selected Peter Baring to succeed him. 6. Nicholas Baring, Peter's brother, who was passed over for the chairmanship and went on to run Commercial Union. 7. Baring's headquarters at Number 8 Bishopsgate. 8. Peter Baring travelled to work each morning on the Central Line, normally unnoticed by his fellow-travellers

9. Andrew Tuckey, Baring's deputy chairman, who had been chosen to succeed Peter Baring, was the principal survivor of the bank's collapse. 10. Christopher Heath, founder of Barings Securities; once Britain's highest-paid worker, he was at home on the race course and the trading floor. 11. Peter Norris, who took over Barings Securities from Heath; considered by colleagues as 'the brightest man in the City'; the only man voluntarily to assume some blame. 12. James Bax, the head of Barings' Singapore operation, and architect of 'Fortress Singapore'. 13. Ron Baker, a talented trader who was bearded, Australian, and, partly because of these attributes, regarded as an outsider. 14. Ocean Towers, Barings' Singapore headquarers, where Bax sat on the twenty-fourth floor, and Leeson worked ten floors beneath him

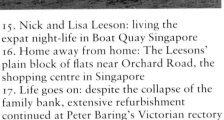

15. Nick and Lisa Leeson: living the
expat night-life in Boat Quay Singapore
16. Home away from home: The Leesons'
plain block of flats near Orchard Road, the
shopping centre in Singapore
17. Life goes on: despite the collapse of the
family bank, extensive refurbishment
continued at Peter Baring's Victorian rectory
outside Hungerford
18. SIMEX on the offensive: Elizabeth Sam,
chairman of the Singapore exchange, with
Koh Ben Seng, head of the Monetary
Authority (right), puts the evidence on show

19. Aad Jacobs, the chairman of ING, announces to the Press that his Dutch bank has bought Barings for £1. (They paid a further £660 million to make its new purchase solvent, and provide it with fresh capital.) Jacobs had asked Barings if it wished to sell four months earlier, and had been sent away with a flea in his ear. Now he claimed 'This is a fair price for a nice bank'

20. Hessel Lindenbergh, ING's man in the City, sits beneath a portrait of Francis Baring, the founder of Barings in 1762; but that pleasure did not last long. The bank's best paintings were soon reclaimed by Lord Northbrook, their rightful owner

21. Prisoner: even in Hoechst prison in Frankfurt, Nick Leeson remained devoted to his baseball cap. Regular visits to a nearby court failed to persuade the German judge that he should not be extradited to Singapore. Although few fellow-prisoners spoke English, Leeson made some friends. His reading material was *Private Eye*, *Viz*, and football magazines. Visits from Lisa were his only real pleasure

23. Celebrity: Lisa Leeson became a public figure. In July 1995, accompanied by a strong presence of television crews and cameramen, she presented a letter from her husband to the Prime Minister in Downing Street. Leeson's argument that he had done no real wrong never carried weight with British politicians, who washed their hands of him

22. Campaigner: Lisa Leeson, who had asked for a solicitor who would help the family 'cope' with her husband's legal problems, proved she was good at coping herself. An adept public performer, she was the main spokesman for the campaign to have Leeson tried in London rather than Singapore. This was Lisa Leeson's debut, at a press conference in London in July 1995

24. Last throw: Sir David Frost's interview with Leeson in his prison cell in Frankfurt was the final attempt to ignite a mass campaign to persuade the law officers and the Serious Fraud Office that Leeson should be tried in a British court. Leeson's lawyer thought the interview might have been more successful if the questions had been tougher

25. Stylist: arriving at Changi Airport to face prosecution in Singapore, Leeson's baseball cap is worn fashionably back-to-front. Under his Adidas sweat-shirt, he wears the light blue strip of Manchester City football club. This laddish image was true to himself, but was not thought to be much help in persuading the Singapore authorities that Leeson was a serious, penitent character

26. Spectators: Lisa Leeson is accompanied by Stephen Pollard, the solicitor from Kingsley Napley in London who conducted Leeson's defence. During the flight, Pollard and Lisa had been allowed to spend only a short period with Leeson. The Singaporean Authorities had got their man, and were doing no one any favours

27. Courthouse: the district court on Havelock Road by Chinatown where Leeson was tried on two counts of forgery and cheating. 28. Alone: Lisa leaves the remand prison after a rare meeting with her husband. 29. Convict: Leeson is driven from the courthouse after having been sentenced to $6\frac{1}{2}$ years in prison for his part in the collapse of Barings.

Singapore International Monetary Exchange Limit

1 Raffles Place #07-00, OUB Centre, Singapore 0104. Tel: 5357382, Telex: RS 38000 SINMEX, Fax: 5357

11 January 95

RECEIVED
12 JAN 1995

0036   Rt

cc: Nleeson
RJ

Baring Futures (Singapore) Pte Ltd
20 Raffles Place
24th Floor Ocean Towers
Singapore 0104

Attention: Mr Simon Dominic Jones

Dear Sir

We refer to the attached information provided by your staff and the telephone conversation as of 5 Jan 94 between your staff and our staff.

Based on the information provided in page 3 of Attachment 1, we note that as of the close of business 28 Dec 94, an initial margin (IM) requirement amount of US$242,180,500 was shown in the US$ account belonging to your customer, Baring Securities Ltd - Customer Segregated Account [BSL-CSA] (a/c no. 99001). We understand from your staff that the IM requirement was the margin requirement of the positions held by the sub-account, a/c no. 88888, of BSL-CSA. Based on the "Daily Activity Statement" as of 28 Dec 94 of a/c no. 88888 (Attachment 2) and a report showing the margin requirement computed by the SPAN margining system (Attachment 3) provided by your staff, we note the IM requirement was actually ¥34,218,050,000 (equivalent to US$342,180,500). We note the above amount of US$342,180,500 was higher than the amount US$242,180,500 reflected in page 3 of Attachment 1 by US$10 million (equivalent to ¥10 billion). Your staff explained that the difference of US$10 million (equivalent to ¥10 billion) was funded by the Yen account of BSL-CSA and the amount ¥10 billion was included in the IM requirement of the Yen account of BSL-CSA. However, the explanation did not appear to be correct as the IM requirement shown in the Yen account of BSL-CSA (page 2 of Attachment 1) was only ¥2,026,239,625. As such, we do not understand how the ¥10 billion could have been included in the margin requirement of the Yen account of BSL-CSA. Your staff then informed us that she needed to check with your Mr Nick Leeson (whom we understand was on leave and was in London) before providing further explanations to the Exchange. Todate, we have yet to receive any further explanation from your staff regarding the above matter.

In addition, based on the information provided so far, it appears to us that your company had financed the trading margin of the positions held by the sub-account no. 88888 of BSL-CSA. If this is really the case, your company has violated SIMEX Rule 822 which prohibits Members from financing the trading margins of their customers. We would also like you to look into the above matter and confirm to the Exchange whether your company had actually financed the trading margins of BSL-CSA. If the above is not the case, please provide documentary evidence to show that your company had not financed the trading margins of BSL-CSA.

Please let us have your reply within two weeks from date hereof.

Yours faithfully

Soo Yu Chuan
Senior Vice President
Audit & Compliance

Enc

Smoking gun: SIMEX's 11 January 1995 letter reveals 88888 account act on 30 December, when he had transferred a sum in yen equivalent to $78 million to his 88888 account. Soo wrote: 'Your staff then informed us that she needed to check with your Mr Leeson (whom we understand was on leave and was in London) before providing further explanations to the exchange.' Soo found this disturbing. 'If your operation system is such that, if the person in overall charge is away, and the assistants are not in a position to provide the information, then we would be concerned.'

But the most serious question posed by Soo was contained in the last paragraph of his letter, which appeared in neither the Board of Banking Supervision's report nor that of the Singapore inspectors. The paragraph stated:

> In addition, based on the information provided so far, it appears to us that your company had financed the trading margin of the positions held by the sub-account no. 88888 of BSL–CSA. If this really is the case, your company has violated SIMEX rule 822, which prohibits members from financing the trading margins of their customers. We would like you to look into the matter and confirm to the exchange whether your company had actually financed the trading margin of BSL–CSA. If the above is not the case, please provide documentary evidence to show that your company had not financed the trading margins of BSL–CSA.

SIMEX was getting close to the truth; without knowing it, Barings was indeed financing the trading account of a 'client' – Leeson himself – and the letter ought to have raised questions about the identity of this client whose account carried a number that did not appear on their systems. His scrawl on Soo's letter suggests that Jones distributed it only to Nick Leeson and Rachel Yong, the financial controller. Leeson was asked to draft a reply. No one in London saw the letter, and when Jones mentioned it later to Hawes, he did so only to jeer at SIMEX, for Soo had made a small, insubstantial and easily detected numerical error. But Soo showed no sense of urgency, either. Since he assumed the 88888 account belonged to a good customer of Barings in London, he allowed Jones two weeks to reply.

A second communication requiring attention arrived on the same day as Soo's letter, 12 January 1995. Tony Hawes was still worried; he had always intended to look more carefully at funding in Singapore. Throughout 1994, he had initiated nothing himself because he felt his treasury department did not have sufficient resources. But in January things began to look up on that front. Hawes and Ian Hopkins, the head of group treasury at Baring Investment Bank, prepared the questions for an inquiry they entitled the 'Singapore Project'. When it was completed, they expected to know why it was that such large and consistent amounts of money sent to Singapore were unreconciled, and were described only as 'loans to clients'. Hawes also intended to find out, once and for all, how the funds sent to Leeson were being used.

Hopkins had hoped that the new Asian regional treasurer – the extra resource for which Hawes was looking – would head up the Singapore Project, but the person he had in mind turned down the job. Consequently, the memorandum outlining the project was sent for action in Singapore to James Bax. This was like asking a gamekeeper to turn poacher. Bax simply passed it on to Nick Leeson and Simon Jones, and asked them to prepare a reply.

Although the simultaneous occurrence of these three developments can only have intensified the pressure on Leeson, he had grown accustomed to dealing with treasurers, auditors and exchange officials. He also appeared to have Simon Jones comfortably in his pocket. Judging by past experience, he could go on coping with these difficulties.

But on 17 January 1995 something happened that Leeson was quite powerless to do anything about. A severe earthquake, measuring 7.2 on the Richter scale, hit Kobe, next door to Osaka. The lasting image of that disaster was the elevated highway that toppled in one piece on to its side, a spectacular example of the damage that would eventually cost more than £50 billion to repair. Although the Kobe earthquake was bound to have serious reverberations in the Japanese economy, no one could be sure what they would be. It could create a building boom and cause shares to rise; on the other hand, the suspension of economic activity in such a vigorous industrial area could cause the market to fall, or else the earthquake might have a psychological impact in which the depression caused by human misery on such a scale brought the market down. These conflicting analyses created uncertainty, and that always triggers greater volatility in the markets. Since Leeson was short-volatility, he needed calm markets – doubt was bad for his position. Sooner or later, the earthquake was going to hit him, too.

Prudent traders kept their heads down after Kobe. The initial reaction in the stock exchanges was one of uncertainty rather than apprehension. In the two days following the earthquake, the Nikkei 225 index fell only 400 points, but for Leeson, that was a move in the wrong direction. He gambled that prices would go up rather than down, plunging into the market on Friday 20 January, building a long position of 10,014 Nikkei 225 futures contracts. He believed that if shares went up, bonds would go down, so he went short Japanese Government Bonds.

On Monday 23 January, the markets decided how to react to the earthquake. The Nikkei 225, as if itself hit by an aftershock, dropped like a stone – by 1,175 points on that day. But Leeson went on buying; by 27 January, his long holding in the Nikkei 225 had risen to 27,158 contracts.

The index was falling, but Leeson was building a huge position that would make pots of money only if the Nikkei 225 went up. It would lose serious money if it went on going down. It was, to say the least, an immense gamble.

The Bank of England's investigators, while admitting that they didn't understand Leeson's motives, none the less indulged in a small speculation of their own. They wondered if Leeson might have been trying to hold up the share market to protect his position in the options market. If the market fell, his clients would exercise their 'put' options, and Leeson would be 'out of the money'. If he could lever the market back up, by taking this large long position in Nikkei 225 futures, he might be 'in the money' again.

There is nothing in Leeson's record as a dealer during the previous thirty months to suggest that he would not try something as silly as this. The movement of a stock-price index in a huge market like Tokyo has a momentum of its own. For one trader to attempt to turn it round is like trying to stop a river in flood: what happens is that you get swept away.

The losses were now building up at a frightening speed. On 23 January alone, Leeson's Nikkei 225 futures position lost £34 million, and his options portfolio had lost £69 million in the few days since the earthquake. The Japanese Government Bonds were doing no better, going up in price when Leeson's position would make money only if they went down.

By now, he had a way of dealing with losses like this. He simply declared another big dividend for Barings. By means of cross-trades between his 88888 accounts and Barings' 92000, he fed £13 million into the firm's profit-and-loss balance. His colleagues were captivated. When he heard that Leeson's revenue in one week in January had been $10 million, Mike Killian said to Ron Baker: 'You know, if he makes $10 million doing arbitrage in a week, what is that? About half a billion dollars a year. That is pretty good doing arbitrage. That guy is a turbo-arbitrageur!' In fact, between 23 and 27 January, when he claimed to have made some £5 million from arbitrage, Leeson had actually lost £47 million.

The task of managing an investment bank is complicated by the fact that senior managers are hardly ever in the same place at the same time. On 23 January, Peter Norris and Ron Baker were in New York; Mary Walz was in Hong Kong; George Maclean was away too; Ian Hopkins was on holiday. The result was poorly attended meetings of the asset and liability committee (ALCO) which had been formed the previous November from the Barings Securities risk committee and Baring Brothers' treasury committee.

Except on Monday, when the members trooped over to head office in Bishopsgate, ALCO met every afternoon around 4 p.m. in a conference room off the main dealing-room in America Square. When they met on 24 January, Tony Hawes was a worried man. The previous day in Singapore, the day the Nikkei had fallen 1,175 points, Barings had had a very lucky escape. Because of Leeson's huge positions, Baring Securities' account at Citibank, out of which SIMEX margins were paid, had been overdrawn. Fortunately, there had been a clerical error, which meant that Citibank had not found out. But in such volatile trading conditions, this might happen again; and the next time they could not rely on a clerical error. If Barings failed to meet margin calls, they would be in default at SIMEX.

Hawes had talked to Mary Walz in Hong Kong about Leeson's positions. She was busy, they did not get along anyway, and now they were at cross-purposes. Hawes thought Walz had 'confirmed that Leeson had been instructed to reduce the size of his positions' (Bank of England report). Walz, though, thought Hawes would be talking directly to Gueler in Tokyo about the problem; indeed, she had warned Gueler to expect the call. This is the first inkling we have that Leeson's managers were moving to curtail his trading.

The next day Tony Hawes raised Barings' margin-call limit at Citibank by $100 million, but he was still concerned that this might prove inadequate if adverse market conditions were to batter Leeson's enormous positions on SIMEX. And he still had no accurate gauge of the potential danger. He knew nothing of the even larger covert positions in the 88888 account, nor of the enormous losses that were building up in it. Nor could he know until the reconciliation of client accounts was completed, and he had been asking about that for months.

When Norris returned from New York on 25 January, Hawes went to see him to outline his worries. Norris took Hawes seriously enough to telephone Ron Baker in New York. He wanted Baker to make sure that Leeson's positions did not cause Barings embarrassment with Citibank in Singapore.

With so many ALCO members on the road, Norris announced that he would prepare an agenda for the meeting the following day. A colleague remembers that he seemed remarkably calm and well organised as he led ALCO through a long agenda. His own notes concentrated on dissecting various kinds of risk, but, in retrospect, the most interesting item was gossip. Various people at Barings had been telephoned with queries about the size of Leeson's positions in Osaka and Singapore. Norris never doubted that the gossip was inaccurate, but he feared that the rumours would harm Barings' good name. He proposed to contact James Bax and the new head of the Tokyo office, William Daniel, to make sure they all rebuffed the rumours with the story that all was well.

The following morning, 27 January, a Barings foreign-exchange trader in London received a call from a former colleague who now worked at the Bank for International Settlements (BIS) in Basle, the central bankers' bank. The Basle trader wanted to know if the rumours were true. What rumours? That Barings could not meet a margin call in Asia.

This news soon reached Norris. 'For the BIS to call was a bit unpleasant,' he told Walz. Walz then rang the traders in Tokyo, who had been fending off enquiries themselves. Walz told them that she had already spoken to Leeson, and the message was: no one in your team should talk to the press. They discussed the rumours, and agreed that what they must be referring to was Barings' house position on the Nikkei in Osaka, which was long 16,700 contracts. That did not concern them. Why should it have done? They knew that Leeson had hedged it with a short position in Singapore. He had told them so.

But the ALCO meeting on 26 January had decided to instruct Leeson not to increase his positions, and, when possible, to reduce them. Detailed instructions were sent on 27 January: no increase in his Nikkei position, and guidelines about dealing in rising or falling markets. When asked to report the positions, Walz confirmed that Barings held a 29 per cent share of the market in the Nikkei in Osaka, and a 26 per cent share of the Japanese Government Bond market in Tokyo. But, of course, the true position was far bigger than that, because of the dealings through the secret account.

If the Barings' risk-managers had decided to curtail Leeson's trading because it was tying up an unhealthy proportion of the group's funding, the decision could have been described as prudent, if somewhat late. But that was not why Leeson was told not to increase his positions. Peter Norris explained his reasoning to Barings' executive committee, attended by Peter Baring and Andrew Tuckey a few days later. The minutes read: '... Because there were some comments about the substantial positions we might be running in Tokyo ... it was decided to reduce this business even though ... [it] was described as completely matched and risk-free. It was still thought prudent ... just to turn it down.' But this was not prudence dictated by risk management: Norris thought risk management was a problem that had been dealt with. This was prudence as a public-relations exercise.

In an aside, the Bank of England report makes a remark about Leeson which is almost flattering. Referring to his options trading, it comments: 'To manage an exposure of the size Leeson constructed is technically and mentally demanding.' The scale of the operation Leeson was running was, frankly, awesome. By the end of January 1995, what he was actually doing was fighting off both SIMEX and Coopers & Lybrand, as well as directing the biggest single futures-and-options operation in the Singapore, Tokyo and Osaka markets. But the strain was building fast. Lisa, his wife, found him morose and unpredictable. She says he was uncommunicative and sleeping badly. 'If I said, "How was it today?" he'd just sort of grunt.'

Simon Jones's reply to Soo Yu Chuan's letter of 11 January, the one in which SIMEX gave Barings two weeks to provide documentary evidence that it was not financing the margins of the 88888 account, was a classic example of evasion. The reply, dated 25 January, was polite, attributing the shortfall found in the margin payment for account number 88888 to a complicated web of inter-company loans. Jones promised that Leeson would provide an overseas contact number when he next went abroad. ('Naturally he would be pleased to reimburse any long-distance telephone charges which you may incur.') But the letter ignored one issue entirely. It contained no other reference to account number 88888, never mind a detailed answer to the suggestion that Barings was financing its margin payments. Still, Leeson knew it would hold SIMEX off for another couple of weeks or so. There was more pressing business at hand.

Drafting correspondence kept Leeson particularly busy that week. By the end of it, he had also finished his reply to Tony Hawes' memorandum of 12 January, the start of his Singapore Project. Leeson's reply dealt with specific questions in vague and general terms. Hawes was dissatisfied with it. But, since he planned to be in Singapore anyway the following week, he did not say so. He dropped a note to Leeson on 28 January, thanking him for the reply. Later, he explained that he was merely keeping his lines of communication open. His colleagues, hearing of this curious thank-you note, suspected that, as a former trader, Hawes had a sneaking admiration for a man who was making so much money.

But if Leeson was playing dumb, no one could answer Hawes' questions. Mary Walz, talking that week on the telephone to Ron Baker, said: '[Leeson] is in an unfortunate position, though, because he's settlements, and he is cash management, and he is the trader. It's a problem because there is nobody else to call but him about it.'

On 27 January, at the end of a frazzled week in Singapore, auditors Coopers & Lybrand could be put off no longer. Having pestered Leeson for two weeks for a new reconciliation that would explain this mysterious sum of 7.778 billion yen, which bore no relation to anything else on the balance sheet, Pang Mui Mui had enlisted the aid of Seet Wee Teong, the audit manager. It was, after all, not a small sum of money. Seet went to Leeson, and, since Coopers' deadline was the end of the following week, demanded an immediate explanation for the discrepancy.

What Seet got was the first version of what became known as the SLK receivable. This did not lead directly to the collapse of Barings, but when the investigators began to sift through the rubble, it came to be seen as a symbol of the two main ingredients in the tale: the recklessness of Leeson's fraud, and the impotence of Barings' management. And, because the story surrounding it seemed to be beyond belief, the SLK receivable provided fertile ground in which conspiracy theories flourished.

First, we need to know exactly what Leeson did, and, after that, exactly how his managers in Singapore and London responded.

The Singapore prosecutors rarely bothered with adjectives, but the story Leeson spun for Seet was cause for a rare exception to be made. It was described as 'ingenious' – as a compliment, I think. Leeson explained that the substantial discrepancy between what appeared on the CONTAC record and on Barings' balance sheet was an OTC (over-the-counter) option trade. It had been brokered, he said, by Baring Futures (Singapore), and written by another branch of the firm, Baring Securities Ltd in London, known as BSL. It involved two clients. The buyer was a New York securities house called Spear, Leeds & Kellogg, generally known by its initials. Although well-established in New York, SLK was not well known in London, but Leeson knew it intimately, since SLK brokers leased one of Barings' SIMEX seats, its trades were cleared by Barings and Leeson admired its traders.

The deal, as Leeson described it, was that SLK had bought 200 lots of Nikkei 225 'call' options from Baring Securities in London. They had been purchased on 1 October, and were due to mature on 30 December. The option price was 777.8 yen, and the total value of the deal was 200 contracts × Y777.8 × Y500, which equalled Y7.778 billion, or £50 million, as near as damn it. This was a big deal, even for an established New York securities firm.

Leeson explained that, since it was an OTC, the premium had never appeared in Baring Futures' reconciliation. As we have seen, a fake deal had been entered into the CONTAC system, and had, therefore, been automatically logged by SIMEX's computerised accounts, even though it had never appeared in Barings' books. There was evidence of it in one place, but not the other. But Seet did not question the grand concept of Leeson's fraud, just its weaker components. What the auditor wanted to know was why the premium had not been paid up once SLK chose not to exercise the option on 30 December.

Leeson replied with a complicated story about margin payments, and how the clients had agreed that the margin would be the same as the premium, so that no money had changed hands when he brokered the deal in October.

To demonstrate that the deal had indeed been done, Leeson displayed the second breathtaking example of the boldness he revealed in January 1995. He handed over a letter from Spear, Leeds & Kellogg. It was dated 1 October 1994, addressed to Leeson, and confirmed the sale of the option. It was, in fact, a crude forgery. The text typeface had a serif; the one used for 'Sincerely yours, Richard Hogan, Managing Director', was sans-serif. The letter would not have convinced a fourteen-year-old suspicious of its authenticity. But Seet never suggested it was not authentic; all he said was that Hogan's 'letter' wasn't proof enough. He told Leeson to produce evidence that SLK would pay the £50 million premium to Baring Futures, and to get confirmation from Baring Securities in London that they knew about the deal.

For a man who had got away with one forgery, a couple more were not a problem. Leeson was now so confident or so desperate that he threw caution to the winds. The next fake was a photocopy of a fax purporting to come from Richard Hogan at SLK, confirming the deal and stating that the premium would be paid by 2 February 1995. Once again the typeface under Hogan's signature was different from the one used for the main text, but the real give-away was the sender's name at the top of the fax. This read: 'From Nick & Lisa Phone no: 737-5463   Feb 03 1995   07.16 a.m. P01'. The accountants accepted it. They never asked why it was that Hogan's good news should have been sent from Leeson's own fax in Singapore.

The third forgery was a fax message on two sheets. The cover sheet announced that the message originated from

Spear, Leeds & Kellogg

120 Broadway, New York, NY 10271 212/433-7000

7917 02 336

1st October 1994

Mr Nick Leeson
Baring Futures (Singapore) Pte Ltd
20 Raffles Place
24th Floor
Singapore 0104

Dear Sir,

      We hereby confirm the following deal entered into today. We purchase :

```
Quantity        :  200
Description     :  Nikkei 225 Call Option
Strike Price    :  19728.34
Premium         :  777.80
Contract Value  :  YEN 50,000
Maturity        :  30th December 1994
```

Sincerely yours,

Richard Hogan
Managing Director

Members New York and American Stock Exchanges

Forgeries: Richard Hogan's signature is in the wrong typeface. In the 'Baker memo' cover sheet only the date is forged. 'Ron' is convincing

BARINGS

Treasury & Trading Dealing Room
8 Bishopsgate, London EC2N 4AE

Fax Message - Cover Sheet

To __Baring Securities - Singapore__

Attention __James Bax / N Leeson__ ✓

Fax Number __010 65 535 8233__   Total No. of pages __2__   (including this one)

From __Ronald Baker__

Date __2·2·95__

Fax: 071-280-1144   Tlx: 883622
Queries regarding this message call
071-280-1833

BARINGS

MEMORANDUM

TO: James Bax   Nick Leeson   FROM: Ronald Baker

DATE: 2nd February 1995

Subject : Audit Confirmation

        As Head of the Financial Products Group I confirm my knowledge and approval of the Nikkei OTC Option deal with Spear Leeds Kellogg.

Ron

Barings' treasury and trading dealing-room at number 8 Bishopsgate in London. The handwriting on the sheet, detailing to whom it had been sent and from whom, was in the neat script of Ron Baker's secretary, and Baker was named as the sender on the fax identification. The date of this earlier message is hard to read, but it looks like 'Oct 94'.

There was no fax identification at all on the second sheet. It was simply headed 'Memorandum', addressed to Bax and Leeson from Baker, and dated 2 February 1995. It read: 'Subject: Audit Confirmation. As Head of the Financial Products Group I confirm my knowledge and approval of the Nikkei OTC Option deal with Spear Leeds Kellogg.' Under a handwritten squiggle was printed the name 'Ron'. This was a more skilful piece of work. Baker had sent a fax to Bax and Leeson on 20 October 1994 reporting the results of a sales conference three days earlier. Only one change had been made to his secretary's covering note (the date was changed to 2.2.95), and she recognised that; she did not, however, recognise the style or template of the characters in the memorandum. Baker thought it was a decent forgery.

Leeson's next job was to convince Seet that the £50 million had indeed been received from SLK. This was not so difficult because he had been doing much the same thing at the end of every month: transferring the losses out of the 88888 account to another Barings account so that 88888 would contain only the small, month-end balance of a real error account. Within hours, at the start of the following month, the balance would be transferred back to the 88888 account. That had become child's play.

Now Leeson asked his settlements office to get the obliging Nisa to call as soon as she got back to work on 2 February after the two-day public holiday for Chinese New Year. He needed her to perform the trick that transformed an account from deficit to credit. Modern banking makes this a simple affair – there are no paying-in slips, queues or tellers. Citibank had located a terminal in the Baring Futures office, and all bank transfers were processed automatically from the office. No money ever changed hands.

There were a number of accounts, for clients and for various Barings subsidiaries, and for different currencies – US dollars, sterling and yen. Around 7.30 that morning, Leeson instructed Nisa to take 7.778 billion yen from the Citibank account number 025, which was for client trades in yen, and transfer it to the 033 account, which was the yen house account.

When Nisa called back to say there were insufficient funds in the 025 account to meet such a large transfer, Leeson told her to make the transfer anyway – no one else would know about it, after all. Having ensured that the transfer would be recorded in the Citibank account, she was then to transfer back from the 033 account however much was needed to restore the true balance. The only control that transactions of this kind required was passwords from two account-holders. Leeson was one, and, on this occasion, Rachel Yong, the financial controller, was the other. She thought it was a routine transfer between two Baring Futures accounts, she said later.

What Leeson needed now was a bank statement to show to the auditors. The difficulty this presented was that the bank statement faxed to him from Citibank showed a transaction between two Barings accounts instead of a deposit from SLK. Scissors and paste again. Leeson copied the original fax and cut out a Citibank ink stamp acknowledging receipt of the funds from the bottom of the page, which he then carefully pasted over the part of the statement which showed that Barings, rather than SLK, had made the payment.

Yong passed the doctored bank statement to Seet's audit team, who duly adjudged that the SLK receivable was a bona fide transaction, and gave an unqualified provisional clearance to Coopers & Lybrand in London. Seet and his auditors had been easily satisfied; Linda and her settlements staff had been wonderfully accommodating. White-collar professional workers in Singapore are dedicated, industrious and loyal, but if this example is any guide, they are also extremely gullible. Leeson had every reason to think that, if he could get away

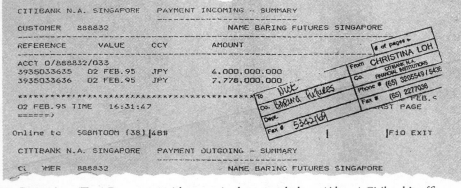

```
CITIBANK N.A. SINGAPORE    PAYMENT INCOMING - SUMMARY
                           ---------------------------------
CUSTOMER   888832                    NAME BARING FUTURES SINGAPORE
------------------------------------------------------------------------
REFERENCE       VALUE       CCY      AMOUNT              BY ORDER OF
------------------------------------------------------------------------
ACCT 0/888832/033
3935033635    02 FEB.95     JPY      4,000,000,000     BARING FUTURES SINGAPORE
3935033636    02 FEB.95     JPY      7,778,000,000     BARING FUTURES SINGAPORE

TRANSACTION IN PROCESS - INFORMATION UNDER RESERVE
3195033027    02 FEB.95     JPY      4,000,000,000     BARING FUTURES SINGAPORE
3195033026    02 FEB.95     JPY      7,778,000,000     BARING FUTURES SINGAPORE



************************************************************** TRANSACTIONS 02 FEB.9
02 FEB.95 TIME   16:31:47                      PAGE 001/001  LAST PAGE
======)

Online to   SGBMTOOM (38) |4B#                         |           |F10 EXIT

CITIBANK N.A. SINGAPORE    PAYMENT OUTGOING - SUMMARY
                           ---------------------------------
CUSTOMER   888832                    NAME BARING FUTURES SINGAPORE
------------------------------------------------------------------------
REFERENCE       VALUE       CCY      AMOUNT              BENEFICIARY
------------------------------------------------------------------------
ACCT 0/888832/033
3095033001    02 FEB.95     JPY              58
3095033002    02 FEB.95     JPY      3,870,585,917
3935033634    02 FEB.95     JPY      7,878,000,000
3935033526    03 FEB.95     JPY        347,810,000     MARGIN
3935033561    03 FEB.95     JPY        597,942,500     MARGIN

TRANSACTION IN PROCESS - INFORMATION UNDER RESERVE
3195033025    02 FEB.95     JPY              58        BARING SEC LTD LDN
3195033023    02 FEB.95     JPY      3,870,585,917     BARING SEC LTD LDN
3195033028    02 FEB.95     JPY      7,878,000,000     BARING FUTURES SINGAPORE



************************************************************** TRANSACTIONS 02 FEB.9
02 FEB.95 TIME   16:32:03                      PAGE 001/001  LAST PAGE
======)

Online to   SGBMTOOM (38) |4B#                         |           |F10 EXIT
```

# of pages ►	
To Nick	From CHRISTINA LOH
Co. Baring Futures	Co. CITIBANK N.A. FINANCIAL INSTITUTIONS
Dept.	Phone # (65) 3205549 / 5436
Fax # 5342169	Fax # (65) 2277036

```
CITIBANK N.A. SINGAPORE    PAYMENT INCOMING - SUMMARY
                           ---------------------------------
CUSTOMER   888832                    NAME BARING FUTURES SINGAPORE
------------------------------------------------------------------------
REFERENCE       VALUE       CCY      AMOUNT
------------------------------------------------------------------------
ACCT 0/888832/033
3935033635    02 FEB.95     JPY      4,000,000,000
3935033636    02 FEB.95     JPY      7,778,000,000
*************************************************
02 FEB.95 TIME   16:31:47                           LAST PAGE
======)

Online to   SGBMTOOM (38) |4B#                         |           |F10 EXIT

CITIBANK N.A. SINGAPORE    PAYMENT OUTGOING - SUMMARY
                           ---------------------------------
CU OMER    888832                    NAME BARING FUTURES SINGAPORE
```

Deception: (Top) Document with stamp in the normal place. (Above) Citibank's office
stamp is moved to hide the true origin of the SLK receivable

with these crude forgeries, there was hardly anything people would not believe.

The behaviour of his bosses in London and Singapore over the SLK receivable did nothing to contradict this view. Simon Jones was the first to hear about it, but at a meeting with Leeson and the auditors on Saturday 28 January, his mind was not on the problem. He said later that the reason he asked no questions about the SLK receivable was that the transaction was so large he assumed it must have been approved by London.

Geoff Broadhurst was the first person in London to learn of it. Seet told his colleagues at Coopers & Lybrand in London about Leeson's story soon after first hearing it himself on 27 January. The news was passed to Broadhurst on 30 January by Duncan Fitzgerald, who was in charge of the Baring Securities audit.

Broadhurst was troubled. For a start, this OTC was not part of Leeson's remit. Furthermore, the name Spear, Leeds & Kellogg was unfamiliar to him. When he checked, he discovered that although Barings' credit unit knew of the firm, SLK's credit limit, it seemed, was only $5 million, not the £50 million involved in this transaction. Broadhurst asked Sajeed Sacranie, Tony Hawes and Tony Gamby what they knew about it. All gave the same answer: not a thing.

Peter Norris, who was out of the office on 30 January, first heard about the SLK receivable the next day. Broadhurst asked if the matter should be raised at the next ALCO meeting. '[Norris's] view was that it would be premature until we actually better understood whether it was a problem,' said Broadhurst.

In Tony Hawes' view it definitely was a problem. He sent Leeson a number of questions via the office e-mail system. This provoked a new bout of office grumbling. Mary Walz, speaking for the financial products group, thought the questions were merely time-consuming. It seemed to her to be another example of Hawes making a nuisance of himself.

Already the issue was sensitive. Tony Gamby, as head of

global settlements, instructed Brenda Granger, who ran futures-and-options settlements, and who was in constant touch with Leeson in Singapore, that, since the matter was being dealt with by senior people in London, she should 'lay off' Nick about the OTC. Granger had also asked whether she ought to check with SLK, but Gamby could not see the point. He told her that not enough details were known about this OTC to enable Granger to ask a sensible question.

Leeson first changed his story on 1 February. The version intended for consumption at Barings, as opposed to Coopers & Lybrand, was revealed in a handwritten note to Simon Jones. Leeson took a staggering risk in the first sentence: 'Large option trade put through the system between SLK and BNP.' Having informed the auditors that the counterparty was Baring Securities Ltd, or BSL, he now told London that it was the Banque National de Paris (BNP). Leeson's gamble was twofold: that either no one would notice, or that Barings would think the auditors had confused BSL and BNP.

While insisting that the transaction had cost Barings nothing, Leeson began, ingeniously, to shoulder the blame.

> ERROR in input of maturity dates. True maturity = 30/12, maturity for BNP Leg of 03/12. Subsequently BNP have received value for the funds of 3/12 and funds have been effectively returned to them over a period during the normal course of business i.e. error not picked up. Therefore the reversal of entries 30/12 has left us with a receivable of JPY 7,778,000.

Deciphering this, the inference is that, instead of SLK having paid the option premium to Banque National de Paris, Baring Futures Singapore had done so – by mistake, of course. The note continued:

> As the trade was to have no impact, referral was not made – so blame me!
> Subsequently received verbal communication that fund will be paid 2.2.95. Expecting written confirmation this evening circa 10 p.m.
> There are obviously a lot of errors that I can be hung on, to

which I will take full responsibility but suggest we tackle the matter with the auditor, show him the receipt of funds value 2.2.95 and confirmations that we will receive this evening of balances and hopefully will make London happy.

The note ended 'see you at 7.30 (p.m.)' and was signed 'Nick'. Simon Jones told the Singapore inspectors he was shocked by Leeson's note. Although it was the second day of the Chinese New Year holiday, 1 February, Jones and Bax were in the office. Jones was worried about recovering the money, Bax about the failure of internal controls. None the less, Jones listened, without comment, as Leeson told the auditors a completely different story the next day. (The auditors were still led to believe that Baring Securities in London was SLK's counterparty.) Jones, who said he had spent a sleepless night worrying, seemed to be finding it hard to concentrate.

On 1 February, Bax had spoken to Norris, describing the SLK receivable as a misbooking of a transaction, or an operational error. Mary Walz spoke to Leeson, who described it as 'just an accounting screw-up'. Tony Gamby, talking to Brenda Granger and Tony Railton, a senior clerk in the settlements department, described it as an 'unauthorised trade' because the credit risk had never been assessed. Gamby's view was the most severe. He added that, since this was a sackable offence, he did not want them gossiping about it. But the line from the top showed a preference for Bax's description of the SLK receivable as an 'operational error'. That is how Broadhurst described it to Walz.

On 3 February, the formal clearance letter from Coopers & Lybrand's Singapore branch still referred to BSL as the counterparty, rather than BNP, Leeson's other candidate for the role. Referring to the forged memo from Ron Baker, the letter stated that Barings in London knew of and had approved the deal. No one in London appears to have seen this letter, however. The BNP–BSL discrepancy went unnoticed.

James Bax was a worried man. On 3 February, he wrote a memorandum addressed to Norris, Broadhurst, Baker,

Hopkins and Gamby. The tone lacked Bax's customary arrogance when dealing with London, which suggests that something had forced Bax to dismantle the defences around Fortress Singapore. From now on, the 'enemy' in London was to be given clear sight of the way operations were conducted. The Bank of England and the Singapore inspectors, who referred to Bax's memo, ignored the full flavour of its language, and the remarkable reference to Nick Leeson's future with Barings. The memo reads:

Subject: SIMEX

As you know recent incidents have highlighted the current operational weaknesses of our SIMEX business and an urgent need for a new approach. The problems can be briefly summarised as follows:

1. The growing volumes traded on SIMEX have meant Nick Leeson can no longer continue to run the trading and settlement roles effectively. In any case it has long been acknowledged that there are control weakness in this arrangement.

2. The growth of this business also means we need to have greater flexibility in funding arrangements for SIMEX margin calls.

I suggest the following course of action.

1. With immediate effect split Nick's role so that he is no longer responsible for the settlement functions. In the past Nick has been unwilling to do this but now appreciates that the demands on him are too much to perform both tasks satisfactorily. He may need some further reassurance that he has a long-term career path with Barings when (or if) arbitrage business declines.

2. Simon Jones will assume responsibility for all futures support functions. Again, previously the nature of the reporting process made this difficult. However, it is critical that we have the proper overview of the business in Singapore.

Bax's memo then outlined changes necessitated by this course of action: Tony Railton from London would go to settlements in the short term; a permanent head of derivatives settlements would be required; a risk-manager would be appointed; and,

Baring Securities (Singapore) Pte Ltd

20 Raffles Place, 24th Floor, Ocean Towers, Singapore 0104

Member of the Stock Exchange of Singapore

FAX TRANSMISSION

To	:	Peter Norris
		Geoff Broadhurst
		Ron Baker
		Ian Hopkins
		Tony Gamby
From	:	James Bax
Date	:	3rd February 1995
Ref	:	JB/015/95/ym
Subject	:	**SIMEX**

As you know recent incidents have highlighted the current operational weaknesses of our SIMEX business and an urgent need for a new approach. The problems can be briefly summarised as follows:

1. The growing volumes traded on SIMEX have meant Nick Leeson can no longer continue to run the trading and settlement roles effectively. In any case it has long been acknowledged that there are control weaknesses in this arrangement.

2. The growth of the business also means we need to have greater flexibility in funding arrangements for SIMEX margin calls.

I suggest the following course of action.

1. With immediate effect split Nick's role so that he is no longer responsible for the settlement functions. In the past Nick has been unwilling to do this but now appreciates that the demands on him are too much to perform both tasks satisfactorily. He may need some further reassurance that he has a long term career path with Barings when, (or if), arbitrage business declines.

2. Simon Jones will assume responsibility for all futures support functions. Again, previously the nature of the reporting process made this difficult. However, it is critical that we have the proper overview of the business in Singapore.

General: 5353688 Dealing: 5395555 Telex: 26881 BARSEC Fax: 5353233

Eureka! Bax finally removes Leeson from the back office

'to free up Simon's time', Bax mentioned that a man named Mark Nelligan might be considered for a job.

When they read the memo in London on 6 February, Norris and Broadhurst were delighted – Norris shouted 'Eureka!' They were less interested in what the subtext of the memo told them about the SLK receivable than in the clear signal that they were going to be free to sack Jones and appoint Mark Nelligan as his successor.

This political victory seems to have overshadowed Bax's admission that, despite having agreed to stop Leeson running the settlements department four months earlier, Jones had done nothing. Leeson's own weight in Singapore is illustrated by Bax's anxiety about his future. Leeson is not spoken of as if he were an employee who was about to be fired; rather, as one who must be persuaded to stay. 'Operational errors' must have been very serious indeed if they required 'an urgent need for a new approach', but Bax did not go into detail; nor did Norris ask him to. Norris and his colleagues still had not grasped that there had been no supervision of Leeson of any sort.

Tony Hawes, who arrived in Singapore on 6 February, had a busy schedule. He had been deputed to reply to another letter from SIMEX, dated 27 January. This time, Simon Jones could not keep it to himself. The letter had to be passed on to London because it asked, politely, whether Barings had enough funds available in Singapore to cope with volatile market conditions. The letter outlined Barings' positions in three futures contracts, the Nikkei, the Eurodollar and the Euroyen, and contrasted them with the funds available to meet margin calls. SIMEX sought guarantees that funds would be available, and Hawes was able to reassure Soo Yu Chuan, their head of audit and compliance, that they were.

But there was something odd about the incompleteness of the SIMEX list of contracts. For some reason that remains unexplained, it did not mention either Japanese Government Bonds or Nikkei 225 options. Had it included the options, someone in London might finally have taken a really hard look at Leeson, because he was no more permitted to write options than he was to broker a massive trade for SLK. Even without knowing about the options, Hawes was still inclined to ask some difficult questions. He was about to discover that some of his colleagues were intent on stopping his inquiry.

Leeson, Bax and Jones told Hawes, was under a lot of strain. That being so, Jones thought it would be better if Hawes addressed any questions through him. He asked for a list to work from, and Hawes duly wrote out his questions. He sent a copy of these to Ian Hopkins in London, which is how Ron Baker came to see them.

Baker had been told that the SLK receivable was an 'accounting error', but the tone of Hawes' questions made it sound worse than that. Hawes wanted to know why Leeson was involved in an OTC trade, and whether the trade had been funded by Baring Securities in London.-Baker went ballistic. His dislike of Hawes, the man he called Forrest Gump, fuelled his attack on the treasury department. To Baker, it looked as if Hawes was trying to pass the blame for treasury mistakes to his financial products group. Baker insisted vehemently that he did not want Hawes to talk to Leeson at all; leave it to Bax, he said. Questioned later about this outburst, Baker told the Bank of England: 'I think I was protecting Leeson . . . from a situation that I felt was premature and ill considered.'

And so the questioning was left to Bax – for the time being, at least. Hawes tried another tack, but when he proposed visiting the Baring Futures (Singapore) offices, situated ten floors below Bax's Baring Securities office, Bax told him not to. Auditors were still going through paperwork in Leeson's office, he said, and their suspicions might be aroused if they saw Hawes rummaging through his files.

Bax had caused a problem in London, too. Annual audits give accountants the opportunity to lecture their clients about the proper way to conduct a business. Coopers & Lybrand in London had a long-standing record of finding fault with Baring Securities in the management letter that always accompanied the annual audit. Normally, managements take this advice in good part, but Bax was worried about it. The SLK deal would

be a strong candidate for a crisp comment from Coopers &
Lybrand in Singapore, and he feared that if anything about the
SLK receivable appeared in the management letter, it might
alert the compliance officers at SIMEX, which was already in
a mood to make trouble. He asked Norris to speak to Coopers
& Lybrand about the problem.

Broadhurst was in Norris's room when he was talking to
Bax about this. Norris called over to him: 'Ask the auditors
not to include any reference to SLK in the management letter.'
Broadhurst, who had never asked the auditors for that kind of
favour before, was uncomfortable. But, he decided, it wasn't
a matter of sweeping the issue under the carpet. It had been
discussed by ALCO, and investigated by Coopers & Lybrand
in Singapore. Broadhurst explained to the Bank of England: 'I
felt it was a very sensitive area . . . potentially, the management
letter might be misinterpreted by someone else who had access
to it.' The only people who knew about this request to Coopers
& Lybrand were Norris, Bax and Broadhurst. Since almost any
outside interpretation would concentrate on the elements of
ignorance, ambiguity and secrecy in the SLK receivable story,
discretion on Coopers & Lybrand's part would come as a relief
to the directors in London as well as in Singapore.

This matter was not raised at the ALCO meeting on 8 February. Discussion about the SLK receivable was recorded
tersely in the minutes: 'PN highlighted a recent operational
error in Singapore due to a trade misposting which took several
weeks to come to light. A full report will be produced by James
Bax at a later stage.' A memorandum from Ian Hopkins to the
management committee gave a fuller account of the discussion.
Hopkins described the 7.778 billion yen as 'an incorrect payment', and noted that no interest had been claimed so far.
'Although our principal was probably never at serious risk, the
episode had brought to a head the need to build a proper
operational infrastructure in the Singapore futures operation,
and particularly to devolve settlement responsibility from Nick
Leeson.' He added that Tony Railton, deputy head of futures

settlements in London, had gone to Singapore to cover in the short term, and 'hopefully' to stay there permanently.

In Singapore, Tony Hawes had been busy. He had visited SIMEX and assured them that they should not be concerned about Barings' commitment to the market. The full resources of the bank were behind its trading operations there. For their part, the compliance officers said he should not worry about their 27 January letter to Jones. It was the kind of thing they sent to all large-position holders. While he was explaining Barings' strategy, Hawes mentioned that Barings was generally short in Singapore and long in Osaka. One of SIMEX's officials interrupted Hawes: 'You are long in Singapore at the moment,' she said.

'No,' insisted Hawes, 'we're short.' But he was troubled by the exchange. Leeson was long – a buyer – in Osaka, so, if his positions were properly hedged, he ought to be short – a seller – in Singapore. If he was long in both markets, Leeson was not arbitraging, he was gambling.

When Hawes finally got to talk to Leeson personally, he checked the position with him. Leeson told Hawes not to worry – SIMEX had phoned him to say they had made a mistake. SIMEX had done no such thing, but Hawes believed him.

Hawes caught up with Leeson on 9 February, shortly before his return to London. Jones acted as chaperone while Hawes went through his list of questions. Bax thought that Leeson had answered satisfactorily; Hawes thought he was being slippery, and said so to the Bank of England inquisitors after the collapse. 'It was quite an extraordinary story, that I did not really believe,' he told them. Leeson had used a new technical description – the third in all – for the SLK receivable deal. This stated that SLK owed BNP £50 million as 'settlement on maturity'. However, Jones, who had now heard all three of Leeson's versions of the tale, had nothing to say about this. The explanation he gave the Singapore inspectors was that this was a period when he was undergoing tremendous personal strain, 'as a result of which he was not in the best frame of mind to perceive such differences'.

The Bank of England report tells us what happened next. '[Hawes] also told us that he had asked for support for Leeson's claims, recalling his request to: "see the entries that it created in the system. So [Leeson] went to get it, and did not come back."' This was the first, but not the last, occasion on which Leeson would leave a meeting saying that he would be back shortly, and not return. Such behaviour might, in a different environment, have been intolerable.

The next day Hawes gave Bax a list of follow-up questions for Leeson, and returned to London. Despite the obstructive and evasive behaviour of Bax and Jones, and his inability to get any sense out of Leeson, Hawes was happy with his week's work. He had left behind him Tony Railton, the senior settlements clerk who had travelled with him from London, in charge of his Singapore Project. Hawes had instructed Railton to get to the bottom of the mysterious millions described as loans to clients but which had never been reconciled with any of Barings' client accounts, in order to settle, once and for all, the way Leeson financed his dealing activities.

In London on 9 February, Broadhurst went to see a senior partner at Coopers & Lybrand to follow up his request that mention of the SLK receivable should be omitted from the management letter in Singapore. When he explained how the Singapore office was being re-organised so that Leeson would no longer run the back office, the auditors were impressed. Duncan Fitzgerald, who was the Coopers man in charge of the Barings audit, decided that the SLK receivable was 'a dead issue'. He did not think any more about it.

The affair rumbled on the following week. Hopkins thought it strange that $80 million of the bank's money had gone walk-about for two months without anyone noticing, never mind claiming interest on the money. Hawes reminded Jones that his inquiries were incomplete, and sent a list of questions he would want answered when he returned to Singapore on 25 February. When Bax saw Hawes' list, he sent a handwritten note to Jones which read: 'Can we not get Nick out of this loop?!! Makes sense you take on TH!'

The language is revealing: Nick Leeson had to be protected, kept from anything that might cause him stress. And Tony Hawes would not stop asking Nick Leeson questions.

IO

Too Much to Bear

A sense of persecution had taken a hold in the Baring Futures (Singapore) office early in 1995. Barings' floor traders in the pit noticed SIMEX officials watching them closely in January, but the person with the strongest sense of persecution was Nick Leeson himself. This was the point at which Leeson began to portray himself not as the architect of his fate, but as a victim of circumstances. 'I don't regard myself as a criminal. I also almost see myself as a victim of what I am, in that I have tried to help people too much,' he told David Frost. The viewers did not see that bit, which was probably just as well.

In another deleted excerpt, Leeson spoke of the frustration he felt as a trader whose huge positions made him an easy target for other traders in Singapore and Osaka. Leeson understood that a falling Tokyo stock market was a disaster for his position in Nikkei-index futures, and for the options he had sold, which would become potential loss-makers, or 'out of the money'. He also knew that the way out was to get out.

> I went in there every day knowing that I had to sell, and, you know, it was quite crazy. You'd be reaching a new level in the futures, it had quite good support, and I would have the opportunity to sell maybe 550 or 1,000 contracts. That sort of size is rarely seen on the screen. It hadn't been traded before ... and you would expect it to get more and more. Somebody would sell 1,000 in front of me, and then I would be just left on the screen.

The market would collapse, and that's just unheard of. So that led to the belief that the phones were tapped.

Here we have a case of a trader blaming everything except himself when things begin to go wrong. Because his positions were so large – his computer password, as we know, was now Superman – Leeson expected the market to do his bidding. But his large positions were unwieldy, and he was in fact following the market, not leading it. Voicing his grievance to David Frost, he went on:

> Also, the exchange called us a couple of times early in 1995 and complained we were cancelling a lot of orders because I was putting bids in the market to try to support it, and then, as the market fell, I would cancel them. I think a lot of people complained that there were a lot of fake orders in the market. They must have checked their records, and [they] said, 'We will suspend you if you do that again.'

Leeson had painted himself into a corner. His problems were of his own making, and his inability to trade freely in Singapore and Osaka was the least of them. What mattered more was Tony Railton's dogged path towards an accurate analysis of his positions.

In retrospect, it is easy to see that everyone would have benefited if Leeson had quit early in January, when paranoia set in and began to loosen what tenuous grip he did have on rational behaviour in the market. The reason he himself gave for staying put is so prosaic that it is disarming. Unlike so many of his remarks to Frost, it may even be true. 'I think I realised that every day when I went back in January, all I was doing was attempting to spread it, or to last a little bit longer, in that family members were visiting. I think my brother came out early in January, and Lisa's sister and her fiancé were due out towards the end of February.' Lisa had always said that they had planned to leave Singapore early in April. By this stage, with such mountainous losses in the 88888 account, Leeson may well have been trying to stave off disaster for such trivial reasons.

Tony Hawes had assured the SIMEX officials he met on 8 February that the entire assets of the Baring Group were available to ensure that Baring Futures in Singapore could meet its liabilities to the exchange. What SIMEX did not know was that Leeson was now fiddling his computer records so that the massive margin calls on his positions would fall drastically. What Hawes did not know was that, in addition to the SIMEX fiddle, Leeson was about to spend the entire assets of the Baring Group, and still leave himself without enough to meet his liabilities.

Leeson's buying spree following the Kobe earthquake had triggered massive margin calls. The margin on Barings' positions was already counted in hundreds of millions of US dollars, and the sums involved were causing comment in Barings' settlements department in London. Brenda Granger, who ran the section specialising in futures and options, talked to Leeson as regularly as anyone in London. But Granger was not a specialist in this particularly complex area, and her colleagues noticed that she lacked the dispassionate attitude expected from settlements clerks. 'Brenda would refer to "my client",' one said. The use of the possessive implied a personal commitment to the trader and that was considered to be sales talk, and was not what was expected of a detached back-office employee.

Moreover, the settlements staff in London were not familiar with the margining system used by SIMEX. Named SPAN, and inherited from the Chicago Mercantile Exchange, it calculates margins continuously. Most other markets must wait until the end of the day before they can raise margins, but with the information SPAN provides, an exchange can deal with volatile trading conditions by calling for margin payments while the market is still open. This is known as 'intra-day margin'. Without fully knowing how it worked, Granger and her staff always obliged when Singapore asked for even more money to meet intra-day margin calls.

These intra-day margin requests had worried Hawes, whose treasury department had to produce the money to meet the calls, when Barings was briefly overdrawn at Citibank on 24

January. For her part, Granger was puzzled by the US dollar requests because they always came in such round sums: half to fund clients, half for house positions. It looked too neat.

While she was trying to pin Leeson down, Granger sent a message to Hawes: 'Awaiting breakdown from my buddy Nick ... (once they creatively allocate the numbers.)' To Leeson, she wrote: 'You are asking me for more money than I can collect in, so it is looking as if I have client debtors, which I do not.' In fact she had one big client debtor, Leeson himself. Leeson replied:

'Brenda, London is the cash cow. You are funding Singapore.' Unfortunately, Granger was joking when she talked about Leeson's creativity. She did as she was told and went on funding Singapore.

But Leeson did understand that he was testing the patience of the paymasters in London, and risking the kind of scrutiny his secret 88888 account would not withstand. In his statement to investigators from the commercial affairs department of the Singapore ministry of finance when he was awaiting trial, he confessed in his usual mixed-tense style: 'I needed to reduce the amount of funding that I am requesting from London on a daily basis, and, therefore, I have to stop the amount of money that I am paying [in margin] to SIMEX.'

Leeson began this new phase of his widening campaign of deception on 26 January 1995. At his first attempt, he reduced the margin call by $162 million. In fact, it proved so easy that he subsequently did it every day. The sums got larger, but the method was always the same: 'simple, but highly effective', noted the Singapore prosecutor, Lawrence Ang.

The prosecutor showed how Leeson manipulated SIMEX's margin system by entering false trades on his CONTAC computer-reporting system. Without going into too much technical detail, what we need to know is that the daily margin call is based on the long position in an account when the market closes. Since a large long position (which is hoping that the market will rise) can be offset by a short position, Leeson simply entered false short purchases. The false short position effectively reduced his long position, and so SIMEX asked for smaller margins.

Lawrence Aug made his case by showing how this manoeuvre worked on just one typical day, 1 February 1995. A false short position of 25,000 Nikkei 225 futures contracts was entered into the CONTAC system, reducing Leeson's real position – 31,184 long contracts – to 7,148 contracts. Once more, the false positions were organised, as were so many of Leeson's phoney deals, by Nisa from the settlements staff. (The Singapore prosecutors, like the inspectors, always seemed to protest a little too much when local staff like Nisa were involved: 'Nisa, being the subordinate and accustomed to carrying out all instructions given by the accused, asked one of the settlements assistants to key in the trade,' they wrote in October 1995.)

Without this false trade, Barings' overall margin call on that day, 1 February, would have been $712 million. Because of it, the call on Barings from SIMEX was $459 million. Having checked that Barings had margins on deposit with SIMEX of $574 million, Leeson then put on an extravagant show of insouciance under pressure. He calculated the difference between the margin already deposited and the false margin call, and put in a claim for a rebate. This was prepared by Nisa and signed by Rachel Yong ('believing it was a routine request', according to the prosecution). Barings was subsequently credited with $115 million, which was useful for meeting future margin calls. Before long, Leeson was depositing $247 million less in margin payments than his real position dictated he should.

Despite this brazen manipulation, Leeson had to keep on pressing London and Tokyo for more funds. The asset and liability committee in London had instructed him to reduce his positions, but his buying spree was unstoppable. There was even the odd, gratifying day on the trading floor. On Monday 30 January, for instance, the Nikkei was up 700 points. By seizing the chance to close out 6,500 contracts, Leeson recovered the money he had lost in that one contract since the Kobe earthquake. But he quickly resumed his losing ways. By the end of the week, his long Nikkei position had shot up from 20,000 to 30,600 contracts.

By February, after a quiet month in January, Leeson had returned to the Nikkei-option pit in a big way. He wrote more than 5,000 straddles, and this made him even more vulnerable in volatile markets. He confessed as much to David Frost: 'I was not offsetting the risk. I was looking for a big return.' What this meant was that he was not hedging against potential loss, as a professional trader would do.

This was no longer a spree, it was more like a frenzy. The Bank of England calculated that the cumulative loss on the secret 88888 account from July 1992 to 6 February 1995 amounted to £253 million. Had he been exposed then, Barings would have been badly wounded, but not bust. After 6 February the market fell persistently. Leeson was mesmerised by it. As his frenzy continued, Barings' chances of survival faded.

Its fate was sealed by the absence of either the people or the systems needed to stop the flow of funds to Singapore. The bank's group treasury was now like a colander, leaking funds to Leeson through a variety of orifices. In London Barings Group treasury paid funds into the London account of Baring Securities (London) Ltd (BSLL), the subsidiary company set up to finance the bank's trading on its own account – the proprietary trading. Funds needed for margin calls on client accounts were transferred from BSLL to Baring Securities Ltd (BSL). The system was this: the first payment advice in group treasury was prepared and signed by a clerk, and then counter-signed by a senior clerk. The same procedure was repeated when a transfer of funds to Singapore was required: a clerk would sign the advice, which would then be countersigned, usually by Brenda Granger, sometimes by assistants of hers in the futures and options settlements department, such as Tony Railton. The paperwork took longer than the transfer of these funds. Computer-operated payment systems like SWIFT – the Society of Worldwide Interbank Financial Telecommunications – make that part easy. BSL or BSLL funds went, via SWIFT, to Baring Futures (Singapore)'s Citibank account in a flash.

Hundreds of millions of pounds were routinely sent to fund Leeson's outrageous gamble, and the routine was never questioned. Tony Gamby, head of global settlements, explained to the Bank of England that payments were subject to various degrees of scrutiny: the trigger for special attention was not the size of the sum involved. Settlements were watchful whenever a transfer was being made from a client's account: then a check call would be made to confirm the transfer. But when transfers were being made from one area of Barings to another – from Baring Securities in London, to Baring Futures (Singapore) for example – there were no checks. It did not seem necessary: where was the risk in transferring funds from one Barings account to another? This job was so straightforward that Barings had traditionally left it to the clerks. The chief operating officer, Geoffrey Barnett, informed the Bank of England that, since he was not involved in 'day-to-day operational issues', he was unfamiliar with the way funds moved throughout the group.

The arrangement that allowed Leeson to start the cover-up of his losses in August 1992 never varied, and was never investigated. He requested funds from London to finance margin calls on client accounts, and London never reconciled those actual accounts with the funds they were sending to finance them. These loans to clients appeared in the solo-consolidated balance sheet – the one everyone but Hawes had difficulty understanding – as 'top-up'.

The 'top-up' Leeson asked for was normally in US dollars, and aroused no suspicions. Tony Railton recalls: 'On the dollars, if they requested the funds, then we paid them.' Brenda Granger remembers: 'They would just say, "Please pay $33 million to our customer account."' On 30 January 1995, the total 'top-up' added up to £150 million. By 24 February, it was more than twice that: £306 million.

Most of this went to pay margin calls on the trading Leeson was doing via his 88888 account. As we have seen, he had deceived the settlements department about this from the start. Remember that at the outset, he had fixed his computer program to erase from the system information that would normally appear on Barings' First Futures reporting program. The only information recorded about his activities was diverted to a margin file, which was a dumping-ground for accounts that did not belong to Barings in London. Brenda Granger, who relied entirely on First Futures, never bothered to look at it. Nor, indeed, did anyone else.

Had she checked that file on 1 February 1995, Granger would have seen that this 88888 account was £320 million in the red that day. But neither she, nor anyone else in London, did check, because there seemed no reason to do so. They believed that Nick Leeson's switching business between Singapore and Osaka was legitimate arbitrage; and very profitable arbitrage, too.

A tiny minority at Barings had moments of doubt, as we know. Mary Walz thought the profits were so good that they might indicate that Leeson was ignoring his position limits during the trading day. Tony Hawes' doubts ebbed and flowed, but when they were flowing, Ron Baker usually managed to turn the tide. Baker liked positive numbers on the balance sheet, and Leeson was providing more positive numbers than any other trader. Baker did not want him roughed up, as Ian Hopkins noted, and later told the Bank of England's investigators. Baker was aware of the vast sums of money involved. 'I knew there were hundreds of millions of dollars involved in the margin calls ... It was not something I felt any responsibility for working out the details of.' These details were left to Mary Walz. When Hawes expressed his doubts, she was perfectly capable of treating him as though he were merely a nuisance.

As banking regulator, the Bank of England should have operated as a backstop, but its supervisors were looking the other way. Had Barings been forced to submit large-exposure reports about its Osaka positions, or had the Bank of England imposed its own rule about refusing to allow a bank to commit more than 25 per cent of its capital to a single customer, the flow of funds might have been halted. But, because Christopher

Thompson, the Bank supervisor, had failed to come to a decision about this for almost eighteen months, the Barings file languished in his in-tray.

The Bank of England began to take an interest again at the beginning of February 1995. Thompson then imposed some unexpectedly severe conditions, which meant that Barings would either have to raise more capital to back its business in Osaka, or reduce its trading volumes. Tony Hawes, who was responsible for applying the regulations, was too busy to see to these conditions straight away. He decided that if the Bank had taken this long to make up its mind, it could wait a few weeks longer.

Leeson's switching business permitted him to plunder the Tokyo office for funds as well. Because SIMEX's system could make margin calls during the day, and because it took longer to transmit funds to Singapore from Tokyo than from London, Baring Securities (Japan) was content to keep a significant excess margin in Singapore. Leeson didn't bank it, he used it to fund another £125 million of margin calls on his new accounts. And besides that surplus, Tokyo was pouring money into the switching business, money mostly borrowed from Japanese commercial banks. Why not? The Tokyo office believed it was risk-free, being for arbitrage only.

At Barings in London, everyone thought Leeson's operation was risk-free. The executive committee believed it: Andrew Tuckey, who was pre-eminent now that Peter Baring was only a few months away from retirement, told friends that the top men at Barings knew Leeson's profits were bound to fall rapidly once other banks discovered how he was making so much money. However, for the time being, Tuckey insisted, they were risk-free.

Leeson is not a critical analyst of his own behaviour, but it is hard to disagree with his version of the attitude at Barings. He told David Frost (and, in this case, his television audience as well):

It was advantageous to me that the senior people in London who were arranging these payments didn't understand the basic administration of futures and options, and that was the biggest failing. Also, without knowing it myself . . . I can actually see now that they wanted to believe in the profits being reported, and therefore they weren't willing to question, or were less inclined to question.

The first bat-squeak of doubt, which arose on 26 January when the Bank for International Settlements checked on a rumour about a missed margin call in Asia, had been stifled. But on 16 February, Jim Peers, the company secretary, was telephoned by a senior director at Schroders, the London merchant bank that had most in common with Barings. Schroders had heard a nasty rumour that an American bank was about to terminate its credit lines to Barings. Apparently, the Americans had heard that a counterparty doing a deal with Barings was about to default on a 20,000-contract position in Osaka. This rumour was discussed by the management committee and dismissed on 20 February. However, the management committee did do something: it decided that the positions in Singapore should be reduced in size. ALCO had reached the same decision more than three weeks earlier. Following ALCO's decision, the positions got bigger. After 20 February they did so again.

Nick Leeson and Tony Railton both already had a shrewd idea that the management committee's decision was too little and too late. They had known each other for some years. Both had learned about futures and options in the settlements department at Morgan Stanley in the late 1980s. Railton had joined Barings six months after Leeson. Unlike Leeson, he seemed content to stay in the back office, where he established a sound reputation. Tony Gamby and Tony Hawes both knew, from experience, how elusive Leeson could be, and how obstructive Simon Jones was, but they thought that Railton might prove tough enough finally to succeed in reconciling those client accounts with their margin calls.

Railton, having arrived in Singapore in the company of Tony Hawes early in February, did not settle down to serious work until a week later, on Monday 13 February. It took him no time at all to uncover the basic flaw in Leeson's trading: since his positions were worth less than he had paid for them, he must be losing money. Railton's first thought was: 'If you close out [sell up] all these positions, there is absolutely no way on God's earth that you could actually return all the yen.'

Despite this discovery, Railton does not seem to have taken the analysis a step further, and questioned whether in fact Leeson was making the profits he said he was making. On 15 February, when Railton began to reconcile the Japanese Government Bond position, Leeson sensed his disquiet. That day, Leeson played his last trick on Barings' books. Calculating that his total loss in futures-trading since 31 December was £170 million, he wiped it out, at a stroke, instructing Nisa to enter the following purchase in the CONTAC system: buy 7,000 JGB contracts at 745 points below the market close. Profit? Exactly £170 million. Of course, the order was never executed on the floor of the exchange, but it had a miraculous effect on the balance in the books. By the next morning, 16 February, the trade was reversed.

Lisa Leeson must have known they would not be staying in Singapore much longer. The couple had sold their Rover and were driving a borrowed Mercedes, and on 15 February Lisa called a removal firm to arrange to have their furniture sent to her parents' home in Kent. But if Leeson was intending to leave Singapore, he did not tell Peter Norris this when they met on 16 February, nor anyone else at Barings.

On 16 February Peter Norris was in Singapore, having arranged to meet there some colleagues from McIntosh Securities, the Australian associate in which Barings held a 19.9 per cent share. He had a full schedule that day, but towards the end of the afternoon he met Leeson in one of the glass-walled offices off the main trading-floor in Baring Securities' twenty-fourth-floor office.

Norris wanted to know what view SIMEX traders took of Barings. After all, Leeson was doing brilliantly, and if he was making so much money, other people must be losing it. Leeson, Norris recounted later, did not have much to say. His recollection was that the meeting lasted five to ten minutes. That was subsequently to become a matter of dispute. The conversation had effectively taken place in semi-public, because the pair of them met in Simon Jones' glass-walled office overlooking the settlements area. At least two of the people who were there swore the meeting lasted longer.

Ten floors below, in the Baring Futures office, Tony Railton was simultaneously looking through the US-dollar funding requests. He had been interested in these for some months, partly because the regular fifty-fifty split between client and house margins was so neat as to be improbable. Talking to Nisa, the senior settlements clerk, Railton discovered that, once the office knew the total margin call in US dollars, they would simply adjust the figures for client and house accounts so that they met the total. Railton introduced a new form of margin request on the spot. He remembers thinking that 'half the stuff I had been advised on as to how the spreadsheet worked did not work . . . The project was becoming more and more complicated the further one went along.'

Railton telephoned his boss, Brenda Granger, who could hear how worried he was. 'I advised Brenda of this, and I said, "I am really stuck now, because we are missing this 14 billion yen."' The problem was quite clearly serious enough for her to inform Tony Gamby immediately.

Tony Gamby had had a hectic fourteen months since being promoted to settlement director of Baring Investment Bank. Much of the first six months on the job had been spent unravelling a dreadful crisis in the New York office, where the American regulator, the Securities and Exchange Commission, was threatening to close down Barings' New York operations. What worried Gamby was that Barings had taken on the profitable but risky business of clearing trades between Wall Street securities houses and Latin American brokers. Since Barings was willing to take the risk in a hazardous business, the service was heavily used, and the settlements department could not cope. Barings wanted this profitable business, but not enough funds had been invested in the information technology needed to run it. The SEC insisted that Barings clear up the settlements mess, and Barings agreed to put up more capital.

In the experience of Barings' branches overseas, men from head office flew in for a couple of days, wrote a report, and nothing happened. But Gamby went on turning up in Manhattan, found the money to pay for new systems, and stayed around until the SEC had been satisfied and the crisis was over. By the summer, he said, he knew Barings Securities' settlements staff in New York better than he knew his own people in London.

Gamby's next preoccupation was Mexico. To relieve the pressure on New York, an office was opened in Mexico City. The settlements system in the new office was unfamiliar, but the old Baring Securities ethos was not dead: as in the old days, they opened the office and hoped for the best. When trading began in November, the errors in settlements were excessive, even for Barings. In January 1995 Gamby and Geoff Broadhurst, the finance director, told Peter Norris that Barings would have to suspend trading in Mexico City. 'We dipped our toe in the water, and pulled it out,' says Gamby. This was unprecedented. With a major settlements problem to sort out, Gamby was still absorbed by Mexico when Brenda Granger reported Tony Railton's findings to him on 17 February.

Gamby is now unable to recall Brenda Granger mentioning a specific sum of money. He understood that Railton had uncovered a serious reconciliation problem, but neither Railton nor Granger suspected fraud. Railton had told Granger he was sure Nick Leeson would come up with an explanation, and that the matter would be resolved once they had had a proper conversation. Gamby assumed that, as a new man in Singapore, Railton simply hadn't got to grips with the system: there was nothing unusual in that. Perhaps he was a little in awe of Leeson, too. In the circumstances, Gamby's advice was that Railton should ask Leeson to help him sort it out. 'There was no fear in my mind that there was anything untoward,' he says. Railton had already had a word with Leeson that Friday, but

Leeson had told him he had other people to see. Leeson suggested they might meet on Sunday, when he got back from Batam.

One of the frustrations of expatriate life in Singapore is the reluctance of the government to allow liberal access to satellite television stations over which it has no control. Among the events not covered by TVS, the Television Corporation of Singapore, are the Five Nations rugby games on alternate Saturdays late in the winter. But the expats have ways of coping, and for the weekend of 18 to 19 February boats had been hired and rooms reserved for a party of twenty-five or so from Singapore at an hotel on the island of Batam, twenty miles south in the Malacca Straits. Batam is in Indonesia, a country that has no inhibitions about satellite television, so a motley crew was going across to watch Wales play England in Cardiff.

Just fifty minutes on the ferry and another three-quarters of an hour on the minibus, and they were as good as back in Blighty, although the time difference meant that the game didn't kick off until 10 p.m. By that time, some members of the party, after a long day on the golf course and some time at the bar, were feeling very cheerful: pissed, actually. Two screens had been set up in the dining-room at the Batam Bay Hotel. Once the game had begun, a member of the party, a schoolmaster from Singapore, became increasingly annoyed by the drunken cries of one man sitting behind him every time England played well. (They were doing very well, in fact, eventually winning by 23–9.) The teacher decided to have a sharp word with the loudmouth at half-time, but when the chance came the drunk was fast asleep, his head slumped on his arms. When Leeson hit the headlines, the teacher told a friend he hadn't met the man. 'You did,' replied his friend. 'Leeson was the one who passed out behind you at the England–Wales game.'

By now, the pressure on Leeson was clearly becoming intolerable. He admitted as much to David Frost.

I was frightened of quantifying the amount [of the loss], you know. I would get faxes in the morning telling me the amount of funding that the girls were requesting, but I was trying desperately not to go to the office so it didn't stare me in the face. I was trying to hide from it. I'd leave the trading-floor rather than go back to the office. I'd grab hold of somebody and take him for lunch somewhere, because going to lunch with him for an hour and a half meant that I didn't have to go to the office for an hour and a half.

He had warned Lisa that they might be leaving Singapore sooner than she had thought. On Monday 20 February, Lisa made a second call to the removal company to tell them this.

That day Leeson was in no mood to meet Railton. Having stood him up on the Sunday, Leeson claimed he was too unwell to meet on Monday. He was not, however, so poorly that he was incapable of building up his short position in Japanese Government Bonds, nor too ill to ask London for £35 million to meet margin calls, nor to place the fictitious trades in the CONTAC system to reduce his margin requirement by £247 million.

On Tuesday 21 February, Railton finally caught up with Leeson for a fascinating meeting, described in lavish detail by the Singapore inspectors.

Mr Railton first recalled that on 21 February 1995, Mr Leeson was still unwell and unable to meet Mr Railton to discuss the problem. During a subsequent interview, Mr Railton recalled that he met Mr Leeson in the late afternoon on that day, for perhaps an hour or so, and that they discussed Mr Railton's future plans, his intention to relocate to Singapore and how he should negotiate his remuneration package for this purpose.

When queried on his lack of urgency in discussing the discrepancy with Mr Leeson, Mr Railton explained that Mr Leeson had sidetracked his initial intention of discussing the matter. Mr Railton pointed out that he was unable to steer the discussion because Mr Leeson was senior to him and potentially his future boss. He also recalled that Mr Leeson had claimed that he was still feeling unwell, and hence not able to discuss an involved issue such as the discrepancy.

All this would have been news to Gamby, who had not yet agreed that Railton should 'relocate' to Singapore, never mind considered how much he should be paid. That Tuesday, Gamby had made desultory enquiries about the state of Railton's investigation, but had not pressed for greater urgency. 'In terms of priorities, it didn't get past third or fourth on my list,' Gamby recalls.

At that meeting Leeson assured Railton that they would discuss the issue the following day. On the Wednesday, Leeson was active again in the market, losing £64 million on Nikkei futures, counting a two-day loss of £33 million in Japanese Government Bonds, and declaring himself too busy to meet Railton until the evening. When they met, Railton at last raised the matter of the yen that had gone missing, and the need for a true reconciliation. Leeson's reply surprised him. 'Yes,' he said, 'I agree with you.' Leeson himself identified the information they needed – and then he put Railton off again, until the next day, Thursday 23 February.

The day Leeson finally conceded defeat began very badly and got worse. In the morning, he was on the hop at SIMEX. The compliance department had summoned him to explain some improper cross-trades conducted by two of his traders the previous day. Leeson's answer was unsatisfactory, and he was told that Barings would be charged with a breach of SIMEX's rule 513.

Arriving on the trading-floor, Leeson found Railton there, insisting on some answers. Leeson had by now managed to put Railton off for six days in a row, and he tried to do so one more time. By talking on the trading-floor, while he was busy executing trades, he made it hard for Railton to concentrate on the subject in hand. Railton gave up, and agreed to meet Leeson at Simon Jones's office in the late afternoon.

The tumult on the floor was real enough. By now SIMEX was trading in Leeson's shadow. His 88888 account controlled 85 per cent of the open interest in Japanese Government Bonds, and almost half the interest in the much more heavily traded Nikkei 225 contracts. When the market was falling, Leeson was losing money; for every 100 points the Nikkei index dropped,

Leeson lost £20 million. And the market was falling fast: by 330 points on 23 February, adding £65 million to his deficit. The JGBs rose by 72, which cost Leeson £61 million, and his options lost a further £18 million. So his loss for that one day was £144 million. Judith Rawnsley reports that Leeson had rushed to the lavatory on several occasions that morning to be sick. It is understandable: he had just become the gold medallist among the world's all-time loss-making traders.

By the time he arrived at Simon Jones's office in the afternoon, Leeson did not want to talk at all. But the news from London suggested that head office might finally be waking from its long sleep. An overnight message from the treasury department for Tony Hawes, who was due to arrive in town that evening, and which must have been intercepted by Simon Jones, said Leeson's funding request on 22 February for $45.5 million was totally incomprehensible. Settlements in London was under the impression that Leeson was reducing his positions, as he had been ordered to do by both the asset and liability committee and the management committee. Yet the message suggested the reverse was happening.

When Railton saw Jones and Leeson conducting an animated conversation in Jones's office, he assumed that the subject was the treasury message. Perhaps it was, but Jones might also have been listening to one of Leeson's last lies as an employee of Barings. He would have to leave the meeting with Jones and Railton, he said, to visit Lisa in hospital: she was suffering from the after-effects of a miscarriage. (Lisa had indeed miscarried at the end of January.) Railton joined them and began, once again to press Leeson for an explanation of the discrepancies and the unreconciled accounts, but Leeson excused himself. He had no answers, and he knew he was going for good.

Leaving Ocean Towers, Leeson met his friend Danny Argyropoulous, the flashy trader from FCT who had been a role model for him. Argyropoulous thought he looked troubled. He drove Leeson to the flat in Anguilla Road, where Leeson knew he would find Lisa, who wasn't in hospital at all. Lisa recalls him saying: 'Let's go away for the weekend. I need to think about things – I'm on the verge of a breakdown.' She pinpoints that suggestion as the first time she knew he was in trouble.

Lisa telephoned her mother in Kent to say they were going to celebrate Nick's birthday over the weekend in Bangkok, in Thailand. Either she was lying, or Leeson had lied to her. When Argyropoulous drove them to Changi Airport, they caught a flight to Kuala Lumpur.

Leeson had left the office between 4 and 4.30 p.m., so Jones and Railton would have expected him back around 5.30, maybe 6 p.m. In his absence they had been joined by Rachel Yong, the financial controller from Baring Securities, and together they chewed over the reconciliation problem. Railton remembers Jones finally admitting that the figures made no sense to him: 'I don't blame you for wanting to speak to him,' Jones said.

Jones, Railton and Yong had begun a random search through Leeson's papers. Recalling the kerfuffle over the SLK receivable, Jones looked through that file. There he found the fax, purportedly from SLK's managing director, but with the 'Nick and Lisa' fax head. It would be rash to jump to conclusions, Jones said. Shortly after 9.30 p.m. (1.30 p.m. in London), he urged them to leave the problem until the morning. Railton did not demur, but if he had not smelled a rat by then, he either had a defective sense of smell or he was as reluctant to offend Jones as he had been to coerce Leeson. After one last telephone conversation with Granger, Railton left the office as well.

Railton had spoken to Brenda Granger during the morning, London time, to report that his conversation with Leeson had been interrupted, but that it would continue shortly. Railton telephoned again, in the early afternoon. This time, Granger told Gamby that Leeson could not be found; she reported that Simon Jones had told Railton that there was no need to raise the alarm that evening. Jones thought they should wait until the morning, to see if Leeson turned up then.

It was 3 p.m. Gamby sat in his office turning over in his mind the events of the previous four days, during which Leeson had persistently evaded Railton's questions. After fifteen minutes, he decided that the story did not sound right. He put on his coat and walked from Bishopsgate to America Square, where he told Peter Norris's assistant, Sajeed Sacranie, that he needed to see Norris immediately. Sacranie said that Norris was in a meeting, and asked what it was about. Gamby replied: 'Leeson may turn up tomorrow, and Railton may have made a Horlicks of the reconciliation. But we haven't been able to track down Leeson, and I'm worried that some money might actually have gone missing.' Sacranie called Norris from his meeting. Norris sensed from Gamby's agitation that the matter must be serious. He told Gamby to call a meeting of all the people involved in his office later in the afternoon when his own meeting was over.

Late in the afternoon, there was already a state of high anxiety in Norris's office, an open-plan room on the fifth floor at America Square. Although it was functional rather than grand, the office was designed in the style of a traditional partners' room, furnished by four desks (Norris's, Richard Greer's, Sajeed Sacranie's and one for visitors), and a large table in the middle. There was plenty of space to accommodate the group that stood around the telephone, listening to incoming calls from Singapore on a loudspeaker. There were Gamby and Granger from settlements; Broadhurst, the financial controller; Sacranie, Norris's assistant; and Mary Walz from financial products. Ron Baker, who was on holiday in Switzerland, spent a lot of time on the telephone to London that evening.

The principal cause of the anxiety was the story that Leeson had vanished. Mary Walz did not yet know enough to assume the worst. She thought it made no sense for Leeson to flee, and remembered hearing that he had been sick. 'I thought it was Nick, not Lisa, in hospital,' she said later. Walz tried to telephone Jones in Singapore, but he was nowhere to be found: Norris's secretary got the telephone numbers of the four biggest hospitals in Singapore, presumably from Bax. All were contacted; none had a patient called Nick Leeson.

Having drawn a blank, they checked Leeson's excuse about

Lisa being in hospital. Walz got hold of Lisa's mother, who confirmed the story about the miscarriage, and added that she had spoken to Lisa a few hours earlier. Her daughter was certainly not in hospital: on the contrary, she and Nick had gone to Thailand for the weekend. So he wasn't going to turn up in Jones's office that night or the next morning.

Norris did his best to remain methodical: list the possibilities, he said, and see how they stand up to the facts. The most frequent misdemeanour in banks like Barings is embezzlement. The group considered that first, but it did not bear much scrutiny. There were no black holes in the bank accounts, and anyway, Leeson did not have signing powers. So theft was out.

They then considered a systems failure: perhaps there were concealed losses as a result of unauthorised trading. That seemed like a good bet, especially to Norris. George Maclean remembers Norris telling him that it was the most likely explanation, when he arrived later, at 7 p.m. But they had no hard information to go on. For the next stage of the investigation they had to rely on Tony Hawes, who had been working in Tokyo and was due to land in Singapore at 1 a.m. local time. Hawes would know what to look for.

Hawes was tired and ready for bed when he got into his room at the Westin Hotel at 2 a.m. What he got instead was a call from Norris in London, instructing him to go straight to the Baring Futures office to check the records and look for any evidence of unauthorised trading. Hawes roused Railton, and the pair of them started work in the deserted office at around 3 a.m.

Meanwhile, in London, it was 7 p.m. The group in Norris's office was resigned to a long night. Norris called Andrew Tuckey, who was being driven to the opera, to tell him there was a serious, though unspecified, problem in Singapore. When George Maclean arrived, Norris told him that the problem seemed to be unauthorised trading. Broadhurst cancelled his squash game; junk food was sent for and picked at.

Broadhurst and Sacranie coped by working, feeding information into a spreadsheet on the screen which showed markets along the top line, and the various contracts down the side. But they were working on the positions that had been openly reported to Barings by Tokyo and Singapore. Based on those, Leeson was, as he said, long in Osaka and short in Singapore. As they tried to justify these positions, anxiety became mixed with frustration. But no one contemplated anything more than a one-off calamity. No one thought Leeson's trading position might prove fatal.

An hour later Tony Hawes came on the open line from Singapore to report slow initial progress. The SLK receivable looked as if it had been manufactured. Bax was giving a helping hand by now. He had tried to rouse Simon Jones, but Jones did not answer his telephone or respond when Bax hammered on his door. He said later that he had been sleeping deeply.

It was 4.30 a.m. Singapore time (8.30 p.m. in London) before they found the equivalent of the Rosetta Stone: the document that exposed Leeson's real positions. This was a computer print-out from SIMEX which quoted all Baring Futures' positions, including an account numbered 88888. 'There were goodness knows how many transactions in it,' Hawes reported, 'all of them seemingly at enormous losses.'

When Hawes began to read out the lists of contracts, Norris suddenly felt sick. The conclusion he reached was instinctive, but accurate: he was sure that Leeson had hidden a large long position in the Nikkei in Singapore. Being long in Singapore and in Osaka meant that Barings was naked in a volatile market. It was a recipe for bankruptcy.

Broadhurst and Sacranie started to feed the new figures into their spreadsheet and soon realised that it was no use subtracting the Singapore position from the Osaka position, as they had been doing earlier. To get the right result, they needed to add up the positions instead. It took them thirty minutes to verify Norris's instinctive explanation. Broadhurst had got the figures on the spreadsheet right, but he had not yet put two and two together. 'It didn't sink in, even at that stage,' he says.

Gamby was taking down the options positions as they came over the line. It was an appalling revelation: a man who was not permitted to trade in options had, in fact, written and sold so many that Gamby was still writing them down half an hour later. It wasn't easy to price the options in London, so it was impossible to quantify the impact of the options-trading. Fernando Gueler could do that. He was woken in Tokyo – for the second time that night – at 4.30 a.m. and told to get to his office at once.

Gueler was not in the mood for this. The previous evening had been hectic: Norris had called to ask if he would become a director of Baring Investment Bank. He didn't think there was any extra money in it, but he was pleased to be appreciated. Gueler then went to a colleague's birthday party, and his good humour had improved when he heard that a trader he really respected planned to join Barings because he thought it was a bank that was getting things right.

So Gueler was cross at being woken for the first time, at 2 a.m., by a call from London to be told that Leeson had 'left'. In his sleepy state, his first thought was that Leeson had left the company to join Morgan Stanley. But no – London wanted him to try to get hold of Leeson in Singapore. He'd put in some calls, but if they couldn't find him, he couldn't, either, he said. And he went back to sleep.

When he climbed into his car later to drive to the office, Gueler was struck by the notion that this might all be a practical joke: that he was being set up because he had been made a director. Another call from Norris at 6 a.m. disabused him of that idea. He was required to calculate the state of Leeson's options, based on figures sent to him via e-mail. Norris's other instruction was not to tell a soul. The system broke down, and the figures had to be faxed, so it was an hour before Gueler began his investigation.

Even before Gueler reported the options loss to London, the mood in Norris's office was sombre. Mary Walz recalled: 'My heart was in my stomach and my stomach was round my ankles. I was as sick as I've felt in my whole life.' Peter Norris said: 'You were watching a group of people seeing their entire professional lives crumble in front of them.' No one's life was crumbling as fast as his: by the small hours of the morning, the calculation of the losses had risen from the sum Gamby had first mentioned ($170 million) to more than £300 million – and they knew there were more losses to come.

Only two explanations were possible: either a customer had reneged, or Leeson had been trading without authority on his own behalf. To get an answer to that question they urgently needed to find Leeson. By midnight in London, the group had another clue as to his whereabouts: a fax from him had arrived at the Barings desk at SIMEX saying that he was taking a day off to spend his birthday in Phuket.

But then a second fax from Leeson arrived at the Singapore office – at 3 p.m., 7 a.m. in London. Handwritten, on notepaper from the Regent Hotel, Kuala Lumpur, it was addressed to Simon Jones and James Bax. It read:

> My sincere apologies for the predicament I have left you in. It was neither my intention or aim for this to happen but the pressures, both business and personal, have become too much to bear and after receiving medical advice, have affected my health to the extent that a breakdown is imminent. In light of my actions I tender my resignation with immediate effect and I will contact you early next week to discuss the best course of action.
> Apologies, Nick.

Bax at once tried to reach Leeson at the Regent, but was told that he had checked out (having paid with his corporate credit card). Norris told Bax to fly to Kuala Lumpur, but it was a tired decision: even if Bax had found Leeson there, and even if Leeson had been able to pin the blame on a client, it was Barings that would have to meet the losses on the exchange.

Gamby and Granger arranged to fly to Singapore to help Hawes. Tuckey had been alerted by 5 a.m.; Peter Baring learned about the disaster an hour later. The board of Barings plc would meet at 8 a.m. Norris called in their lawyers, Slaughter and May, and prepared to face the music.

the Regent
KUALA LUMPUR

A FOUR SEASONS · REGENT HOTEL

160, Jalan Bukit Bintang, 55100 Kuala Lumpur, Malaysia.
Telephone (60-3) 241-8000. Telex XXXX. Telefax (60-3) 242-1441
Malaysia Toll Free Reservation 800-8006

TELEX		FACSIMILE
	Our Fax Number is 03-242 1441	(65) - 534 - 2169
TELEX NUMBER	ANSWER BACK	AREA CODE · FAX NUMBER
COUNTRY		Singapore
		COUNTRY

ATTN: Simon Jones James Bax   DATE: 24th February 1995

FROM: Nick Leeson   TOTAL PAGES: One (including cover page)

MESSAGES

Simon James

        My sincere apologies for the predicament that I have left you in. It was neither my intention or aim for this to happen but the pressures, both business and personal have become too much to bear and after receiving medical advice have affected my health to the extent that a breakdown is imminent. In light of my actions I tender my resignation with immediate effect and will contact you early next week to discuss the best course of action

Apologies
NL

A REGENT INTERNATIONAL HOTEL

Resignation: Leeson's final fax to Bax

11

Have I Bought Barings?

Bankers in the City of London work longer hours now than they once did, and most of them were still in their offices at 5 p.m. on a Friday evening late in February when a message came from the Bank of England's deputy governor to the City's top men. Rupert Pennant-Rea would be grateful if they would attend a meeting at the Bank at 5.30 p.m. No hint was given of the subject, but these men did not question the summons. When the Bank of England calls them in at such short notice, it is because there is a financial crisis. This message from Pennant-Rea marked the start of a weekend which would have profound implications for all of the City's famous merchant banks – not just Barings, but Warburgs, Schroders and Kleinwort Benson, too. The reputation of the Bank of England was about to come under severe scrutiny; even the power of capitalism itself was tested that weekend. 'It struck at the heart of the City,' is how Andrew Buxton, the chairman of Barclays, put it. As the months went by and the participants forgot some of the details, the drama itself nevertheless remained as vivid in their minds as when they lived through it.

For most of them, the Bank of England's fortress-like building in Threadneedle Street is a short walk away. The big commercial banks – known both as the clearers, because they clear the cheques that flow through the monetary system, and as high-street banks, because that is where they are to be found – have huddled around the Bank for 100 years, as if to make sure they do not lose sight of each other. When one of the merchant bankers, George Mallinkrodt, entered the Bank that Friday, he bumped into Peter Baring. 'What are they up to?' Mallinkrodt asked. Baring wasn't telling – not even a colleague from Schroders.

The only bank with headquarters outside the City was the Abbey National, miles away in Baker Street, on the site of number 222, where Sherlock Holmes grappled with dastardly crimes. As Christopher Tugendhat, the chairman, left for the Bank, he remarked to a colleague that he thought he'd better take his hat – he suspected he might be going to a funeral.

Despite the rumours in the Bank for International Settlements, the gossip that had been picked up by Schroders, and the speculation about Barings' Japanese positions, the Bank of England had had no hint of trouble at Barings. The governor, Eddie George, had left London that Friday morning for a skiing holiday in Avoriaz in Switzerland, and in his absence the weekly meeting of the Bank's executive committee had been taken by the deputy governor, Rupert Pennant-Rea. At about 11.30 a.m. Pennant-Rea had been called out of the meeting to take a telephone call. On his return, he said he had been talking to Peter Baring: apparently, there was a serious problem in Singapore. He was coming in shortly to discuss it. Since it would clearly involve the banking supervisors, Michael Foot, the head of that department, was alerted, though he had no idea what it might be about. 'It could be a waste of time, but you might look in,' Foot said to a colleague.

After an agonising board meeting at Barings, Peter Baring arrived at the Bank of England at noon. He had an extraordinary story to tell. He believed Barings was the victim of a very substantial fraud in the bank's Singapore operation. He didn't know whether it involved one person or several, but a man named Nick Leeson, who was manager of Barings' futures-trading operation there, had gone missing. They did not know exactly how much money was involved, but there was a big hole in the accounts, maybe as much as £400 million, a sum amounting to more than the capital of Barings Bank. If this was so, the bank was insolvent. Bankrupt. They were talking about ruin.

A participant at that first meeting recalls that, while Peter Baring was quite collected, Andrew Tuckey and Peter Norris seemed on the verge of tears. They were in a state of shock. 'The news came as a bolt from the blue,' says Brian Quinn, one of four executive directors at the Bank of England and the senior man responsible for banking supervision.

Quinn is a small Glaswegian, the son of a shipyard worker and brother of a trade-union official, who speaks with no trace of an English accent. He cuts a distinctive figure, with silver hair and black eyebrows. Quinn had lived through the two earlier crises that had scarred the Bank's reputation: the bail-out of Johnson Matthey bankers in 1983, and the crash in 1991 of BCCI, the bank dubbed the Bank of Crooks and Cocaine International. Unlike some of his colleagues, he had survived both disasters.

'I didn't understand the Barings crisis properly at that stage, and I wanted to get an idea of the nature and dimensions of the case,' Quinn says. 'There are bank crises where things turn out worse than they seem at the beginning, and others where the opposite is true.' Quinn, Michael Foot and his senior supervisors started brainstorming. What, precisely, were the issues involved? How would the crisis affect markets in London and abroad? And, not least, who would pass the bad news on to 'the other end of town' – the Bank's euphemism for the treasury in Whitehall. This all went ahead without the benefit of Christopher Thompson, the supervisor who knew Barings best. He was away.

One thing was clear. Pennant-Rea telephoned Sir Terry Burns, the treasury's permanent secretary, and told him that the Bank of England would not be recommending that any public money should be spent to bail out Barings. That was exactly what Burns wanted to hear.

Another of Quinn's tasks was to put Pennant-Rea through a crash-course in crisis management. Pennant-Rea had been appointed deputy governor on Eddie George's promotion to governor in January 1993. He was an astonishing choice: although he had worked in the Bank in the 1970s, he had subsequently become a distinguished journalist and editor of the *Economist*. He was therefore an outsider – and not only by trade: like Andrew Tuckey, Pennant-Rea was born and brought up in Rhodesia. Unlike Tuckey, however he had no instinctive respect for the institutions of the British establishment. One of his colleagues at the *Economist* was Sarah Hogg, who had moved on to 10 Downing Street to run John Major's kitchen cabinet. The general assumption was that it was she who had picked Pennant-Rea for the Bank, maybe to keep Downing Street in touch, perhaps to act as the grit in the oyster. As it was, Pennant-Rea's economic intelligence had hardly been called upon at all. Eddie George had wanted a thorough re-organisation of the Bank's staff. That meant redundancies, and the governor cast his deputy as his hatchet man. Pennant-Rea had personally informed those who were to be made redundant of their fate, and his own fate was to be cordially disliked for it.

Quinn went through the drill with Pennant-Rea: get the governor back from holiday immediately; find out the implications for bank supervisors in other countries; list our options, including the possibility of a rescue exercise, which would have to be discussed with the City's bankers. Quinn suggested that they should all be called in at five o'clock. 'Speak to them in general terms; say there's a problem and we're thinking about it. Warm them up,' he advised.

Only the British-owned banks were invited, a fact which appeared to ignore the seismic changes in the City of London since Big Bang in 1985. This had meant embracing American, European and Japanese banks, and by 1995 the operations of Goldman Sachs and Salomon Brothers, Deutsche Bank and Daiwa, Morgan Stanley and Merrill Lynch dwarfed those of the City's native merchant banks and brokers. In the global market, too, these foreign banks were larger than the British clearing banks.

The basis of the Bank of England's reasoning was a law of

numbers that applies to bank-rescue operations: 'The bigger it gets, the harder it gets,' says Quinn. Self-interest was a motive, too; if the collapse of Barings threatened the British banking system, posing what is called systemic risk, the British banks would be more anxious to sign on for a lifeboat operation than would the City's big foreign players.

In the first-floor committee room at the Bank of England, shortly after 5 p.m. that Friday, Rupert Pennant-Rea opened with a speech that sounded like an editorial he might have written in the *Economist*. He was intellectually single-minded and emotionally uncompromising. He explained that Barings had been the victim of a 'massive fraud', and that, as far as was known, the losses amounted to roughly £400 million. The Bank of England hoped that a bail-out would be organised, but there was no question of any public money being made available, by either the treasury or the Bank. Pennant-Rea told friends later that he felt like the old-fashioned bank manager who says, 'I will give you every help except money.' From the very start, it was clear that this was not going to be a repeat of the celebrated Barings bail-out of 1890, which the governor of the Bank of England both orchestrated and helped to finance.

Sir Nicholas Goodison, head of the Trustee Savings Bank, who knew what Barings' capital amounted to, gasped when he heard that the loss was £400 million. He knew the bank was bust. Peter Birch, from the Abbey National, also felt his heart sink. A couple of years earlier, the Abbey National had established a joint venture with Barings to trade derivatives. The venture had not been a success, and Birch had decided to end it, having found Barings pompous, arrogant and ferociously political. ('It was a jungle; you succeed by being ruthless,' he noted.) Birch knew the Abbey National had no involvement in Barings' Far East trading. None the less, the fact that they were linked in a joint venture made him apprehensive.

The merchant bankers were more sympathetic: 'After all, we're in the same blood group,' explains George Mallinkrodt of Schroders. He appreciated that fraud was one thing even the most prudent of banks could not always protect itself against. 'I took Peter Baring's explanation at face value,' he says. Pennant-Rea declared that since the problem was fraud, saving Barings was largely a matter of recapitalising the bank. Since the Bank of England was not proposing to do that, the bankers present were going to have to stump up the money to bring Barings back to life.

The obstacle to this plan was the absence of proper figures. 'In any fraud case, you don't believe any number unless it's been checked by people who are not connected with the fraud,' says Michael Foot, the head supervisor. Goodison pressed Pennant-Rea and Quinn about the extent of the liabilities. 'They tend to grow as you're looking at them,' he explained later.

Goodison, the clearing banker, doubted whether the Bank of England could solve the crisis, but Mallinkrodt, the merchant banker, was fairly optimistic. His understanding of the discussion was that, if the London bankers came up with the new equity, Pennant-Rea had committed the Bank of England to finding a way of capping Barings' liabilities by arranging for a bank or finance house to take over all the existing positions in the market, whatever they were. That cap had to be in place when the markets opened in Tokyo on Monday morning. The deadline for saving Barings was 10 p.m. GMT on Sunday evening.

Misunderstandings and resentments began here. Mallinkrodt's inference might have been that the Bank had committed itself to providing the cap as its contribution to the rescue, but the Bank's minutes of the meeting are more ambiguous, describing the cap as one of two options, the other being the sale of Barings to a rival bank.

The Bank's method rather than its objectives was what worried Sir David Scholey of S. G. Warburg. One of the City's grandees with a seat on the court of the Bank of England, Scholey felt uneasy as he returned to his office at Warburgs. He shared the genuine shock that had been felt around the table, but Pennant-Rea, perhaps because he was new to the job, had not capitalised on it. Once they knew about the problem, the pace should have picked up and been maintained, but Pennant-Rea, having asked the bankers to let him know if they had any ideas, sent them home. Had it been Scholey's meeting, he would have let the participants get some expert advice and then he would have locked the doors until a plan had been hammered out.

This criticism reflects different priorities. Scholey thirsted for action; the supervisors pursued the facts. 'There were 101 questions and we spent the next forty-eight hours trying to answer them. Talking further on Friday night would have been a waste of breath,' says Quinn.

When Eddie George arrived at the door of his chalet in Avoriaz, the telephone was ringing. George didn't even unpack: a taxi took him back to Geneva Airport and he caught the first flight to London, reaching his house in Dulwich at 10.30 p.m. on Friday. He made a number of calls as soon as he got home. 'I reckoned it was odds-against from Friday night, really. I knew it was going to be uphill all the way,' he said a few months later.

George Mallinkrodt of Schroders, had told Peter Baring on Friday evening as they left Threadneedle Street to let him know if Barings needed any help. Baring had telephoned at eight on the Saturday morning to take up the offer. Peter Baring had always told his fellow merchant bankers how lucky his firm was: since its capital was owned by the Baring Foundation, the bank was simply not for sale, ever. Now he was asking Schroders to advise on the disposal of the bank to the highest bidder.

Mallinkrodt's offer was not motivated by friendship alone. If Barings failed, the City of London would suffer from the fall-out, and the most vulnerable of all would be the merchant banks. If a depositor's money was not safe in Barings, depositors might wonder why it should be secure in Warburgs, or Rothschilds, or Kleinwort Benson, or Schroders.

Win Bischoff, Schroders' chairman, took personal charge of the team that went into Barings on Saturday morning to put a rough value on the assets. The bankrupt securities business was, of course, one of three different operations at the bank. There was also Tuckey's corporate finance department (the merchant-banking arm), and a prosperous asset-management business. At a guess, Baring Asset Management was worth anything between £400 million and £500 million.

Potential buyers came sniffing round the same day. ABM–Amro, a Dutch bank which had a long relationship with Barings, expressed an interest in the whole package; securities houses, like Merrill Lynch, were interested only in the profitable bit. But the interest was real enough: John Heimann, the man in charge of Merrill Lynch's international operations, was woken at 5 a.m. on Saturday morning in New York City by a call from the London office. He caught the day flight from JFK to Heathrow.

Since a piecemeal sale would not, by itself, rescue Barings, Bischoff also began talks about temporary equity for Barings, so that it would have sufficient assets to open for business on the Monday. This was to be drawn, he hoped, from the bankers who had been at the Bank of England on Friday evening. He sounded them out on Saturday and found that, while there were reservations, the mood was optimistic. Mallinkrodt did not move from his telephone all day ('When you have a crisis like this, you don't go to the races'). He briefed City eminences like Sir Evelyn Rothschild, who was in Singapore, of all places, but had to find out from London what was happening a few blocks away from his hotel.

Schroders saw that the top management at Barings was pushing hard to get a sale. But this conviction was not evident further down the hierarchy. There the Bank of England's supervisors found people in shock, and often got a palsied response when they asked for internal documents. Nobody yet knew exactly how much Leeson had lost.

The different time zones were a complicating factor. When Quinn and his colleagues telephoned the Monetary Authority of Singapore (MAS) on Friday, everyone had gone home. 'I called the home telephone numbers of people I knew in Singapore, but I had to leave messages: "Call back. This is urgent,"' says Quinn.

At 3 a.m. on Saturday, the first response to these messages woke up David Reid, who supervised Singaporean banks in London. Reid told his MAS contact that there was a problem with a British bank in Singapore. He was flying out later that morning to brief them, and to consult about various options. The local man, who had no idea that there was a crisis in Singapore, was anxious to know which bank Reid was talking about. Reid would not say, not on an open line. 'Telephones can be tapped, and we were desperately keen to keep this as tight as possible,' he said later. MAS, upset at not being told immediately, subsequently never showed much enthusiasm for helping with the bail-out.

First thing on Saturday morning Rupert Pennant-Rea got on the telephone and started trying to organise the cap. He began at the top of a list of chairmen and chief executives of the world's leading banks and securities houses. To each he explained the problem, and the proposed solution: he wanted someone to take over Barings' positions, at a price. The bankers were polite but cagey; most said they could not decide anything without first consulting their derivatives specialists. They would want to know the size of the liabilities, and of the fee. Pennant-Rea was in no position on Saturday to answer either question.

Eddie George talks about problem-solving as a question of putting a ferret down a hole to see what it comes up with. On Saturday morning George's ferret was aimed in the direction of Japan. Relations between the Bank of England and the Bank of Japan and its patron, the ministry of finance, are not intimate, as they are with the Federal Reserve in Washington DC, but they both belong to the freemasonry of central bankers, and are part of a network that is often good for a discreet favour.

Michael Foot had already spoken to the Bank of Japan's duty officer in London on Friday evening, asking him to look in at Threadneedle Street on Saturday morning. The Bank of England's idea was to get Japanese support for a plan to contain

Barings' losses when the financial markets opened in Osaka and Tokyo on Monday morning. The Bank wanted to be able to declare that the game was over by unilaterally closing out all Leeson's positions. That would freeze profits (owed to the various counterparties) and losses (owed entirely to Barings) where they had stood on Friday evening. George explains: 'Since the Nikkei was the crucial thing, we thought that, if the market was driven down, the people who suffered would be the Japanese themselves.' The Japanese authorities had to be persuaded that bailing out Barings was enlightened self-interest.

A second ferret went down another hole that morning. Quinn had been given the impression that there might be only one or two counterparties involved in Leeson's trading. The Baring positions were huge: £3.6 billion long (as buyers) in the Nikkei 225, £8.7 billion short (as sellers) in Japanese Government Bonds and £4.6 billion short in European contracts. The search to find the counterparties began. When found, they were to be asked by the Bank of England to co-operate: by agreeing to close out their positions first thing on Monday morning, they would get a premium on the existing profit.

It was a clever idea, but not very practical. It was inherently improbable that there would only be a couple of counterparties for such large positions. Securities houses like Bankers Trust, Goldman Sachs and Morgan Stanley told the Bank their own big positions in the Far East, unlike those of Barings, were hedged.

The Bank of Japan and the ministry of finance in Tokyo did not prove helpful, either. Without pressure from these two bodies, the Japanese markets would not bend their rules, and unless the rules were bent (positions had to be closed before the markets opened), the Bank's plans would founder. The Japanese ministry of finance's London representative went to the Bank on Saturday and was given the message first hand. But friendly persuasion was not working. When Quinn eventually talked directly to the deputy governor of the Bank of Japan, he learned that there was no way of co-opting officials at the ministry of finance. (In Tokyo, the Bank of Japan proposes, but the ministry of finance disposes.) The previous December, the bail-out of two credit unions in Tokyo had led to a public outcry, and the ministry of finance had been bruised by the episode. Quinn recalls: 'They just didn't want to get involved in any rescue exercise, far less one in which a UK bank was involved.'

George describes the state of play on Saturday evening: 'The failure to find a large counterparty meant there was no solution in the marketplace. We went up and down, but I still thought it was odds against saving Barings.'

Saving Barings involved raising around £400 million in the form of temporary equity from the British banks. But because the Bank would need to cap Barings' losses before serious talks about new investment got under way, the City of London's top bankers were not asked back to the Bank of England for further talks until 10 a.m. on Sunday. As the Bank was anxious to avoid media attention the bankers were asked to enter through the back door in Lothbury.

But it was too late. On Saturday afternoon, Charles Moore, the editor of the *Sunday Telegraph*, had received a call from an old friend with good Asian contacts who said it looked as if Barings was ruined. Moore passed the news on to his City staff, whose initial reaction was that it couldn't possibly be true. But within ten minutes the story had been confirmed, and it appeared on the front page of the *Sunday Telegraph*'s first edition. This goes to press at 6.30 p.m., and since first editions circulate quickly among rival newspapers, all of them knew about it by 8 p.m. In fact the *Sunday Telegraph* had only just scooped *The Sunday Times*, which learned of the story from the legendary City editor Sir Patrick Sergeant. He had been tipped off by his son-in-law in Hong Kong – apparently, the Barings' debacle was common knowledge in Hong Kong's futures market by Saturday morning.

The omens on Sunday morning were mixed. On one hand, when Sir Nicholas Goodison of the TSB, John Bond of the Midland and Andrew Buxton, the Barclays chairman, arrived simultaneously at the back door of the Bank of England, it was closed. There was no doorman and no bell. On the other hand, when they walked round to the front of the building, they spotted a limousine parked outside with the licence number BRU 1, and a label on the windscreen which read 'Brunei Carriage Company'. Barings' best single client was certainly not the Queen, nor even a fabulously rich Saudi sheik, but the Sultan of Brunei. The thought of enlisting that fortune in a bail-out made everyone more hopeful.

Shortly before the governor was due to start the meeting, bad news came from Barings. Ploughing through files in Singapore on Saturday, Tony Hawes and Tony Gamby had finally calculated the likely cost of closing out losses in Leeson's options positions. Quinn's wariness about the size of the losses was vindicated: instead of £400 million, the deficit now seemed likely to be around £600 million, maybe more. 'One of the problems was that Barings kept finding little bits of paper in bottom drawers,' says Andrew Buxton.

The British bankers went back to the dark first-floor committee-room, its high ceiling painted in two shades of blue, with a fine chandelier and gilded, decorative plasterwork. An Augustus John portrait of Montagu Norman, the bank's most famous and most notorious governor, stared down from the wall. Like every other important room in the Bank, it has a clock. When the room falls silent, you can hear time ticking away.

This was not the kind of crisis Eddie George relished. Banking supervision was a bit of a distraction, frankly; something he liked to be able to delegate. He preferred high-profile monetary-policy meetings with the chancellor of the exchequer. George is a professional central banker who joined the Bank of England directly from Cambridge University, where he was spotted by a Bank recruiter playing a disciplined hand of bridge. Having become only the second governor to be drawn from the Bank's staff, he had one more ambition: to establish the independence of the Bank of England from the treasury in setting interest rates, a power that had gone to the treasury when the Bank was nationalised in 1945. It was a bold objective, but one towards which he had been making progress.

After George announced to the meeting the latest score on the losses, the dreadful details of Barings' Singapore disaster were outlined by Peter Baring and Andrew Tuckey. They said Leeson had been authorised only as a clerk executing orders for clients and doing routine arbitrage between SIMEX and Osaka. They could not have known what he was up to.

As the story unfolded, however, the catastrophic failure in Barings' internal management controls became obvious. A banker at the table detected a change in atmosphere. At the outset, it had been sympathetic and supportive: after all, Baring and Tuckey were among friends. The first frost came after Peter Norris's presentation of Barings' financial position, which was designed to show that it was worth a lot more than the temporary equity the banks were being asked to provide. Norris, who was exhausted, gravely misjudged the audience. 'He talked as though he was making a pitch to a company like British Telecom. "We're the best," he said – no hint of humility at all,' recalled one of the merchant bankers. The presentation included an outline of the 1994 balance sheet, which revealed that bonuses for the year would come to more than £100 million. These were hardened bankers, not easily shocked, but most were genuinely staggered when they learned the size of Barings' bonuses.

A detailed account of this Sunday in Threadneedle Street, written immediately after the event by a participant who insists on anonymity, records: 'Perhaps the most revealing fact was that the so-called SIMEX business ... had contributed £41 million of pre-profit share and £18 million after. In other words, the employees had enjoyed 55 per cent of the profits. I suspect that others shared my view that this extraordinary bonus arrangement was at the root of the problem that Barings had encountered.'

The distaste felt by the bankers did not lessen their desire to save Barings, but a bail-out was growing more problematic. Not only had the losses surged by 50 per cent overnight, but the Bank of England still had to find a way to cap them – the essential pre-condition if the banks were to finance the bail-out. Since the cap was proving the harder part, Barings agreed to pay a premium, or fee, in return for the cap: $250 million was set aside. Experienced bankers wondered whether it would be enough. When the markets opened in the Far East later on Sunday night London time, Barings' positions would make the futures markets a speculator's delight. Since prices could go down, the assumption was that giant hedge funds, like George Soros's Quantum fund, would take short positions that would send the market plummeting. A fee of $250 million would cover only the first 4 per cent of any fall. A devastating drop of as much as 10 per cent could not be ruled out.

There had, none the less, been a couple of candidates for the role of white knight. Derivatives specialists from investment banks like J. P. Morgan and Crédit Suisse First Boston were familiar with the technicalities of unwinding large market positions. They were mercenaries attracted by the prospect of a good fee. But they had their own conditions. Since a few rules would need bending for such massive deals to be done effectively, they would need help from the Japanese and Singapore exchanges. Michael Foot, who knew about the talks with Bank of Japan and the MAS, confessed that, while these sounded like relatively small favours, neither Tokyo nor Singapore were offering favours of any kind. 'It felt a bit like the infantry at war. It's fine for the generals in the rear to order an advance of 50 yards, but it's more difficult than they know,' says one of the negotiators.

Eddie George had another idea. Perhaps, he said, the London banks should provide the cap themselves. David Scholey was keen, and Barclays and the Midland had an idea of how it might be done: they could form a consortium, and appoint one or two members to manage the closure of Leeson's positions. Scholey thought he knew how to distribute the risk among the banks. But again there was a condition: the Bank of England would have to agree to protect the consortium against a staggering fall in the Japanese market – a fall of more than, say, 10 per cent. That revived the matter of spending public money on the bail-out. On Sunday morning, the governor was being very cagey about that.

But the plan was torpedoed before it was properly afloat, for an acutely embarrassing reason. The anonymous recorder of events noted: 'It is perhaps salient to observe that there was a glaring lack of knowledge about this type of business and the inherent risks among a representative cross-section of leading British bankers.' Because of their ignorance of futures markets, they took fright.

George gave them a straw to grasp at. Reporting that Barings had come up with another possible rescuer, he referred to 'an Islamic family fortune'. Despite the presence of the BRU 1 numberplate in Threadneedle Street, he was naming no names.

With relief, the British bankers turned from the problem of the cap to the option they knew something about: raising money to lend at good rates of interest to companies threatened by bankruptcy. That the size of the loan had risen to £600 million overnight seemed to worry none of them. The adrenaline was running now, and, as they discussed it among themselves, a leader emerged. No one asked him specially, but Andrew Buxton, chairman of Barclays, simply assumed the role. His attitude to raising money is matter-of-fact. 'Money occupies a special place in an Englishman's heart, but what people don't realise is that to a banker money is a commodity like a pair of socks. Some amounts look big, but the amount itself isn't frightening at all.'

Buxton did some mental arithmetic based on a rough formula worked out by Schroders. He needed £50 to £60 million each from the big clearers, Barclays, NatWest and the Midland, and £40 million from Lloyds, the Abbey National and the TSB. Most of the merchant banks were asked for £30 million, and the rest for between £10 and £20 million. The first £500 million was easy; the rest had to be wrung out of the TSB and Kleinwort Benson (neither objected in principle, but thought they had been placed in the wrong category and wanted to cough up less). The most reluctant participant was Standard Chartered: Patrick Gilmore, its managing director, and Peter Wood, the finance director, were the only bankers present to plead lack of authority.

The Abbey National's Peter Birch recalls Buxton's forthright response: 'He said, "Am I going to tell the governor the three of you won't contribute? This is UK Ltd, and we've all got to contribute. I'm going to put you down anyway."' Buxton thought he'd said this privately, but Birch remembers being impressed; he had had an image of Buxton as a beleaguered chairman of Barclays. Now he saw him as a cricketer who had played every stroke in the book and was 100 not out at the close of play.

When Barings' losses were revised up to £650 million, Buxton simply stated that they would all have to chip in an extra 10 per cent. No one demurred. They weren't doing it for nothing, of course: the terms were 5 per cent interest immediately and 1 per cent a month thereafter – 17 per cent in a full year. Even so, George Mallinkrodt of Schroders thought that watching fourteen banks round the table putting up such a massive sum to save a merchant bank was the most elating moment of his career.

The clearers were less sentimental. The only row round the table started when they indulged in a remarkable speculation about the future of Barings. What if the bank was saved, and then eventually sold at a profit: how would this be divided? They would certainly each want a share. One fastidious merchant banker later complained to the governor about this undignified display of greed.

Conditions were attached to the bankers' proposed big Barings loan: obviously they would not proceed without a cap; and they were dubious about the Baring bonuses, amounting to £105 million, which were due to be paid the next day, 27 February. Andrew Buxton's first reaction was that they should not be paid at all. Peter Baring spoke out in favour of them, and most of the other bankers could see that there was a case to be made for them.

In the old days, young men joined a bank and spent their working lives there. Barings Bank had been typical; that was one of its problems. The new breed of clever bankers and traders were more like mercenaries, hiring out their labour to the highest bidder. If Barings did not pay the 1995 bonus, the best of their staff would be clearing their desks and moving on. This would reduce the value of the company into which the other banks were proposing to invest £650 million. Looked at that way, making a principled stand on Barings' bonuses was cutting off their noses to spite their faces.

Being a confirmed City man himself, Buxton saw the force of the argument and gave in. The deal was that no bonuses would be paid the following day, or to the top executives who were intimately involved in the debacle; those that were paid would be spread out through the year.

Eddie George and Rupert Pennant-Rea had slipped out at lunchtime to see Kenneth Clarke, the chancellor of the exchequer. There was no question of Clarke's refusing to put up public money for the bail-out, because the governor had not asked for it. But George and the chancellor agreed that only if the risk was 'systemic' was there a case for financing a bail-out. This meant that the collapse of Barings would have to be seen to undermine the whole British banking system and the global markets before George would intervene, and he had already decided that Barings was not big enough to have any profound, or systemic, effect.

Not all the bankers round the table that morning agreed with this view. The next day, the Barings collapse could lead to chaos in derivatives markets; moreover, such a dramatic bank failure would have a detrimental effect on all the banks' share prices. For their part, the merchant bankers thought that almost any price was worth paying to save a merchant bank. But George had not been speaking to the chancellor as their representative. He knew his own mind and spoke it. 'Go tell that to the taxpayer,' was his sharp response some months later to the suggestion that saving a merchant bank was a proper use of public funds.

* * *

George had a smile on his face when he met the bankers after lunch, and it had nothing to do with his trip to Downing Street. He now thought that, maybe, there was a buyer for Barings after all, as the bankers had already guessed. Since Brunei's oil revenue goes into the Sultan's bank balance, the Sultan is widely assumed to be the richest man in the world – even if he does have to finance the whole government all by himself. The Sultan was also a client of Baring Asset Management. In fact, he was BAM's biggest single client by far, having deposited perhaps 10 per cent of the £35 billion under its management. The Queen's account was puny in comparison.

John Bolsover, who ran BAM, had managed to persuade the Brunei Investment Authority's London representatives that Barings was a good buy, and had conducted the negotiations himself. The Bank of England wanted to be sure that it was made clear that Barings, and not the Bank of England, were the vendors and would take legal responsibility for anything that was said. Besides that, Eddie George did not think his intervention would help: 'If I'd rung the Sultan and said, "How would you like to take out these options?" he wouldn't have known what the hell I was talking about.'

George's improved humour reflected the attractiveness of the deal that was being negotiated. Acting on the Sultan's behalf, the Brunei Investment Authority would agree to cap Barings' positions in Singapore and Osaka for a fee of $200 million. On top of that, it would pump £300 million of new equity into Barings. This would soon be converted into a 50.1 per cent holding, giving the Sultan control. The Sultan's investment would reduce the contribution from the British banks from £650 million to a much more manageable £350 million, and the likelihood was that the Sultan would eventually buy them out, too. Naturally, the banks were enthusiastic. Perhaps the wish was father to the thought.

The longer they waited in the Bank of England for firm news, the greater the difficulties seemed. Michael Foot realised that, by assuming Barings' market positions, the Sultan would be required to raise large sums of ready cash to meet margin calls on SIMEX and in Osaka the following day. Not even the richest man in the world can summon up hundreds of millions in cash quite that quickly. There was too much risk and not enough time.

David Scholey recalled the Johnson Matthey crisis in 1983, when the Bank of England's negotiators wasted time on a deal that eventually fell through. He felt it might well be happening all over again, and he was right. At 8.30 p.m., the governor called the bankers together for the last time to tell them that there was no deal with the Sultan. Time was the problem. The Sydney futures market was about to open, and the Tokyo stock exchange would be open in an hour and a half. But the crucial factor was the time in Brunei: 8 p.m. in London was 2 a.m. there.

Later on, George Mallinkrodt remarked on the difficulty of getting people to make a decision at that time in the morning. A more detailed and subversive account of what happened in Brunei surfaced soon afterwards on Wall Street. According to this story, the reason the deal fell through was that the Brunei Investment Authority could not agree final details without the consent of the Sultan himself. By the time they were ready for him to scrutinise these, he had gone to bed. And when the Sultan of Brunei goes to sleep, no one wakes him up. The most doleful detail in this account is that when the Sultan awoke on Monday morning, his first question was, 'Have I bought Barings?'

So, late on Sunday evening, Eddie George announced that there was no alternative but to declare Barings bust, and to call in the administrators. A statement was prepared declaring that Barings' problem was unique, not generic: in other words, 'Don't panic, chaps.' Peter Baring thanked his colleagues, knowing that they would soon be his former colleagues. Peter Norris was unable to hold back his tears.

As they dispersed, John Craven of Morgan Grenfell was keenly aware of the irony involved. At a lunch he had had with Peter Baring and Andrew Tuckey shortly after Morgan Grenfell had been taken over by Deutsche Bank, they had patronised him. It could, they said, never happen to Barings.

George Mallinkrodt thought the timing of the collapse was the crucial factor. Derivatives had recently acquired a bad name. He was sure that six months earlier, a cap for Barings' exposure would have been found. But episodes like Bankers Trust (the case of Gibson Greetings Inc), and Merrill Lynch (the case of Orange County, California) earlier in 1995 had left a legacy of fearful ignorance, and a weekend was not long enough to dispel it. 'We were pretty close to solving it. If we'd had another twenty-four hours, this would not have happened,' he says.

On the Sunday night, David Scholey of Warburgs looked in on the Bank of England's exhausted team of officials eating pizza in the ground-floor committee-room. He reassured them that they had done all they could. The Bank's resources had been over-stretched, and they had been expected to do too many things at once. But Scholey was full of foreboding for the wider consequences of the failed bail-out.

Looking at him at Threadneedle Street that day, the other bankers thought they saw a rattled man. Scholey himself had confided his fear to friends that weekend; that the collapse of Barings could spell the end of the City of London's merchant banks. He was not sure how long it would take, but he was acutely aware of a German precedent. Before the collapse of the Bank Herstatt in 1974, there had been fifteen German private banks; now there are only two.

One repercussion of the bankruptcy of Barings was obvious to all the other merchant bankers who had been at the Bank. Before they left, George assured them that he had spoken to the Midland Bank and to Lloyds, and that outside funds would be raised if there should be a run on their deposits the following day. But, with the collapse of Barings, the other merchant banks knew in their bones that they could no longer rely on the Bank of England to look after their interests. For two centuries, the Bank had been like a mother hen protecting her chicks. A long historical relationship had now ended. The disaster would alter the way the City of London saw the Bank in the future.

Eddie George understood that the authority of the Bank of

England would be damaged by the failure of the bail-out. 'There is an exaggerated expectation about what any financial regulator can achieve,' he says. After Johnson Matthey and the scandalous bankruptcy of BCCI, Barings was the third well-publicised bank failure since 1978, when the Bank of England had been given legal powers to regulate them.

In fact, the collapse of Barings was a moment when the City of London re-defined itself. Ever since Big Bang, its image as a quintessentially English place, nourished by its history and yet flexible enough to welcome new ideas and new men, had been changing. Now the emphasis had switched entirely to the new men and their money. The collapse of Barings, and the prospect of the sale of other merchant banks, wrenched the City from its roots.

The City may be surrounded by London, but it no longer really belongs there. The new City of London has more in common with Wall Street and Marunouchi in Tokyo than with Glasgow or Birmingham. Everything in the City has its price, and patriotism is not worth very much. One Bank of England official who negotiated with the Wall Street securities houses about providing the cap says: 'If the price of the cap had been high enough, they'd all have come in.' But it wasn't high enough, and they didn't. Another noted: 'If the liabilities had been £500 million, as we originally thought, we'd have been able to cap the losses.' But the losses grew too big, and they didn't.

The global financial system did not care enough about Barings to pay the price of saving it. Michael Foot relates the episode to the philosophy that underlies the system: 'Capitalism, which, like us, the bankers espouse, did not come up with a solution. Nobody would punt on that scale for that possible return.'

The odd thing is that the speculators did not run wild, and markets in the Far East did not collapse when they opened on Monday morning. Any bank or securities house that had had the guts to take the big gamble could have picked up Barings, if not for a song, at least at a sale price.

12

In Denial

Courtiers reported to their friends in the City that the Duke of Edinburgh, who often gets furious, was furious with the directors of Barings. They had put his wife's funds at risk.

The fate of the Queen's savings was one factor that drew more attention to the Barings collapse than to any other City crisis. Her Majesty also takes advice from Morgan Grenfell, and from Rowe and Pitman (about stocks and shares), but Barings was regarded as Her banker, and Baring Asset Management invested Her money.

Only the 5 per cent of it that all prudent investors keep in cash was at risk – if Barings had gone into liquidation, Her Majesty would have applied to the Depositors' Protection Fund, which would eventually have awarded her £15,000 of the first £20,000 that she had lost. But word soon seeped out in the right quarters that the Queen's account was ring-fenced. Indeed, the same courtiers reported that the Queen had no intention of punishing Barings. Her account would stay where it was.

Compared to the leading characters in the drama, the Queen displayed regal composure. The rest were in denial. The day the administrators moved in, Peter Baring, breaking his rule about not speaking to journalists, gave a memorable interview to the editor and banking editor of the *Financial Times*, in which he declared that Barings had been the victim of fraud.

What could Leeson have had in mind? asked the *FT*.

It is difficult to get a fix on the motivation of this fellow. But we share the view that the creation of a substantial hidden long position was the aim of the operation, by someone who no doubt is out there with a substantial short.

Let us suppose the associate approached our trader and said, 'You should build up a long hidden position at Barings so great that when Barings discover it, they cannot possibly sustain it and remain solvent.

'I, meanwhile, will build up a short position, and when Barings duly fails, I will have a wonderful opportunity to cover my short at a profit.'

The pair from the *Financial Times* reported, without comment, that Mr Baring said this seemed to him to be a credible account of events. Since this view denied any possibility that Barings' management might share any responsibility for the collapse, Peter Baring was virtually alone in believing it. His best friends thought that he should have stuck to his rule about not talking to the press.

William Rees-Mogg thundered in *The Times* that the collapse of Barings was the fault of the Bank of England. Comparing it to the sinking of the British battleship the *Hood* in the Second World War, Rees-Mogg wrote: 'At one moment in time, it is unthinkable: at the next it has happened.'

Rees-Mogg denied that the failure was at all the fault of Barings. He had, he wrote, known several of the leading figures at Barings over the past generation. 'Barings has not been a badly run bank, but a good one, highly professional, relatively altruistic, realistic, rather conservative. The parallel of the *Hood* again comes to mind. On the bridge, in the engine room, manning the guns, there is an admirable professional crew. One shell penetrates the magazine and the ship is lost.' He accused the Bank of England of a 'grotesque and dangerous error' in refusing to save Barings, no matter what the price.

Nick Leeson also denied that it was all his fault. When he gave his side of the story, he blamed the Bank of England for the size of Barings' loss. (Eddie George put the damage at £860 million. Later on, the Board of Banking Supervision revised it to £869 million.) Leeson outlined his reasoning in his interview with David Frost. Watching television in his hotel room on the Friday night, the day after he had left Singapore, he saw the market had been firm that day. 'I thought, they've had a great day to get out and the market's only down by 300 points. At that stage I believed they had unwound 60, 70 per cent of the position.'

But Barings could not unwind any positions on Friday. That was done by the exchanges, starting on Monday. Leeson claimed the difference between his accumulated loss on the previous Thursday, the day he had fled, and the eventual loss was £535 million.

> I think the Bank of England definitely mishandled the situation. I mean, they told ... every market participant, 'There is going to be a big sell order on the Monday,' and they're certainly guilty of the market being down 1,000 or 1,200 points on the Monday. I think everybody would agree that to unwind the position over that 1,200-point movement, rather than at the bottom of it, would result in a lower loss. I have to put my hands up, I'm the guy who caused the £325 million loss that led to the £860 million loss. But whether it had to be £860 million, I'm not so sure. I don't think so. I think it could have been better handled.

In the first few days after the collapse, only one person took any blame. That was Peter Norris. He had hardly stopped working since the Thursday afternoon. When the bail-out failed to materialise on the Sunday night, he returned to his office and began telephoning Barings' offices abroad, starting with Tokyo. It was 6 a.m. on Monday there when he talked to William Daniel. 'He told me that because money due to Baring Securities Japan from London and Singapore could not be sent, basically we were bankrupt; it was quite an emotional conversation,' Daniel said later. He passed on the news to the Tokyo stock exchange, and all the Barings' terminals were switched off within minutes. As Norris worked grimly on, this action was repeated all over the world.

At Barings in London there was a feeling of positive anger

at the way Leeson's positions had been closed out in Singapore. The losses seemed to be multiplying faster than was right. The options portfolio, for example, which showed a loss of around $410 million on Monday, was taken over by a single, unnamed purchaser showing a deficit of $500 million, which was added to the sum of Barings' debt. The loss on the Nikkei 225 futures seemed to have been bumped up by about $30 million.

But lots of traders, especially in the United States, were cross with SIMEX. So angry, in fact, that some even contemplated pulling the plug on the Singaporean market. The person who saved the day was a thirty-nine-year-old lawyer from Long Island in New York called Mary Shapiro. In October 1994, she had been sworn in as chairman of the Commodities Futures Trading Commission – the CFTC – which is the futures-and-options regulator in the United States. Within weeks, the president of the Chicago Board of Trade, Tom Donovan, boasted to his board that he wouldn't 'be intimidated by some blonde five-foot-two-inch girl'. Asked to comment, Shapiro replied: 'I'm five-foot-five.'

Shapiro had gone to her office in Washington DC on Sunday afternoon, and by 5 p.m. she knew Barings wasn't going to make it. The worry was that the markets in the Far East would go into free-fall – 'a fall of maybe as much as 10 per cent', she had thought – that that would have an impact on American markets the next day. As it turned out, this did not happen. In Tokyo, the Nikkei 225 fell by 800 points in the morning, but recovered 150 points in the afternoon. On SIMEX, the Nikkei 225 futures followed the same trend, but the movement was more exaggerated: they fell by 1,050 points at first, but finished only 645 points – or 3.8 per cent – down on the day. But the crisis that Mary Shapiro had to face was not caused by the behaviour of the stock index. American futures-traders had $350 million at risk as a result of the Barings collapse, and a lot of that money might be about to go down the drain. It was panic stations.

What SIMEX did on Monday to control downward pressure on Nikkei 225 futures was to double the margin requirement for that one contract. Firms that had been paying 15 per cent of a contract's value as margin were now called on for 30 per cent; moreover, the exchange refused to release margin paid by American clients trading through Barings. But, behaving in their customarily secretive way, neither SIMEX nor its regulator, the Monetary Authority of Singapore (MAS), would explain the reason why. The margins might have been sensibly doubled as a deterrent to speculation; alternatively, the money might have been appropriated by SIMEX to offset Barings' losses, and to shore up the clearing-house. American finance houses like Merrill Lynch and futures-traders like Leo Melamed in Chicago were damned if they were going to let SIMEX use their money to bail itself out of trouble.

An exchange's reputation depends mainly on the integrity of the clearing-house, which collects debts, pays out winners and makes the margin calls. When a clearing-house comes under pressure, it sets alarm bells ringing. 'I don't think it occurred to SIMEX that some American trading-houses would be unwilling to meet their margin calls,' says Shapiro. 'But if they hadn't met them, their positions would have been liquidated. Thousands of Nikkei contracts would have been dumped on the market, with devastating implications. SIMEX could have failed, and that would have cast doubt on all the futures markets.'

Relations between the Chicago Mercantile Exchange and SIMEX were deteriorating fast. 'We tried to calm them down,' says Shapiro, but the American firms wanted more than reassurance. At lunchtime on Monday in Washington, she suddenly realised that unless they got guarantees from Singapore about the safety of their money, some US traders would quit SIMEX. Washington is fourteen hours behind Singapore, so it was 3 a.m. in Singapore when Shapiro decided she had to act. Undeterred by the hour, she woke up Ko Beng Seng, the chairman of the MAS, to tell him how serious the situation was.

Ko Beng Seng is a dour and powerful official, used to being treated with deference, but he dressed quickly and drove to his office. In the small hours of the morning, the MAS released a statement through the CFTC in Washington DC, which gave the assurance that all customer margin deposits were secure. The message got to New York City just in time to stop Merrill Lynch announcing that it would not meet margin calls in Singapore.

Japan – where most of the American clients' margin money had gone – proved a more difficult nut to crack. Barings had been in the habit of placing the money in an omnibus account along with funds it supplied to meet margin calls on its own proprietary-trading accounts. But omnibus accounts were being treated by the administrators in London, Ernst and Young, as part of Barings' assets. Consequently, it looked as though money belonging to American clients might end up being distributed among Barings creditors. The traders went to law; Mary Shapiro, meanwhile, went to war.

Arriving at the CFTC at 7 a.m. each day, she immediately called London repeatedly to make American fears abundantly clear to the Bank of England, the Securities and Investment Board and the Securities and Futures Authority. It was an uphill struggle. Shapiro imagined them saying, 'It's that American woman again, rattling the bars.' Eric Bettelheim, who represented the American traders, asserts that there was a strong smell of 'fuck the USA'. The emphasis, he says, was on protecting the City of London.

But this was a stirring period in English legal history. In the office of a solicitor rather than his own court, and at 4 a.m. rather than mid-morning, which had never happened before, Sir Richard Scott, then vice-chancellor of the chancery division of the High Court, heard the case for a mandatory injunction to stop Ernst and Young impounding American money. Scott eventually told the administrators to release the American customer positions, but relief was slow in coming. Having won the case in London, the CTFC had to win it all over again in Japan, where the courts were refusing to release American clients' margin funds. It was then the turn of Japanese officials to be woken in the middle of the night by Shapiro calling from Washington DC. Three weeks passed before the American traders got their money out of the frozen Barings accounts in Japan, but they got all $350 million of it.

Plenty of bankers were by now sniffing round the carcass of Barings. The asset-management business, with £35 billion under management, was clearly a desirable acquisition. Although its value was diminished by the uncertainty that now attached to the name, BAM was valued at about £500 million. Besides NatWest, Morgan Stanley and the Union Bank of Switzerland were looking it over. The Barings corporate finance department also had a good reputation in the City, and two of the British high-street banks, the Midland and NatWest, were interested in that. The problem was the securities business. Would anyone want to take on that?

Ernst and Young, the administrators, who were acting as agents for the sale, were anxious to dispose of the bank as a going concern. Although Barings bonds would become virtually worthless, a sale would guarantee that none of the customers lost money. Compared with a clearing bank, Barings had only a handful of account-holders – some 3,000 in all. But the deposits of those customers were much bigger than those of the clients of a high-street bank, averaging £500,000 each, and the customers included local authorities, churches and colleges as well as wealthy individuals such as the Queen and the Sultan of Brunei. Prospective purchasers who were willing to negotiate the acquisition of all three divisions of Barings would be on the inside track.

ABM–Amro, an Amsterdam-based bank which had been rapidly expanding its foreign operations, had talked to Schroders about a sale even before the administrators moved in late on the evening of Sunday 26 February. ABM–Amro's plans did not include the securities arm, but it had forged an alliance with Smith Barney, a Wall Street broking firm that was impatient to expand – even into Barings Securities. ABM–Amro remained near the top of the list of potential purchasers.

A second Dutch bank, ING, was barely mentioned as a

potential purchaser for the first three days. Andrew Tuckey, Barings' deputy chairman, must have found this odd, because the previous November, Aad Jacobs, ING's chairman, had been to see him in London and expressed an interest in buying the bank.

ING, the Internationale Nederlanden Groep, was a new name in international banking. Formed in 1991 by the merger of an old insurance company, a banking group and the recently privatised Dutch Postbank, ING was conscious of crucial gaps in its range of services. Although it was strong in emerging markets in areas like Latin America, it lacked clout in merchant banking, and did comparatively little in the way of asset management. In 1994, Jacobs had ordered a study to be made of London's merchant banks to see which would best complement ING. Barings was top of the list.

In his meeting with Andrew Tuckey, Jacobs had not gone as far as to put a price on Barings, but he had decided that if Tuckey showed interest, he would propose that they should co-operate. Tuckey was accustomed to approaches of this kind and dealt with them in a peremptory manner. So Jacobs left empty-handed – but he did say that, if Barings was ever for sale, ING would be interested.

At the time the idea must have seemed preposterous to the top echelon at Barings. The only alliance they had ever contemplated was with a firm which was, if anything, even more blue-blooded than Barings itself. This was not some Johnny-come-lately Dutch bank but the celebrated City stockbrokers Cazenove. Though no negotiations had taken place, Barings had approached Cazenove twice, first in 1985 and again in 1994. On the second occasion, Tuckey had asked Mark Loveday, Cazenove's senior partner, to talk to Barings before anyone else if they ever considered surrendering their independence. A good relationship with Cazenove, Tuckey said, was fundamental to Barings' business.

By the mid-1990s, however, the Dutch banks were not taking no for an answer any more. Theirs is an affluent country with a strong, stable currency. The domestic business is what

bankers call 'mature', which means that it has reached satu-
ration level and any expansion has to take place abroad. The
initial investment needed to get a foothold in France, Germany
or the UK was too big, so ING concentrated on a bold counter-
cyclical strategy. When the major New York and London banks
took fright in Latin America, ING would move in and assume
the risk, mopping up old debts at a good price. They had
also established the largest banking network in eastern Europe.
Dutch banks had had a reputation for deep-dyed conservatism,
but this entrepreneurism was reminiscent of the old days, before
the French Revolution, when Amsterdam had been Europe's
leading financial centre, and when the once-celebrated Hope
Brothers bank became the first international banker to recognise Sir Francis Baring's skills.

Aad Jacobs was given no special intelligence from London
about the Barings crisis. The news was already in the papers
when he heard about it on 26 February. Calling for the Barings
file from his office, he put the purchase on the agenda of the
board meeting the following day, and soon convinced his colleagues that, instead of picking different parts of Barings, ING
should gain the initiative by bidding for the whole group.

By Thursday, Ernst and Young had awarded ING exclusive
negotiating rights. When the Dutch asked for more time, it was
granted. A bid was ready by Sunday. On Monday, it was
cleared by the High Court and approved by the Bank of England; Hessel Lindenbergh moved right in to run it in London.
A profound sigh of relief gusted through the streets of the City
of London: Barings' huge bank loans would be paid off, the
counterparties would take their profits and the depositors'
money was safe. The grumpy lion which is ING's trademark
had a smile on its face.

ING bought Barings for a token £1, but the real cost was
at least £660 million. This figure was arrived at by deducting
Barings' capital (£440 million) from trading losses (£860 million), and then adding to that deficit (£420 million) an injection
of new capital (£240 million). The Bank of England calculated
Leeson's total loss at £869 million; add in foreign exchange

losses and SIMEX costs and the grand total is really £927 million. But: 'This is a fair price for a nice bank,' said Jacobs.

Both those adjectives were soon being called into question. One reason why ING had had such a smooth ride was that it had agreed to honour the bonuses to Barings' staff, due to be paid on 27 February. But because these bonuses had been based on Leeson's phoney profits, they had been set at a false level. When the Bank of England worked out the real level of Barings' profits, after the Singapore contribution had been stripped away, the figures were staggering. In the unaudited returns for 1994, Barings' profit before tax and bonuses was £204.8 million. Halve that, and you have the bonus pool – £102.4 million. But the real profit for 1994 was only £19.8 million. Half of that, £9.9 million, is all there was for the bonuses.

ING actually paid out between £90 and £95 million (executive directors and the managers directly implicated in the collapse got no bonus at all). The £80-million difference can be interpreted in two ways. Either it was the bribe ING had to pay the people it wanted to keep at Barings, or it was the Nicholas Leeson Memorial Fund: an unearned, undeserved £80 million bonanza acquired by one man's fraud, forgery and deception.

ING sweetened the bitter taste the sale left at the charitable Baring Foundation by making a one-off contribution of £10 million to allow it to meet commitments already made for 1995. After that, the foundation would have to get by on an annual budget of £1.5 million. But the people who were most entitled to be furious at the sums going into the bulging pockets of Barings' staff were the holders of £100 million of their bonds. Granting the administrators permission to sell to ING, the judge, Sir Richard Scott, expressed sympathy with the bond-holders. They might, he thought, have got more of their money back if Barings had gone into liquidation instead. As it was, the bond-holders did less well than the foundation: ING offered to pay 5p in the pound, with a distant and vague promise of a further £20 million. Had there been any real gentlemen left at

Barings, they would have donated their bonuses to the bond-holders; but there weren't.

Jacobs and ING had reason to feel a bit sorry for themselves as well. As the Board of Banking Supervision later confirmed, Leeson's losses were actually higher than £860 million. Worse still, the Inland Revenue presented the Dutch with an entirely unexpected tax demand for millions more to cover stamp duty. The price thus began to look a lot less 'fair'; moreover, with its emphasis on a ruthless bonus culture, 'nice' was not the word that sprang to mind to describe Barings.

One last piece of bad news was wonderfully symbolic. Barings' name had always been associated with fine paintings, and the bank's history had been displayed on its walls. The two finest pictures in the collection were by the eminent British portrait-painter Sir Thomas Lawrence, who worked in the late eighteenth and early nineteenth centuries. As mentioned in Chapter 2, Sir Francis Baring, the founder of the bank, had commissioned Lawrence to paint two portraits of himself: one of him alone, and another with his brother, John, and a Mr Wall, one of the partners. The second painting, in which Sir Francis is looking away from the two men with his hand raised to his ear, is quite a famous one. There were also five excellent Dutch landscapes and church interiors, which had been part of Sir Francis's own collection.

Directors outside the family had always assumed that the paintings belonged to the bank. In the late 1980s, they were delighted when a re-appraisal of the collection valued them in millions. However, the paintings had been inherited by the Northbrooks, the branch of the family which traces its line directly to Sir Francis Baring. Early in the twentieth century, Lord Northbrook had lent the collection to the bank to be hung in the head office in Bishopsgate.

The present Lord Northbrook, another Francis, worked at Barings for a few years in the 1980s without ever feeling at home there. Like Leonard Ingrams, he thought his name had not helped his career in the bank – rather the reverse, in fact. When he was having a new house built on old Barings property at Micheldever near Winchester, he had the principal rooms designed to provide a suitable setting for the family portraits, to Peter Baring's bitter disappointment. While the prospects of a bail-out of Barings were being debated at the Bank of England, Francis Northbrook was hastily checking that he could prove his title to the paintings. His lawyer duly presented evidence of his ownership, and Ernst and Young had to remove the collection from the inventory of Barings' most desirable assets.

So Lord Northbrook took the paintings home. With the collapse of the bank, they were the only part of the founder's legacy that remained in the hands of the family.

13

Hung Out to Dry

When she telephoned London from Frankfurt at 7.30 a.m. on 3 March, Lisa Leeson was lucky to find John Clitheroe, the senior partner of Kingsley Napley, at his desk. The British consul in Frankfurt had given her the telephone numbers of a list of London solicitors, among them the firm of Kingsley Napley, which specialised in white-collar crime. Clitheroe remembers the conversation exactly. Lisa Leeson asked if he could help them cope with their problem. Clitheroe was impressed by her use of the word 'cope' rather than 'defend' or 'get him off', and judged her to be a sensible young woman. But coping was the order of the day, because it had never been Leeson's intention to be arrested and imprisoned in Frankfurt rather than London.

Nick and Lisa Leeson had been scheduled to leave their hideaway, a comfortable beach hotel called the Shangri-La Tanjung Aru in Kota Kinabalu, on the evening of Monday 27 February. Lisa had a return ticket to Singapore, and Nick had planned to go to Thailand to wait until Lisa's sister and her fiancé arrived there on holiday from England. On that Monday, however, Leeson glimpsed a *Borneo Times* report about the collapse of a British bank. He hoped it wasn't Barings, but when Lisa bought a paper he saw that it was. Back in their room, Lisa telephoned her mother in Kent. (It was always Lisa's mother who got the call, never Nick's father.) With masterly understatement, her mother said: 'Ooh, Lisa, there's been a lot of press interest.'

The Times had in fact run a front-page piece headlined: 'ROGUE TRADER AND WIFE FLEE POLICE IN YACHT'. 'Like a latter-day Lord Jim, Nick Leeson is seeking an escape in the Far East. But whether he finds the sanctuary that restored the self-respect of Joseph Conrad's European outcast remains to be seen.'

What Leeson actually did was check in at the Shangri-La for another night and consider his strategy. After speaking to an unnamed friend in Singapore, he decided against the Lord Jim option. He told David Frost: 'The first thing I wanted to do . . . was to get to a country where I was comfortable with the legal advice that I would be receiving, and that meant Europe, Australia or New Zealand . . . The big fear was Lisa ending up in jail, and that was just something I didn't want to happen.'

So instead of striking out for the South Pacific, the Leesons opted for a prompt return to London. First thing on Tuesday, they checked out, paying their £500 bill in cash, and made for the airport. Flights to Brunei and all the connections to Europe were fully booked, so they returned to the town centre and bought two tickets on the Royal Brunei Airlines flight to Frankfurt the following day. That cost £2,600, and, once again, Leeson paid cash.

On the Wednesday they returned to the airport for their flight. Leeson, fearing he would be stopped at customs, was jumpy. Once he had survived that, there was still an eight-hour stop-over at Brunei Airport to contend with. 'I had a baseball cap on, and I was carrying a small rucksack which I always had in front of me to disguise myself. In Kota Kinabalu there were no televisions, but at Brunei everywhere you looked was television, so we . . . [found] a little day-care place where you could get a bed, and just checked in for eight hours. Lisa went out and got a few cups of tea and a book.'

It was while they were resting in Brunei that the penny finally dropped in Kota Kinabalu. A ticketing clerk at the Royal Brunei Airlines office recognised Leeson on the television news. The local police were called, but the name Leeson meant nothing to them. The local paper, the Sabah *Daily Express*, was quicker off the mark, but by the time their story had been confirmed, the Leesons' plane was just taking off on the second leg of its flight from Bangkok to Dubai. Still, the paper's story was a world scoop: 'A triumph for Malaysian journalism,' said an assistant editor, modestly.

Leeson, in a window seat, was surrounded by passengers reading newspapers with his photograph on the front pages. He concentrated on looking inconspicuous: 'I had my baseball cap on my head and the blanket almost stuck into the hat,' he told Frost. Lisa thought he was making his attempts to disguise himself too obvious, but no one on the flight recognised him. It wouldn't have mattered much if they had. The news flashed from Bangkok to Singapore, and the police had plenty of time to file an international arrest warrant before flight BI 535 reached Frankfurt, shortly after 6 a.m. local time the following morning.

There the German border police were in a heightened state of alert, but acting on incomplete information. Thinking that a Singapore arrest-warrant meant Leeson must be on a flight from Singapore, they boarded the first plane from there, which was en route to New York. Failing to find Leeson among the disembarking passengers, the guards unceremoniously woke those sleeping on board to demand identification. Some passengers pointed out that, since an aircraft in transit was not on German territory, the police had no right to insist. Uninterested in the niceties of the law, the police told them to produce their passports or be frogmarched to the terminal.

On the flight from Brunei, which arrived a little later, the passengers were told there would be a passport check at the exit door. Lisa gave a vivid description of what happened next, to Angela Lambert of the *Independent*. 'Nick said, "Oh Lisa, you've got to be strong." As we walked off the plane, they noticed "Leeson" on my passport and said, "Where's your husband?" Nick was right behind me.'

The pair were formally arrested and taken to another part

of the airport. 'Nick said, "Will there be press?" and when they said yes, he said, "Could we go a different way?" and they said no. Suddenly there were all these flashes and people calling us by our names and this American chap running alongside us to ask us questions. It was all over in a few seconds but I couldn't believe the number of photographers . . . it was terrifying.' The police informed Lisa that they would be detaining Nick overnight, and told her she should say goodbye.

In spite of what was waiting for him in Frankfurt, Leeson's mood was one of relief. Being arrested there, however, was not part of his game plan. He believed he would be put on the next flight to Heathrow, and kept asking his German guard when that would be.

In fact, his detention in Germany was a stroke of bad luck. If his ticket had showed his destination as London, there would have been a case for sending him on. At Heathrow, he would have been arrested and held overnight in the cells before appearing at Bow Street the next morning. Extradition cases are heard there by the chief metropolitan magistrate, who would probably have remanded him in custody. But after a couple of days, when his family and friends had got the sureties together, it is likely that he would have been granted conditional bail. Leeson would have been obliged to surrender his passport, but since extradition hearings invariably drag on, he could have contemplated his defence in the comfort of Lisa's house. He might well have been returned to Singapore eventually in any case, since the *actus reus* – the guilty act – of the alleged crime had taken place there, but there would have been a chance of having the case against him heard by a British court, where *mens rea* – the guilty mind – could have been a factor. In the mean time, Leeson would have been free to go to some football matches rather than having to watch them on television in a jail at Hoechst on the outskirts of Frankfurt.

John Clitheroe had handed the Leeson file to Stephen Pollard, a junior colleague at Kingsley Napley. Pollard was better qualified than most solicitors to take on the case, partly because he had appeared before regulatory tribunals and knew a future from an option. But another reason for the choice is that, like many barristers, but unlike most solicitors, Pollard is not fazed by public scrutiny; in fact, he relishes it.

Pollard was born in London, but his family moved north and he went to Manchester Grammar School. The northern accent is still audible. As a teenager, he wanted to be a barrister. His tutor in English, which he read at Pembroke College, Oxford, commented on his well-organised, lawyer-like approach. But he became a solicitor instead because, he says, he liked having proper clients instead of just representing someone at a trial. He is lean and precise, and wears fashionable, round spectacles. A suspicion of the southern ways of the London establishment, a legacy of his Mancunian upbringing, means that he is usually found on the side of the defence.

Pollard fought Leeson's case on two fronts, in Germany and in London. In Frankfurt, the Singaporean commercial affairs department initiated extradition proceedings based on twelve charges: four of forgery, and eight of manipulation and deception. If convicted of all of them, Leeson could, theoretically, find himself facing a maximum prison sentence of eighty-four years, probably in Changi jail which, with its echoes of the terrible Japanese prisoner-of-war camp of the same name, still makes the British shudder. What was striking about the charges is that they were so specific, and all twelve of them related to episodes that happened after 6 January 1995.

Pollard seized on the fact that the full story of the collapse of Barings would not emerge from this narrow approach as the best way of meeting his client's instructions, which were to get him out of the clutches of the Germans and the Singaporeans and back for trial in England. In London, the case came within the jurisdiction of the Serious Fraud Office, and, although its own investigation was under way, no request went to Germany for Leeson's extradition. The Germans were expecting one, and, since both countries belong to the European Union, all the British had to do was ask. That being the case, the Leeson defence would have to go public. A public-relations consultant named Rodney Tyler was co-opted to advise on the media campaign. Tyler's byline was on the first interview given by Leeson, priced at £50,000 and bought by the *Sun*. The accompanying pictures showed him river-rafting in Kota Kinabalu and the headline read: 'DO I LOOK LIKE A MAN WHO'S JUST SUNK ONE OF BRITAIN'S TOP BANKS?' The photograph gave no answer to that question.

Pollard and Tyler decided they must establish the Leesons as sympathetic characters, and not, therefore, as high-flying millionaires who drove a Porsche and sailed a yacht. The message was that Nick Leeson drove a Rover, until the cost of running it in Singapore had forced him to sell it; that the one substantial bonus he had ever received had been 'only' £130,000. The line was hammered home in a press statement: 'Mr and Mrs Leeson are not wealthy people from a wealthy background. They are struggling to fund Mr Leeson's fight against extradition to Singapore themselves. They are not receiving help from any rich benefactor.' This distinguished them – by implication – from the Barings and the bank's staff.

This picture of Leeson cut no ice at the Serious Fraud Office. Although it was getting no help from Singapore, the SFO completed its own preliminary inquiry at the end of May. It concluded that Leeson could be successfully charged in an English court under Section 17 of the Theft Act. Considering that his losses had led to the bankruptcy of Barings, this sounded like small beer, and was not considered sufficient reason to commence proceedings.

To engage the interest of the SFO, Pollard tried to tempt James Kellock, the SFO's case lawyer, to take a greater interest. First, Pollard said Leeson was willing to be interviewed unconditionally by the SFO. (He had already refused to talk to Bank of England investigators.) When this produced no response, Pollard's next move was to submit to the SFO a seventy-five-page statement prepared by Leeson in his cell. In this document he confessed to five charges of false accounting; but its real purpose was to persuade the SFO that the indictment should be broadened to take in the reasons for the collapse of Barings. George Staple, the head of the SFO, was unmoved. Having talked to his colleagues and consulted the attorney-general, Staple accepted that, while it would be possible to bring a case against Leeson in London, Singapore, on balance, had a better claim.

Lisa Leeson made her debut in her brief career as a public campaigner on 12 July. A press conference began a publicity blitz designed to persuade the authorities to change their minds and bring Leeson home for trial. Lisa's look was austere: short, straight blonde hair, white blouse and coloured scarf. Behind her sat her parents. The main feature at the conference was a letter from Leeson, addressed to the 'British media'. ('Mr Leeson is happy for you to put in the name of your paper,' Pollard told the rows of reporters.) In this communication, Leeson conceded that he had acted unwisely and had exceeded his authority, but he came up with a motive: 'The biggest crime I am guilty of is trying to protect people and ensure that the bonuses they expected were paid, and it is this that led to the escalation of the problem, and the offences of which I now stand accused.'

As it turned out, this unlikely story was an irrelevance, because Lisa stole the show. Tears ran down her cheeks as she spoke of her husband being sent to 'a show trial' in Singapore, and of the threat of a maximum eighty-four-year jail sentence. Her father wiped away a tear, too. The journalists asked if Nick was being thrown to the wolves. Lisa replied: 'Obviously. To close things down, he's been hung out to dry.' She had told the *Sun* earlier that she did not believe he had been acting alone. 'If Barings were sending the money up to Nick to trade with, then I'm sure they must have had a bit of an inkling.'

It was all put across as a simple case: to save the blushes of the former management of Barings, of the City of London, and of the Bank of England, Leeson was to stand trial in a faraway place where his human rights could be trampled on. According to this argument, Nick Leeson was the victim of an establishment cover-up.

14

Witch-Hunt

In mid-July 1995, a week after the publication of the report of the first of two inquiries into the collapse of Barings, Lord Kingsdown, who as Robin Leigh-Pemberton had been Eddie George's predecessor as governor of the Bank of England, was asked what he thought of the affair. His reply, overheard at a dinner party, was that if Peter Baring had told *him* that everything was OK at Barings, he would have believed him. It was one old Etonian speaking of another: the authentic voice of that old-boy network, the City establishment.

The present governor, Eddie George, responds sharply to the suggestion that an old-boy net runs the City of London. Although he went to a public school himself (Dulwich), George does not encourage such an ethos within the Bank of England. He points to the scarcity of old Etonians at the Bank as evidence of its meritocratic character. But establishments and old-boy networks are not susceptible of clear definition and statistical analysis. They exist partly in the mind – and in the mind of most people, the governor of the Bank of England is at the very heart of the British establishment.

The year had begun well for George. He had used 1994, the Bank of England's 300th anniversary, to intensify his campaign for independence from the treasury, and to free the bank to fight more effectively against inflation. In 1995, George could reasonably have expected to win a few more skirmishes in the struggle for autonomy, and to confirm the success of his term as governor thus far. It was not to be.

In the months after the collapse of Barings, the Bank of England became a target for a growing volume of abuse. The Bank had received mixed notices for its handling of the attempted bail-out (good from the *Financial Times* and the clearing banks; bad from *The Times* and the merchant banks). But the critics continued to insist that George should not have let Barings fail. Commentators in Parliament and the press said that the Bank's supervisors should have prevented the failure in the first place, and, when the report of the Board of Banking Supervision came out in July, popular opinion dismissed it as a cover-up – an establishment cover-up.

Moreover, in 1995 the Bank of England began to appear accident-prone. A month after the Barings bankruptcy, George lost his deputy governor. Rupert Pennant-Rea discovered that there really is no fury like a woman scorned, when his former mistress, an Irish journalist named Mary Ellen Synon, exposed their affair in the *Sunday Mirror*. Had it not been for the comical revelation that they had made love on the floor of the governor's changing-room, Pennant-Rea might have survived. This small, first-floor office, where the governor and his deputy do a quick change from business suit into black tie before dinner, was such a bizarre location for a dalliance that the tabloid papers developed an unusual interest in the Bank of England. This focus of attention was the specific reason Pennant-Rea gave for his resignation. Kenneth Clarke, the chancellor of the exchequer, did not think it a good enough one, but no one at the Bank appears to have tried to stop Pennant-Rea from going.

Unlike a merchant bank, the Bank of England has statutory powers under the Banking Act which buttress its power as the regulator of the banking system. But, like a merchant bank, its authority also rests on its reputation. When the Bank is admired, it can get its way without recourse to its legal clout. It was Eddie George's judgement that, by tarnishing the Bank's reputation, the Barings debacle had 'seriously' undermined its authority; and the deputy governor's resignation added another dimension to the problem. 'I want to avoid the possibility of the Bank being damaged by some foolish mistakes I made, albeit more than a year ago.' Pennant-Rea wrote in his resignation letter. But instead his departure further weakened the Bank's confidence and its cool, both of which were under strain.

The Bank of England got no credit at all for announcing immediately after the Barings collapse that there would be a formal inquiry. On the contrary, the bank was accused of acting as judge and jury. The reason why is clear from the first page of the printed report, which took the form of a letter from the Board of Banking Supervision's investigators. It was addressed to the Bank of England, and the contents explained that a copy of its report was attached, and that the board expected it to be passed on to the chancellor of the exchequer. The letter was signed by Sir Alan Hardcastle, one of the board's members, and by its chairman, E. A. J. George. Not only was the governor effectively writing to himself, but he was also a key witness with a profound interest in the outcome of the inquiry.

Kenneth Clarke saw off the demands of the government opposition for an independent inquiry, but the Bank did offer one concession. As a mark of its sensitivity to criticism, the role of the Bank of England itself in Barings' collapse would be investigated by the six independent members of the Board of Banking Supervision. This body existed as a watchdog, advising and, where necessary, reproaching the Bank's regulators. As a watchdog, however, it had never barked.

The best argument in favour of an internal inquiry was that it could be conducted more quickly than an outside job, and everyone – the chancellor himself, the House of Commons, the City, ING and the whole banking industry – was in a hurry to see the report. But fermenting in the guts of public opinion was the belief that the establishment was organising a whitewash.

The principal scourge of the Bank of England is a Labour MP called Brian Sedgemore, who has been chiding the Bank for years. He had a field day on 5 April 1995, when Eddie

George visited the House of Commons. George appeared before the treasury and civil-service select committee, which had transformed a study of financial-services regulation into an examination of the Barings collapse. Sedgemore is a committee member. A large, shambling man, he picked his nose and yawned while waiting for his turn to speak. When he did, he taunted George with a number of leaked Barings documents, one of which described how subsidiaries of the bank had lent £330 million of Barings' own funds to Baring Futures in Singapore. The exchange between them developed as follows:

Sedgemore: 'Am I not right in thinking that if you transfer the whole of a company's shareholders' capital, the Bank of England has to be notified?'

George: 'The Bank of England has to be notified as a matter of law if a company wishes to advance more than 25 per cent of its capital to a single counterparty.'

Sedgemore: 'My question, Mr George, is this: were you notified?'

George: 'I could be absolutely certain [in telling] you that we did not know as of 27 February that [£330 million] was advanced this way.'

Sedgemore: 'So effectively you are saying to the committee quite honestly that you have a supervisory system which is incapable of informing the Bank of England that a sum in excess of the whole of the shareholders' capital has been transferred out of the country. Is there not something wrong with the supervisory system?'

George: 'We do not know day by day the details of every exposure taken.'

Sedgemore: 'We are talking about rather a lot of money, Mr George, in relation to the size of the bank.'

George: 'Of course we are, but how can we be certain to know about the large amount of money unless we are monitoring every day the small amounts of money? It is a criminal offence—'

Sedgemore: 'Or unless the internal or external auditors tell you. It is a criminal offence . . . ?'

George: 'It is a criminal offence not to inform us; to advance this money without notifying us.'

Soon after this exchange, a City grandee, who paused to gossip with a journalist, was asked what was on his mind. 'What worries me,' he replied, 'is whether we can keep Peter Baring out of jail.' It was an astonishing prospect, but it conformed to the inference that was generally drawn from George's answer to Sedgemore's question. The course of action would be dictated by the report's conclusions, and this heightened anticipation, as weeks went by and deadlines were passed. The report finally appeared on 18 July.

The news of the resignation of Christopher Thompson, the supervisor who had given Barings a nod and a wink, leaked out shortly before the publication of the report. He had been accused of 'an error of judgement' in granting Barings its 'informal concession' – discussed in Chapter 7 – to exceed the 25 per cent limit on the Osaka stock exchange. The authors of the report declared that they could not determine whether the delay in imposing that 25 per cent limit was a factor in the collapse, but the existence of the 'informal concession' let Barings' management off the hook. They could hardly be prosecuted for an action that had been condoned by the banking regulator.

The report went further: since Barings did not know the exact use to which the funds going to Singapore were put, it was unlikely that an offence under Section 38 of the Banking Act had been committed by them in London. This might have proved a winning defence, but it would have been more satisfying if this had been the judgement of a court of law rather than of the Board of Banking Supervision.

The report received a bad press. The leader in the *Financial Times* accused the Board of Banking Supervision of being 'woefully soft on the Bank of England'; in the *Daily Telegraph*, the editorial-writer concluded: 'If Mr Leeson goes to prison while the former board of Barings continues going to Glyndebourne, this sorry saga will leave the bitterest of tastes.' The report was a substantial document – 337 A4-sized pages – and newspaper reporters did not have enough time to study the whole thing.

Their reaction was based mainly on the Bank's press release and Eddie George's press conference. George's line was that, despite the Barings saga, banking regulation was better ordered in Britain than in ... well, France, for instance. He could see no good reason why the Bank of England should hand over bank regulation to an independent body ('changing the brass plate doesn't achieve anything'). Thompson had not been sacked; his decision to resign had been personal. 'He decided he wouldn't have the confidence of the people around him,' said George. There would, he added briskly, be no further resignations.

The Bank of England's press release blamed Barings' collapse on the catastrophic activities of one individual, and on a failure of Barings' management and internal controls of the most basic kind. Considerable emphasis was given to the report's conclusion that, on the information available to it, there was no evidence to show that the Bank of England could have done anything to prevent the disaster. 'We do not believe the Bank was aware of the substantial transfer of funds ... We consider the Bank reasonably placed reliance on local regulators ... [The Bank] was entitled to place reliance on the explanations given by management as to the profitability of these operations ...'

But the message – 'It wasn't me, Guv' – was inelegant, and it hid the report's virtues. In spite of being denied access to documents held in Singapore, the investigators produced a thorough piece of work – although this appraisal could be made only after weeks of study. Because an index, as well as a narrative style, was absent, the only people who fully appreciated the report were a few obsessive students of the affair, and some of the victims of the collapse – some of the bond-holders, and twenty-one Barings people sacked in May by ING, which had grown tired of waiting for the report to appear.

In fact, the report's long dissection of the role of Christopher Thompson's 'informal concession' was a damning indictment of the Bank of England, but, because it was couched in technical terms, it went largely unnoticed. There was much else to criticise. Diane Abbott, a Labour member of the treasury and civil-service committee, accused the Bank of possessing second-rate intelligence about markets (there was no point in 'spending money buying drinks in bars', replied George), and of not understanding derivatives markets ('We have to work hard to keep up,' admitted the governor). Warburgs and Kleinwort Benson were by this time losing their fight for an independent life, and at least one of the British bankers was regretting the decisions not to bail out Barings. For reasons of prudence – admirable in a banker, I suppose – this critic does not wish to be identified. Occasionally, anonymity in return for strong opinions is a fair swap.

> We were wrong to close the door so finally on Sunday evening. We should have said, 'Let's leave it for a few days; see how it goes in the markets,' which is what the Dutch did. They played it brilliantly. Having done nothing for three days, they then said they were interested; forty-eight hours later they said 'We're not ready yet.' By the time they were ready, the open-ended positions were almost closed out. We jumped to conclusions on the Sunday, and we should have waited. Then British institutions should have got together and bought Barings. The French have let Crédit Lyonnais run its losses for years, but we Anglo-Saxons always say, 'Do it now – the market's opening in half an hour.' We fell for that Sunday-evening deadline hook, line and sinker.

The banker concludes: 'It shouldn't be a regulator who decides whether a bank should be saved or not.' His argument is that as bank regulators care only about the integrity of the banking system, they will not save a bank unless its failure threatens that system, even if the banking industry itself is damaged by the failure, as the British-owned merchant banks were.

With the benefit of hindsight, it is possible to see how Barings might have been 'saved' for London. If the Bank of England had been willing to guarantee a consortium of British banks against catastrophic falls of more than 10 per cent when Far Eastern markets opened on 27 February, the banks could have agreed to cap Barings' losses themselves. Once the losses had been capped, the banks could have proceeded to re-capitalise Barings. The bankers did not see this solution at the time, partly because of the refusal of the Bank of England to view it as one.

The growing disenchantment prompted some bitter criticism of the Bank of England as banking regulator. Our anonymous banker had become a severe judge, comparing the Bank's style unfavourably with Moody's and Standard and Poors, the privately owned agencies that rate the creditworthiness of banks and businesses.

> The trouble with the Bank of England is that its experience is narrow, and pay is uncompetitive. The ratings agencies employ highly qualified analysts with broad business experience. They're stickier, and better informed than the Bank. When Moody's come to see us – and we have to pay them to give us a rating – we rehearse beforehand. They spend a whole day with us, and they niggle and niggle. You don't like them, but you respect them, and when they've gone you deserve a stiff gin and tonic.

His colleagues do not bother to prepare so scrupulously for a visit from the Bank of England, however. 'You spend three hours with them; they're likeable people, and it feels like a day out at the seaside.' You can see why he doesn't want to be named.

The regulators at the Bank have a reply to this criticism. Brian Quinn correctly points out that no ratings agency found fault with Barings. Eddie George boasts that the regulators have a reputation in the City for being too rigorous and intrusive. Whatever the case, though, this anonymous attack was only one of many made at the time.

When George made his second appearance at the treasury and civil-service committee, he appeared to lose his cool. At the end of a line of hostile questioning, he wagged his finger at the MPs: 'You have got to take account of the fact that if there is a witch-hunt every time something goes wrong, it is going to make it very difficult to get people to do the job,' he said. George intended to make a general point about recruiting bank supervisors, but the MPs were engaged in a Quinn-hunt rather than a witch-hunt, and Sedgemore was at the head of the posse.

Brian Quinn is softly spoken, patient, stubborn and committed, so much so that attacks on him seem indistinguishable from attacks on the Bank itself. He fights them off fiercely. He was at George's side and did not seek his protection when Sedgemore said: 'Maybe we should put your head on the platter.' Instead Quinn responded that he was responsible for the system of banking supervision, and if the system had failed, or if policies or internal guidelines had been shown to be wrong, he would have resigned. But what had gone wrong, he said, was merely the way in which the system had been implemented, so he did not feel compelled to go.

Soon after this ordeal, he talked to me in his comfortable room in the Bank. I told him that, having read about the part played in the downfall of Barings by Christopher Thompson's informal concessions, I had been struck by similarities between the Bank of England and Barings. Decisions were not minuted, no one else knew about them – and it sometimes took fifteen months to make one. Quinn was provoked by the comparison.

I couldn't agree less. After BCCI [in 1991], we've been moving progressively away from the cup-of-tea-type approach. We have a manual that sets out management guidelines, and says who is responsible for what. Contrast that with Barings: you could not find an organisation chart there. Nobody was responsible for Leeson. In our way of doing things, everything is absolutely clear. Circumstances in which you refer up the line are clear; delegated authority is spelled out. That's been in place since 1993. I presided over that. Every conversation we have with a bank is minuted; every interview is recorded; every telephone call is logged. We're a very different institution than we were. We're moving in a more intrusive direction, and we will go on doing so.

But it is precisely this intrusion that was lacking in the case of Christopher Thompson and Barings. Quinn argues: 'We had to discover whether that machine had broken down or not.

We looked to see if this was an isolated case. It was.' There is no doubt that Quinn believes that to be true, and indeed, it may well be. But his critics didn't believe him.

They thought his best course of action was resignation. But resignation, which would inevitably be seen as an admission of error, is not part of the Bank of England's disciplinary culture. An outsider who served a term in a senior position at the Bank remarks: 'The hierarchy works on constructive ambiguity. They're responsible – until something goes wrong.' Quinn remained unrepentant. Until his retirement in February 1996, which had been planned over a year earlier, he insisted there was nothing wrong with the system.

In public, the Bank of England was reluctant to admit failure of any kind. This hard, public face was, perhaps, an indication of the wound left by the Barings debacle on the Bank's inner confidence: the top men insisted so strongly that they were not at fault that it seemed as if they were trying to convince themselves that this was the case. But this strict defensive posture did relax a little as the months went by. In the summer, Eddie George sat behind his desk in the governor's office and considered again whether there was anything the Bank could or should have done, but hadn't.

'No,' he said. A pause. 'No, I really don't,' he repeated. A further pause. Then he said: 'No, that's not right. We could have homed in much harder and said, "Where is all this profit coming from? From the Far East? What do you think?" Actually, we did ask the questions, but we could have pressed them harder; so could the management, the auditor and the Securities and Futures Authority.' But there was also, George added, a convincing historical explanation for Leeson's profits: they were, after all, in the tradition of Christopher Heath and the Japanese warrants. 'Of course, we could have said right at the beginning that putting together a bank with a securities operation would lead to a change in its culture. But with hindsight, you say to yourself you should have pressed harder.'

Barings was not pressed hard, however, and the Bank of

England had to live with the consequences. If its strategy really had been, as some of its critics claimed, to connive in a cynical establishment cover-up of the collapse, it had been a fiasco. The Bank of England's performance as the Grand Panjandrum of the City's regulators got lousy reviews.

Things were no better on the economic front. The chancellor of the exchequer, Kenneth Clarke, was unmoved by George's campaign for higher interest rates. Not much was heard now about independence for the Bank of England. The year that had started so well left George chastened.

Once the Board of Banking Supervision's report was out of the way, George took comfort from one aspect of this dreadful affair. At his press conference, he said that he could not exclude the possibility that something nasty would emerge from the woodshed: the second of the two inquiries into the collapse, by the Singapore inspectors, had still to be published. However, George declared: 'I would be quite surprised if it isn't the last word. I would be very surprised if a whole new dimension emerges.'

The Singapore inspectors proved yet another disappointment in Eddie George's own *annus horribilis*.

15

Panic, Ignorance, Greed

There are three possible explanations for the collapse of Barings. It was either a conspiracy, a cover-up or a cock-up.

An early instance of the conspiracy theory came from eighteen-year-old Sarah Leeson in an interview with the *Watford Observer*: 'I think there is something dodgy going on at Barings and they are trying to cover it up. Nick is being blamed for everything. It is not just Nick, if Nick at all. One person can't lose all that money, and they're playing on his background, making him the scapegoat because of his upbringing.'

The Bank of England's inquiry came down heavily in favour of the cock-up theory. Adjudging the lack of controls within Barings to be 'absolute', the report stated: 'It was this lack of effective controls which provided Leeson with the opportunity to undertake his unauthorised trading activities, and reduced the likelihood of their detection.'

The whole line-up of Barings' senior managers was implicated by the Bank in this failure: old bankers, like Geoffrey Barnett, George Maclean, Ian Hopkins and Tony Hawes; and younger Turks, Peter Norris, Ron Baker, Mary Walz, Geoff Broadhurst, Tony Gamby and Brenda Granger. As chief executive officer, Norris was singled out in London for the most consistent censure.

In Singapore, James Bax was criticised as having 'failed to concern himself with', and Simon Jones as seeming to have 'taken no significant steps [to end]', Leeson's control of trading and the back office in Baring Futures. The only people let off lightly by the Bank of England inquiry were Barings' most senior executives. The report concluded that Andrew Tuckey and Peter Baring were responsible merely for failing to assess critically the huge profits coming from Baring Futures in Singapore. The inference is that they had been a bit greedy, but no worse than that.

Only one paragraph in the Bank if England's inquiry hinted at something more serious than a cock-up. On the subject of the SLK receivable, the report stated:

> The appreciation by certain members of the management that there were very unsatisfactory features relating to this transaction is, we consider, illustrated by the fact that Broadhurst (at the request of Norris, who had himself been so requested by Bax) asked Coopers & Lybrand in London that no reference to the transaction should be made in the auditors' management letter for Baring Futures (Singapore). We consider it was inappropriate for Broadhurst, Norris and Bax to have caused this request to be made, which was done with a view to attempting to avoid potential problems with the regulators of BFS in Singapore.

'Very unsatisfactory features' and 'inappropriate' action do not add up to a conspiracy, although they might be factors in a cover-up. Indeed, the Bank of England's tepid conclusion was treated by many critics as a judgement by the toffs for the toffs. Many people remained sceptical: just because the Bank did not find any evidence of conspiracy, it didn't mean there hadn't been one. The story was so improbable: a twenty-eight-year-old trader fiddling and forging, undiscovered for thirty-two months, asking for and receiving £869 million with which to gamble, and losing every penny of it. It seemed inconceivable that Leeson could have been acting alone.

The spectre of a serious cover-up, even of a conspiracy, was first raised inside Barings itself. During the two weeks after the collapse, the level of stress remained barely tolerable. Administrators, crawling over the office, had to be told where the files were and how the place worked. Prickliness in personal relationships was exaggerated by the sense of failure. Ron Baker sat alone in his office. Mary Walz, whose desk was on the trading-floor at the Bishopsgate office, had hardly anyone to talk to.

Walz began to re-construct the events leading to the debacle. She talked to Brenda Granger and Tony Railton about their discoveries in Singapore. She delved into the SLK receivable, and into Peter Norris's trip to Singapore in February – a journey neither she nor Baker had known anything about. 'I was, to say the least, a bit curious about how all this could have happened, but then I thought "Who wouldn't be?"' She was surprised that more people seemed not to be surprised.

What she did not know was that Gamby and Broadhurst had also been harbouring their own doubts. While uncertainty cloaked the whole Leeson story, almost everyone connected with Baring Securities, from before as well as after Christopher Heath's dismissal, was happy to contribute indicative items to support one theory or another. During the summer of 1995, I made a collection of these.

Item 1. When news of Leeson's disappearance came from Simon Jones's office on 23 February, Tony Gamby was astonished at the speed with which Peter Norris saw to the heart of the problem. While Gamby, Broadhurst and Sacranie were only just starting to absorb the scale of Leeson's transactions on the 88888 account, Norris was directing the investigation with remarkable speed and precision. Gamby's first impression was that Norris was not surprised by the fact of Leeson's unauthorised dealing, though he might have been by the scale of it.

Item 2. A week earlier, on 16 February, when Norris had been visiting Singapore, a colleague who knew him well from London swore that he had seen Norris talking to Leeson for more than two hours in a glass-walled office in Baring Securities' Singapore premises. With hindsight, the implication seemed to be that the two of them had been discussing Leeson's huge trading positions. After all, these were already common gossip in Tokyo, Hong Kong and the Bank for International Settlements in Basle.

Supporting this claim was the fact that Leeson sent an e-mail message on 20 February to Tony Hawes stating that, 'following my conversation with Peter Norris, James Bax and Simon Jones', he proposed to delay giving Hawes answers to the hard questions he had been asking.

Item 3. Norris appeared to have a motive. Duff and Trotter, the company run by his first wife, Louise, had ceased trading during the recession of the early 1990s, and Norris had assumed responsibility for some of its debt. His £1 million bonus for 1994, due to be announced on 27 February, would have come in handy. But once Leeson's losses were exposed, that bonus would, of course, not be paid.

Item 4. Former colleagues and contemporaries at Charterhouse recalled Norris's reputation as a fierce gambler. As we have seen when he was at school his grandparents had taken him racing. He loved it, and kept a betting-book for seven years, turning in a profit in three of them. Indeed, until he realised he didn't have enough money for it, Norris's ambition was to train horses, and this passion never deserted him. Many good stories about Norris had a racing theme. For example, Norris once gave a colleague a good tip for the following day. When the horse failed to finish in the first three, the out-of-pocket colleague commiserated with him. 'Don't worry,' Norris said. 'I walked the course in the morning and, when I realised the going was soft, I cancelled my bet.' To the proponents of a conspiracy theory, Norris's passion for gambling suggested that a great gamble with Barings' future might not be inconceivable.

Because it contained some facts, the single most influential contribution to the conspiracy theory was the SLK receivable. As we already know from Chapter 9, this was a complex matter. To recap briefly, Leeson had had to raise 7.778 billion yen (£50 million), and had done that by fabricating an over-the-counter option trade between the Wall Street firm of Spear, Leeds and Kellogg and – depending on who he was talking to – either Baring Securities London or the Banque Nationale de Paris. To satisfy the accountants, and the anxious managers in

Singapore and London, Leeson had produced bogus documents to make it appear as if Barings' local Citibank account had received the £50 million from SLK. To convince the accountants that he had been acting properly, Leeson had also forged a memorandum purporting to come from Ron Baker, his boss in London, 'confirming' Baker's knowledge of, and approval of, the OTC option deal with SLK.

Item 5 in support of a conspiracy theory came from Ron Baker. During the investigations into the collapse, he was shown two documents that he later claimed were among the most shocking things he had seen in his life. The Serious Fraud Office possessed a copy of the forged memorandum, signed 'Ron', that Leeson produced for the auditors. And the Bank of England's investigators showed him a copy of the letter written by SIMEX's Mr Soo to Simon Jones on 11 January 1995 – the letter that ought to have made it clear to Jones that a client account number 88888 was being improperly financed by Barings.

Baker places special emphasis on an affidavit sworn by James Bax as part of the Bank of England investigation. It read: 'Leeson told Simon [Jones] he would provide the auditors . . . with the confirmations that the financial products group . . . had approved the trade.' But, Baker points out, Leeson had confessed to Jones that the trade was unauthorised, and Bax had been informed of this. If this was the case, Bax ought to have known that the information in 'Baker's' memorandum was untrue. Had this conflict between two pieces of evidence been reported to London, Baker says, he would himself have been the target of an investigation. But it was not, and no one questioned him about his 'authorisation'.

Baker, putting two and two together, convinced himself that someone other than Leeson must have known that the SLK receivable was disquieting evidence of potential fraud. But Baker had no hard evidence, and so never made his allegations public.

Baker's speculations may well have had a decisive effect on one of the inquiry teams. Those in Barings who had suspicious minds had not been impressed by the Bank of England's gentlemanly style of investigation. Having been interviewed by the Singapore inspectors, Walz felt they showed a greater willingness to question and dig. Other former colleagues who had been persuaded by ING to help the Singapore inspectors agreed with her, though they had not enjoyed being interviewed. It was like a fierce cross-examination in a criminal court.

Even before publication of the Bank of England's report, it had become clear that the Singapore inspectors were casting a critical eye over the Barings story. An article in the *Financial Times* by Nicholas Denton and John Gapper on 7 July 1995, which first publicised questions about the roles of Peter Norris and James Bax, was inspired by the Singapore inspectors' investigation.

What the inspectors were probing was whether Norris and Bax had known about Leeson's enormous trading losses well before 23 February. If that were the case, since neither Norris nor Bax had stopped him trading, they also became responsible for the collapse of Barings. If there was something nasty in the woodshed, it looked as if this was it.

The Singapore inspectors' report, published in October 1995, became the principal sourcebook for the conspiracy theory. The inspectors, Michael Lim and Nicky Tan, both partners in Price Waterhouse in Singapore, were so intrigued by the SLK receivable that they devoted thirty of their 155 pages of text to it. The tone of the report they submitted to the minister for finance is quite unlike an accountant's unemotional analysis. It more closely resembles the heated closing address of a prosecuting counsel.

The case is based on a judgement of Norris's character. Because they do not accept his version of events, the inspectors say that Norris was untruthful. Having established that to their satisfaction, they then proceed to make their case by means of pronouncements.

The inspectors assert that Norris talked to Leeson for ninety minutes in Singapore on 16 February.

They assert that Leeson's e-mail message to Tony Hawes on

20 February followed discussions about the SLK receivable between Leeson on the one hand, and Norris, Bax and Jones on the other.

They assert that Norris, after talking with Leeson, discouraged efforts to reduce Barings' futures positions in Singapore in the days before the collapse.

They assert that Bax's fears about a critical reaction from Singapore's regulators to any reference to the SLK receivable in the auditors' report were simply incomprehensible.

And they also assert that, since Bax also gave evidence that was 'false in material respects', he was a co-conspirator with Norris. (No mention is made of Simon Jones in the climax to the inspectors' report.)

The two accountants then address the question of motive. First, they had to decide whether this was an isolated case of unauthorised trading, as Baker suggested, or whether it was part of a wider pattern of deception.

The notion that Norris might have been protecting Leeson because of his astounding profits is dismissed as unlikely. 'If this had been viewed as an unauthorised trade in isolation, then it would have been an act of recklessness on Mr Norris's part to frustrate the investigation into the SLK receivable.' The reason for this was that senior management knew – or should have known – of the unsatisfactory state of affairs at Baring Futures in Singapore.

In the judgement of the inspectors, the consequences of the conspiracy were fatal. 'Had Mr Norris and Mr Bax not taken such steps [to frustrate an investigation], and, as a result of proper investigations, the flow of funds to BFS had been curtailed, this may have averted the collapse of the Barings Group.'

The inspectors report that Norris had asked them what motive he could possibly have had for taking such a monumental risk. 'A plausible motive can readily be conjectured,' wrote Lim and Tan.

[Norris's] predecessor had left [Baring Securities] when it had incurred £11 million of losses. In those circumstances, Mr Norris clearly had an interest to conceal the much larger losses that the Baring Group had incurred via account 88888 in the course of the three years that Mr Leeson had been in Singapore. This would have supplied Mr Norris with an adequate motive to suppress the nature of the problem, to discourage other investigations, and to ensure that the problem was not reported in a way that would have attracted widespread attention.

The final section of the inspectors' report on the SLK receivable is headed 'Inferences and Findings'. Careful reading suggests that it is stronger on the former than the latter.

Publication of the report whipped up a storm about where the real responsibility for the collapse of Barings lay. Drawing attention away from Leeson and SIMEX, it put Norris and Bax in the dock. And if the Singaporeans had their way, that might literally be the case.

Richard Hu, Singapore's finance minister, told the *Financial Times* that charges would be pursued if substantive evidence could be found. 'It would be very difficult to believe senior Barings executives, particularly Mr Norris and the financial controllers in London, knew nothing of the potential for collapse ... We have never held back from prosecuting an individual, whether he is a Singaporean or a foreigner ... I don't think the British government would expect us to pull back for political reasons.'

This was in mid-October, almost nine months after the collapse of the bank. Grave charges against Norris and Bax – and less grave charges against Jones and Broadhurst – were being freely made. The nightmare would not go away, and the former executives targeted by the conspiracy theorists became disconsolate.

When I first put the conspiracy theory to Norris, early in the summer of 1995 before the Singapore inspectors' report appeared, he was unfazed. He regarded the SLK receivable as a management problem only, and the Bank of England inquiry had reached much the same conclusion. Norris admitted that the SLK receivable had been handled extremely badly. 'I didn't give it enough attention, and I probably got impatient about it. That's the thing I feel least proud about.'

But early in the autumn, more substantial evidence was accumulating, and there was a strong rumour, before the transmission of Leeson's televised interview with David Frost, that Leeson would be implicating his bosses at Barings. I sought out Norris urgently then, interrupting his seaside holiday, to repeat the charges to him. By September he was more concerned, and took them seriously, answering each one in turn.

Of Tony Gamby's observation that he had been suspiciously quick to spot Leeson's fraud on 23 February (item 1 in support of the conspiracy theory), Norris replied: 'I was a lot sharper than anyone else who was there that night. I suppose coping with pressure is why I was chief executive officer.' Gamby, who interrogated Norris a couple of times in the weeks after the collapse, now believes that he did not know Leeson's dealing was unauthorised.

On the meeting with Leeson in Singapore on 16 February (item 2) – which witnesses claimed had lasted between ninety minutes and two hours, and which Norris insisted took between five and ten minutes – he commented: 'I said to [Leeson], "If we're making all this money, the counterparties must be losing it," and I asked him what the market thought about us. That's all.'

As for the testimony of the London colleague who said he had seen Norris talking to Leeson at length, Norris replied: 'He wasn't even there. He arrived the next day.' The colleague continues to insist that he was there, but has mislaid his diary.

But why did Norris not raise SLK with Leeson that day? Surely it was too important a topic to ignore? 'We'd agreed that Bax would investigate it. It didn't seem like an outstanding problem.' Norris was in Singapore to hold a conference with the top executives from McIntosh Securities, an Australian firm in which Barings had a 19.9 per cent holding. While he was in Singapore, it was Australia that was on his mind.

Of the e-mail message sent by Leeson to Hawes on 20 February, suggesting that Norris had agreed to put off Hawes and the awkward questions about SLK, Norris commented: 'That was a bare-faced lie. But Leeson was in the habit of concocting spurious authority for what he was doing.'

On item 3 – the idea that he might have delayed exposing Leeson so as to guarantee his £1 million bonus to pay off his last Duff and Trotter debts – Norris points out that bonuses were not paid in cash. They were announced on 27 February 1995, and then paid in instalments during the year. Consequently, delaying the discovery of Leeson's frauds would have been of no benefit to him. But even if the bonuses had been paid on the nail, 'I'd have been the stupidest man in the City to think I could get away with that,' he says.

The Singapore inspectors' report had appeared by the time I next spoke to Norris about the conspiracy theory. By now his face was pale and strained, and he seemed greyer. At one moment he stopped talking, and blurted out, 'This is torment.'

Norris did not believe Ron Baker could seriously be suggesting that anyone in London had known, or even suspected, that the SLK receivable was a phoney deal (item 5 in the conspiracy theory). Norris states unequivocally that he himself did not suspect it was forged.

The case made against him by the Singapore inspectors was, said Norris, 'laughable'. But their report was no laughing matter for him: if the commercial affairs department did decide to bring charges against Barings' managers, the report would be produced as evidence. For Norris, the single issue that made it easy to dismiss the whole report as a farrago was the suggestion that he had deliberately covered up Leeson's losses because he wished to avoid being compared with his predecessor, who had presided over an £11 million loss. The inspectors were accusing Norris of covering up a loss of hundreds of millions of pounds. 'That is not remotely the same circumstance. It is Armageddon. The comparison they draw is laughable, and the motivation is ludicrous.'

The charges of conspiracy and cover-up made no sense to Norris, who reacted to them with a combination of anger and frustration: 'If any of it were true, it would mean that I had spent months lying to the asset and liability committee, to the management committee and to the main board.'

His former colleagues, some of whom had never sympathised with Norris, began to do so now. Friends began to speak up, too. Andrew Fraser, who had lived through the complete history of Baring Securities, described Norris as 'straight, ethical, intelligent'. Having observed him at work, Fraser judged that Norris would raise an issue only when he knew all the facts about it; if this is so, it would explain why he did not want the asset and liability committee to discuss the SLK receivable until he had got a full report from Bax.

As far as the conspiracy theory is concerned, the most influential witness for the defence was Leeson himself. In his interview with David Frost, he said that he had not colluded with any Barings manager. Interviewed by the Serious Fraud Office, he again made no statements on which a case for conspiracy could be based. Moreover, Leeson sabotaged one important item in the conspiracy theory by confirming Norris's account of the brief duration of their meeting in Singapore on 16 February. Of course, if Leeson and Norris had conspired, Leeson might well support Norris's account in any case, but Leeson would have had a powerful motive for admitting to such a collusion. It would have clinched his campaign to have his case tried in England, and his lawyers could have used a long Norris–Leeson meeting in Singapore to fuel that campaign.

But Leeson's evidence on this one point has a wider significance. In their report, the inspectors simply asserted that Norris had lied about the length of the meeting. If he did not, it does not inspire much confidence in the other claims they make on the question of Norris's complicity.

The inspectors' theory finally breaks down with James Bax's memo of 3 February 1995, which explained that Leeson's control of trading and the back office could no longer continue. Had London been conspiring with Singapore, it is highly improbable that Norris and Broadhurst would have cried 'Eureka!' when they saw the memo as the long-awaited pretext to dump Simon Jones. If Norris in London and Bax in

Singapore really did know about Leeson's losses, it is even more unlikely that they would have been considering reassuring Leeson about his 'long-term career path with Barings'.

True conspirators trying to cover up the losses in Leeson's 88888 account might have hoped that a dramatic reversal in market prices would wipe out bad losses and set matters right. But Leeson's losses were too big for that, and discovery was inevitable. Even for a mad gambler, this was a bet beyond all reason, especially since built-in delays in the bonus-payment system meant that these gamblers would not collect their winnings in cash on the nail. Moreover, it is hard to see what co-conspirators would have had to gain. Perhaps, as managers who had proved inefficient, they feared the sack? But when Leeson's losses were exploding, the best way for anyone at Barings to secure their future was to expose him, and as fast as possible.

A strong case against a conspiracy theory is the existence of the theory itself. It is normally wheeled out when an event is particularly difficult to explain in any other way. The possibility of a conspiracy helps the participants to convince themselves that they were not to blame; it turns them into victims of circumstances outside their control. It helps outsiders stick to their prejudices: establishment whitewash or working-class plot can both be supported by a conspiracy theory.

Yet the absence of a full-blown conspiracy does not necessarily mean that there was no cover-up of any kind. There was. Even the Bank of England hinted as much. It was a management cover-up, designed purely to keep SIMEX officials in the dark, and off the backs of the Singapore office. There is copious evidence that James Bax did ask Norris to request that Coopers & Lybrand in London keep any mention of the SLK irregularity out of their covering letter to the management in Singapore. Broadhurst did pass on Bax's request to Coopers & Lybrand. They were all afraid of the wrath of Singapore's regulators if they discovered that Leeson had acted improperly by broking an unauthorised OTC transaction. Norris, by agreeing to pass on Bax's request to the auditors, was a party to that cover-up.

As Norris's messenger in London, Broadhurst was a bit-part player in that cover-up. This deception was a serious irregularity, but it is not a hanging offence.

Another version of the cover-up theory surfaced in Singapore during Leeson's trial. Without going as far as the Singapore inspectors, John Koh, his lawyer, took the case further than the Bank of England did. Koh stated: 'His immediate bosses, Simon Jones and James Bax, were aware of this important balance-sheet discrepancy, as were many senior executives of Barings in London ... The bosses knew something was amiss but took no action. They compromised to obtain a clean audit bill of health.' Koh did not explain the nature of the compromise, nor who knew what, or when. But, during the whole judicial process, this was the only charge Leeson levelled at his bosses.

James Bax, detained in Singapore and unable to speak directly to me, or to other unauthorised researchers, went out of his way to deny the allegation of a management cover-up. Through Richards Butler, his London solicitors, Bax stated that he was not involved in a cover-up with regard to the SLK receivable, but the interpretation of his response depends on how you define the word 'cover-up' in this context. My case is based on undisputed facts that have appeared in reports by both the Bank of England and the Singapore inspectors. Besides that, there is the Tony Hawes' evidence, also referred to by the Singapore inspectors, that Bax asked him not to talk directly to Leeson, and to suppress his urge to trawl through the papers in Leeson's office.

Some fundamental questions still remain unanswered. The most perplexing concern the role of Simon Jones. He did not act on, or even pass on, the SIMEX letter of 11 January, which should have made it clear that Leeson was improperly funding a client account with Barings' own money. Despite the fact that the money was coming from London and Tokyo, Jones did not alert either office to the existence of the SIMEX letter. When he did eventually mention it to Tony Hawes, he did so only to make fun of an error in SIMEX's margin calculations. He did not refer to the 88888 account.

There is an assertion in the Singapore inspectors' report which seems more firmly based than many others. It concerns Jones's role in the discovery of the SLK receivable. The inspectors wrote:

> If, as we believe to be the case, the nature of the transaction as understood by Coopers & Lybrand Singapore was explained to Mr Jones, then it is not credible that Mr Jones, who had the previous day:
> (i) had the benefit of a lengthy briefing by Mr Leeson, which was at variance with the explanation given by C&L Singapore;
> (ii) conveyed the version presented to him and his concerns arising from this, to Mr Bax; and
> (iii) spent a sleepless night worrying about the SLK receivable and the risks faced by BFS,
> did not realise that Mr Leeson had told the auditors a wholly different story than that which he had told Mr Jones the previous day.

When the inspectors asked Jones why it was that he had listened to two, maybe three, versions of Leeson's story, apparently without comment, Jones replied that he was under tremendous personal strain at the time, 'as a result of which he was not in the best frame of mind to perceive such differences'. Because Jones, like Bax, was incommunicado in Singapore in the months after the publication of the inspectors' report, it was impossible to investigate his part any further. The fact that he allowed both the SIMEX letter and Leeson's conflicting explanations of the SLK receivable to remain uninvestigated still needs to be explained.

But the truth is that it was not necessary to conspire to bring about the collapse of Barings. Given the instability created by Leeson's crazy trading, the people who ran it were perfectly capable of presiding over that themselves. The bankruptcy of Barings was the biggest cock-up in the history of British banking, and it enabled Nicholas Leeson to become the biggest trading disaster in the history of financial markets. In fifth place in the all-time list of disasters is Joseph Jett, who created phantom profits that cost Kidder Peabody $350 million. Fourth is Howard Rubin, who ignored instructions and lost $377 million in mortgage-backed derivatives in New York in 1987. Two Japanese share second place. Toshihide Iguchi, Daiwa's securities trader in New York, lost $1.1 billion, as did the lesser-known Yukihusu Fujita, who speculated in currencies on behalf of a Japanese subsidiary of Shell. With losses of $1.4 billion, Leeson is streets ahead of his rivals.

To understand why Barings' bankruptcy was a cock-up of such monumental proportions, we need to recall the three motives cited by Roger Geissler, the New York trader, as those that drive financial markets. 'PIG,' he says. 'Panic, ignorance, greed.'

Panic gripped the participants at the end. They did not know where Leeson was, nor how much he had lost, nor how he could have lost it. But there was an earlier instance of panic, and this one set in motion the collapse of the whole edifice.

The first panic occurred when Baring Securities, after years of fat profits, first lost money in 1992. For a trading organisation, losses of £11 million were embarrassing, but they were certainly not ruinous. They could have been the pretext for a management re-organisation, the dropping of some surplus staff, and the tying-up of some of the loose ends that had never bothered Christopher Heath too much.

Instead the losses became the pretext for a takeover, masterminded by Andrew Tuckey, of Heath's turbulent empire. Baring Brothers had taken fright at Baring Securities. Although the old Baring bankers liked the money Heath's people made, they could not stand his style, and they refused to appreciate that the style was part of the secret of making the money.

Tuckey and the bankers dreamed of a securities business that was risk-averse. To bind two competing cultures into a harmonious whole necessitated the removal of Heath and most of his top men. These were replaced by a corporate financier, Peter Norris, and by specialists in treasury, finance and settlements from Baring Brothers, the firm's banking arm. But the upheaval had the force of an earthquake, and the new organisation had not properly settled down when it fell apart. That was the legacy of panic.

The ignorance was a by-product of the original panic. In some cases – such as putting Ron Baker in charge of equity derivatives – executives were asked to manage in areas that they did not fully understand. Other executives, like Tony Gamby in the settlements department, were capable of running a tight ship, but they were not given the means to do it.

There is no excuse for ignorance in derivatives markets. The language may be strange at first, but they are not a mystery. These markets do consume a great deal of a firm's capital, however, and they can bounce about unpredictably. Risk management is the means of countering these dangers, but there was no effective risk management in Barings' securities operation. Because the senior executives foolishly believed that they were not taking any risks in Singapore and Tokyo, they did not impose a risk-management system. Under Heath's regime, risk management was rudimentary, but at least it was taken seriously. Under the new regime, it was not.

Ignorance was what allowed Leeson to play his game for thirty-two months. Had Barings purchased a system that enabled the settlements department in London to reconcile trades made in any part of the world with clients' orders from any part of the world, instead of relying on branch offices like Singapore for the information, Leeson's fraudulent use of the 88888 account would have been exposed within months, if not weeks. Such a system, known as BRAINS, would have cost about £10 million. Barings did give it the go-ahead, but too late – in January 1995. Consider the savings that would have been made if BRAINS had been in use earlier.

Tony Hawes, suspecting that all was not well in Singapore for well over a year, saw the need for reconciliation of clients' accounts with the margin funds sent from London and Tokyo. But he lacked either the decisiveness or the seniority required to make it happen. Coopers & Lybrand did not reconcile the accounts, either. The Bank of England was sharp about the audit: 'We do not consider that C&L London performed sufficient tests to satisfy themselves that the controls over payment of margin and the associated accounting balances were operating effectively.' No control systems, no authoritative management, not enough help from the auditors: that was the legacy of ignorance.

Greed is the easiest of the three motives to understand. In the old days, most of the Baring family – especially those who worked in the bank – were very comfortably off. Their motives were a blend of influence in the City, social position and a bit of public service. The clerks were not greedy because they were in no position to be. Big Bang in 1985 altered that, and the fast growth of derivatives markets in the late 1980s changed it beyond recognition. Having transferred their last shares to the Baring Foundation, the directors now relied on bonuses to earn good money. But much of the firm's profit now depended on the people who had once performed the function of the clerks. And bonuses were a more democratic form of payment than dividends – everyone expected one.

The golden years of Christopher Heath altered the expectations of all Barings' employees once and for all. Half of the firm's pre-tax profits went towards bonuses, and for eight years in a row these profits were terrific. In an industry in which real talent is always scarce, bonuses became a bargaining tool, contributing to the natural instinct to ask for more. As a result of Leeson's phoney bonanza in 1994, fifty-eight Barings employees were due to receive bonuses of between £250,000 and £499,999, and five were to get between £500,000 and £749,999. Andrew Tuckey, Peter Baring, Peter Norris and Ron Baker were due to receive more than three-quarters of a million pounds on top of their salaries, with Tuckey (£1,650,000) at the top of the heap.

Everyone involved in the Barings debacle instantly denies that these swollen bonuses had anything to do with the collapse of the bank. This is nonsense. No one wanted to upset the goose that was laying so many golden eggs. James Baker's internal-audit report had emphasised the importance of keeping Leeson, and when Fernando Gueler initially heard that Leeson had 'gone', his first thought was that he had 'gone' to Morgan Stanley. A man who has been told that he is to receive a bonus of, say, £450,000, wants to be sure that the money keeps on coming in.

Defenders of the City of London's pay structure state that earnings in London must be high because financial services is a global industry. But these earnings, far from lending stability to the City, make their own contribution to instability.

'A modern morality tale' is how David Frost described the story of Nick Leeson and the collapse of Barings. Since morality tales deal with the triumph of good over evil, there ought to be some good guys involved. It is hard to find any heroes in this story.

16

'I Am Guilty, Your Honour'

In the summer of 1995, the opinions held by readers of the *Sun* about the collapse of Barings were no less strong than those of the readers of the *Financial Times*. Public opinion shifted, grew hot, cooled down, but it never faded. After the Bank of England published its report, public opinion settled into the view that Barings' management was to blame. When ING finally summarily dismissed twenty-one men and women in London, Singapore and Tokyo at the end of July, there was no sympathy for them. But it wasn't Barings' management that had lost hundreds of millions of pounds – Leeson had done that all by himself. At least, the general assumption was that he had been acting alone.

Not everyone believed that. Peter Baring had suggested that Leeson was a part not of an internal conspiracy, but of an outside conspiracy to bankrupt Barings. The theory was that a Mr Big had held positions which mirrored Leeson's. When Leeson was long, Mr Big was short; when Leeson's positions were liquidated, Mr Big would be walking off with profits of hundreds of millions of pounds. Unfortunately, the facts refused to support this theory. Dealing records in the Singapore and Osaka exchanges revealed some sizeable positions held by US firms like Goldman Sachs and Dean Whitter, but the contracts were spread widely among the familiar traders. Lots of people had made money out of Barings' losses.

However, this did not rule out the possibility that Leeson

had benefited personally. The administrators, Ernst and Young, and the new owners, ING, went on investigating leads about the alleged whereabouts of Leeson's secret bank accounts. Tips flowed in. One emerged during one of the legal battles over turf rights between the Bank of England and the Singapore inspectors. To encourage co-operation, the Bank of England's solicitors gave an example of information that only the Bank could provide. This concerned a tip-off about assets Leeson held in South Africa. The Singapore judge thought the tip too speculative to qualify as a bargaining-tool. But no one has yet fully studied Leeson's trading records since 1992.

A stir was caused by a paragraph in the Singapore inspectors' report about a trading firm called First Continental Trading. Leeson's friend Danny Argyropoulous, the man who had driven him and Lisa to Changi Airport on 22 February, worked for FCT. This was a Chicago-based company whose owner, Roger Carlsson, had used his own money to guarantee the company's relationship with Barings. FCT had its own membership on SIMEX and an office in Singapore, but its trades were cleared – settled – through Baring Futures. Relationships between the two companies were close in Tokyo as well as in Singapore.

The Singapore inspectors stated that Leeson made price adjustments in favour of FCT in Singapore of the kind that he had made to boost Barings' profits in London and Japan: in other words, that he would surreptitiously give FCT a profit on a deal and absorb the loss in his 88888 account. The report said that on six occasions between June and November 1994, Leeson adjusted the price of Japanese Government Bond deals in Argyropoulous's favour, to the tune of £106,000. But the story did not add up. The next sentence read: 'There were, however, five occasions in the same period where the price adjustments were to the detriment of FCT.' Since the price of these adjustments came to £75,500, the 'profit' to FCT of £30,000 hardly makes Argyropoulous Mr Big. When I read that paragraph to Roger Geissler, my New York mentor, he was of the opinion that such transactions could easily arise from a normal business relationship on the trading-floor.

Indeed, the evidence points in this direction, rather than towards a conspiracy to defraud.

Leeson insists that he has no secret bank accounts. And certainly Lisa's behaviour while he was in prison in Frankfurt gave no hint of private funds: she worked in a teashop in Maidstone in Kent. There are market-watchers who believe that it is not possible for Leeson to have lost money as persistently as he did; that he must have been deliberately taking the loss in the 88888 account and feeding the profit to a third party. In many cases, we know this to be true – but the third party was Barings.

It would be reckless of me to assert that there is no hidden cache of money – Leeson might prove to be cleverer and more devious than he seems. But the discovery of lost millions would be astounding.

The subject of conspiracy should not be abandoned before we expose one that actually worked. This is, perhaps, more accurately described as a counter-conspiracy, or a conspiracy of silence. All the conspirators are Singaporeans.

Singaporeans are capable of proxility on a grand scale. Their submission to the German court backing the request of the Singapore commercial affairs department for Leeson's extradition on twelve fairly straightforward charges of fraud, forgery and breach of trust was 1,000 pages long. In public, however, the Singaporean authorities are monumentally tight-lipped. Koh Ben Seng, the head of the Monetary Authority of Singapore, could teach central-bankers' courses in uncommunicativeness. His one public comment was 136 words long, including the words, 'That is the end of my statement.'

In Singapore, powerful people speak on their terms only, and they dictate both the content and the timing of their pronouncements. This is due in part to an obsession with secrecy; in part to the absence of public pressure and criticism. So no adverse comment was ever made about the way the Singaporean government handled Leeson and the collapse of Barings. But there was plenty to hide.

It is impossible not to admire the energy and dedication of the officials of the Singaporean state. Only ten weeks after Barings folded, the chairman of SIMEX, Elizabeth Sam, popped up in London at a derivatives conference to boast that in the first five months of 1995, the average daily volume on SIMEX was *up* by 17 per cent on the year before. Not bad, considering that for three of those months there had been no Leeson to bump up the figures. 'In the larger historical context, the Barings crisis proved to be a minor one,' she said.

Sam, a small, lively woman who is at ease with the predominantly male ethos of the futures markets, was on the road again three months later. At another futures-industry conference, in Burgenstock in Switzerland, her message was that the Barings collapse was the fault of their management: had they understood the business, they would not have unquestioningly remitted such huge funds to meet Leeson's margin calls.

The report of the Singapore inspectors elaborated on Sam's theme. While it made the gravest assertions about the integrity of Barings' senior management, towards Leeson it took an unaccountably conciliatory tone. Referring to their inability to speak to him, the inspectors said: 'In view of Mr Leeson's position, *which can be appreciated*, the findings . . . were perforce reached without the benefit of his version of the relevant events.' Since a political motive can be ascribed to many events that happen in Singapore, one plausible explanation for this would be a conspiracy theory along the following lines: Sam's speech-making offensive, and the inspectors' focus on Norris and Bax, were intended to shift scrutiny away from Singapore to London.

Singapore is anxious to protect its reputation as an international monetary centre, and SIMEX has become important in the global financial market. Its reputation for integrity is important to the spirit of Singapore, which may explain why the inspectors' criticism of SIMEX was so mild. For example, they did not investigate why it was that Leeson was allowed to build huge positions in the most heavily traded contracts on the exchange.

Rule 1502, section D, of SIMEX's hefty, four-inch-thick rulebook is headed 'Position Limits' and states: 'A person shall not own or control more than 1,000 contracts net long or net short in all contract months combined.' Section F, headed 'Exemptions', reads: 'The Board may from time to time provide exemptions to the foregoing position limits.' By the time he fled, Leeson controlled 49 per cent of all SIMEX's contracts in the Nikkei 225. This vast holding amounted to more than 55,399 contracts. Leeson had not reported all of these to SIMEX, but the exchange did know about 23,039 of them.

The Singapore inspectors commented: 'Based on the positions reported to SIMEX, it appeared that Baring Futures (Singapore) had exceeded its approved limit on a few occasions. However, SIMEX relied on the facts that margins were being met in full, and did not raise the matter with BFS.'

But Leeson had exceeded the exchange's rules in Nikkei options as well, holding five times more than the permitted limit. In the JGB contract, his declared holding was almost three times over the limit. SIMEX had borrowed the rulebook from the Chicago Mercantile Exchange, but it did not copy its rule-enforcement. Chicago rarely grants exemptions to position limits, and when it does so it monitors the positions daily.

SIMEX officials also tolerated Leeson's persistent cross-trading after the market closed for the day. This was the sleight of hand that Leeson used to boost the profit-and-loss account of Barings in London and Tokyo, at the expense of the 88888 account. Barings' traders in Tokyo had been curious about the way trading volumes on SIMEX would suddenly rise thirty minutes after the formal close to reflect the volume of business Leeson had already reported to them. SIMEX turned a blind eye to Leeson's cross-trades until February 1995, and even then intervened only after other traders had complained that Leeson was breaking the rules.

The most damaging criticism of SIMEX, however, is that it knew more about Leeson's 88888 account than anyone apart from Leeson himself. On the basis of what SIMEX knew, it should have asked for more details about ultimate ownership and the clients' intentions. Just like Barings' management, SIMEX accepted at face value Leeson's explanation that these were client accounts. Like that of Barings' management, SIMEX's behaviour was influenced by a reluctance to criticise the goose that was laying the golden egg.

In futures markets, volume matters most. Volume makes the market efficient; it attracts new business; it swells revenues. That is why Barings won SIMEX awards for Leeson's trading; why the exchange officials spoke of him in such glowing terms, and helped him through little local difficulties, like his arrest for mooning. Without SIMEX's indulgence, Leeson could never have got away with his grand deception.

After the event, SIMEX asked a committee of luminaries from the world's futures markets to advise them on tougher rules. Little publicity was given to the report of this blue-chip committee, but the resultant battery of rule changes on SIMEX in October 1995 was a tacit admission of the lapses that had opened the way for Leeson.

The other group of Singaporeans without whom Leeson's fraud would not have been possible was his staff at Baring Futures. By the time he left, they had been playing the game with him for years. On the floor they always gave a tick – the preferential price – to Tokyo and got on with the cross-trades. In the office, Leeson's assistants in the settlements department keyed in his instructions to alter bank balances and mislead SIMEX. In a hard-driven investigation, they would have been fiercely cross-examined to discover whether they had been true accessories.

But Lawrence Ang, who brought the case against Leeson, was even more tolerant and avuncular towards the staff than Leeson himself. Ang's case carefully exempted them from any responsibility for the crime.

'Linda, being the subordinate of the accused, performed the operation as instructed.'

'Yong authorised the transfer as she perceived this transaction to be just a routine transaction.'

'Nisa, being the subordinate and accustomed to carrying out

all instructions given by the accused, asked one of the settlements assistants to key the false entry.'

The impression given here is that of a society in which unquestioning obedience to authority is the natural order of things, and in which deceitful foreigners take advantage of the good nature of the local population. The only exceptions to this are those working in the private sector. Lawrence Ang threw Coopers & Lybrand's auditors in Singapore to the wolves by quoting the Singapore prosecution's cross-examination of Leeson about the auditors' technique in the case of the 7.778 yen SLK receivable. 'I can't get a bank statement to show that the money is from SLK because I don't have the bank printing documentation. So I am going to show them a receipt of 7.778 and take the risk that they are not very good at their jobs, because if an auditor in England received 7.778 billion, they would check where it came from.'

By the time the Singaporean authorities got their hands on Leeson himself, they had conscientiously prepared the grounds for his trial. The message from all the agencies of the state was the same. Singapore was the victim, Leeson was the agent – but the blame lay with senior Barings' executives like Norris and Bax.

In London, the campaign to claw Leeson out of the clutches of Singapore was an entertaining diversion in a long, hot summer. Lisa Leeson became a celebrity, asked by chat shows to give her opinion on matters far removed from extradition treaties and futures-and-options markets. Stephen Pollard's advocacy was intended to give life to the idea that only a trial in London would enable the whole story to come out. This was a beguiling prospect: a long Old Bailey affair with all the participants in the witness box, and the lawyers inexorably sorting out truth from fiction.

But when he was questioned by Marcel Berlins, a broadcaster on legal affairs, Pollard tripped and almost fell. He had told Berlins that Leeson would plead guilty to charges of false accounting if he were brought to trial in London. In that case,

Berlins said, the trial would last only a day or so. Pollard hurriedly replied that, even if there were no adversarial trial, Leeson's plea of mitigation could last a whole day, and would tell the whole story. Well, not quite: what it would tell would be Leeson's side of the whole story.

All summer, newspapers competed for the first exclusive interview with Leeson. As an outsider, Pollard was fascinated by the competitive zeal of the British press. One of the requests for an interview may explain why. 'Of course, the whole basis of a publication would be the provision of exclusive material from your client, setting out why he feels he should be returned and his feelings on other relevant subject matters. We would also require the right to syndicate such material worldwide and to advertise and publicise the story, at our discretion.' Money was not actually mentioned, but there was no disguising the strong commercial motive.

Pollard was hoping for a spontaneous uprising of public opinion, as there had been in the case of Private Lee Clegg, the British soldier who had received a long jail sentence after a fatal incident in Northern Ireland. For that to happen, Pollard needed the backing of the broadsheet newspapers, which would lend respectability to the campaign. Leeson had been keen all along to tell his version of the story in a number of selected newspaper interviews.

Then Sir David Frost expressed an interest in a television interview, and everything changed. Here was a man who talked to presidents and prime ministers, a man with an international reputation who could command a huge TV audience. Frost offered an hour of prime viewing-time on the BBC, and syndication to one of the American networks before the programme was sold on to television stations all over the world. Though Frost stood to make a small fortune through syndication, and he did not pay Leeson a penny, the idea was irresistible. *The Frost Interview* was something money could not buy. Pollard and his campaigners were full of hope: a legitimate, no-holds-barred conversation in which Leeson could admit to dishonesty, confess that he was not proud of it, but say that, until the very end, he had still hoped to recover the situation. Had he been on remand in a British prison, no such revelations could even have been contemplated.

David Frost is a man of furious energy. Breakfast in the Savoy; first cigar of the day as the chauffeur drives him to his office off Kensington High Street. Usually someone is sitting on the sofa in the outer officer waiting to talk to him when he arrives. He always has four or five things on the go, and grabs whatever expert advice he can get to speed them on. I remembered a particularly good interview he had conducted thirty years earlier with an insurance shark called Emil Savundra. This relied heavily on questions provided by interested journalists. I suggested that he might like to repeat the process, and he eagerly agreed to a meeting. As I outlined the case against Leeson, drawn from the Bank of England's report and various other sources, Frost's enthusiasm was so great that I was infected by it. After ninety minutes, I was full of hope that Frost would ask the questions that I had suggested – the questions I wanted to ask Leeson myself. We parted full of bonhomie, and I looked forward to seeing a copy of the unedited text of the interview.

Leeson had got used to answering questions by the time he met Frost in Frankfurt on 4 September. The Serious Fraud Office had changed its mind and decided to interview him after all. SFO investigators had been with him the week before Frost's recording, and they were due to return when it was over. Frost's two-hour session with Leeson was edited down to half that length for the broadcast on 11 September. The first thing to be said is that they got on remarkably well together. One of Frost's former colleagues unkindly remarked that this was because they shared an interest in celebrity and money, but that does not explain the sympathy Frost showed Leeson. He treated him throughout as though he were the underdog. 'Very well put, very well put,' he exclaimed after one answer. Leeson set out his (false) version of the origin of trading in the 88888 account, but Frost's probing never revealed Leeson's cavalier attitude to the truth. The tone of the interview is vividly expressed in this excerpt, as are the faintly different flavours of what was transmitted and what was not. Those parts not broadcast are printed in italics.

Leeson: '*I don't regard myself as a criminal. I also almost see myself as being a victim of what I am in that I have tried to help people too much. I know that hasn't caused £860 millionworth of losses, but it's the initial thing* . . . There's been a few errors . . . I'll put my hands up to that, but the unauthorised [trading] is a by-product of that. It's not like Nick Leeson wanted to do some unauthorised trading, which is what I read in the papers . . . *and it's just so far from the point and completely wrong* . . . I just hope this changes people's impressions of me, which is so very important. Not just for me, but for everybody who knows me . . . Hopefully this will change the public's understanding of me, and perhaps what happened. Although you know it's pretty deep.'

Frost: '*Absolutely*. What would be your message now to the bond-holders at Barings?'

Leeson: 'It's, it's you know, everything that I, you know, it's a very difficult thing. As I explained my state of mind earlier, you know I have to keep myself on an even keel, so it's, you know, in asking questions like that, they bring back bad memories, and you know I feel complete remorse. I'm very sorry for them . . . and I will do whatever I can to help them in their claims . . . [but] I don't have a pot of gold that I've hidden away somewhere, so it's not as if I can pay them, but I'm very, very sorry. I mean if I could have my time again, I wouldn't have gone to Singapore in April '92. *As much as I feel sorry for them I also have to keep my own mental situation pretty sane, which means that, whilst I think about it, I can't let it eat me up too much.*'

Frost: '*Absolutely.*'

The Frost Interview had a mixed reception. Plenty of viewers fell for Leeson's boyish charm, and thought that he was being made a scapegoat for Barings' failure. But no body of public opinion formed in support of Leeson, as it had done for Private Clegg. The lofty view of the performance was expressed by Alan Bennett, who had a little dig at it in his diary for 1995: 'The papers are full of Leeson's self-justifications, but nobody seems to question the propriety of broadcasting such an interview in the first place; and, like so many of the interviews Frost is involved with, it's a pretty seedy affair.'

Frost's enthusiasm was not diminished by criticism or reproach. He declared that Leeson was 'fascinating', and announced that he proposed to produce 'Leeson: the film'. This would, he said, be a modern morality tale with flashes of comedy, in which Hugh Grant, star of *Four Weddings and a Funeral*, would play Leeson – 'He'd be absolutely perfect for this.' (In fact, Grant had already played a bit part in the story: he once drove a van for Duff and Trotter, the company run by Peter Norris's wife.) The *Mail on Sunday* put Frost's proposal on their front page: 'Leeson, 28, could pick up a large fee for the £20 million film and a share of the profits – earning him up to £3 million.'

At the Frankfurt Book Fair in the middle of October, Ed Victor, who had become Leeson's literary agent, pulled off a real coup. Victor managed to jack up the price of Leeson's story to £450,000, Little, Brown coming in as the highest bidders. After Victor had deducted his 15 per cent, there would be plenty left to pay for the ghost who would write the book (a journalist named Oliver Whitley), to meet some of the legal bills, and to leave some spare cash for Lisa. *The Sunday Times* headlined a story about the exploitation of the story: 'LEESON TO MAKE £3 MILLION AS THE MEDIA MOGULS MOVE IN.'

Pollard was appalled. Although it might cover some of his firm's costs, the commercialisation of Leeson was not going to help the defence. He insisted that Ed Victor should tone down the triumphalism after the gratifying Frankfurt sale.

The money might have been rolling in, but the campaign to have Leeson tried in London was faltering. *The Frost Interview* had disappointed Pollard, who thought his client would have looked better if Frost had asked harder questions. 'The interview had less legitimacy than it deserved because of the perception that Frost had gone easy on him,' he said.

Having studied the transcript of its own interviews with

Leeson, lawyers at the Serious Fraud Office decided nothing in it altered the previous decision not to compete with the Singaporeans for Leeson's extradition. By the end of September, Pollard saw that it was time for a change of tactics.

Even before the regional high court in Frankfurt ruled, on 3 October, that Leeson should be returned to face trial on eleven charges, confidential discussions about a deal had begun in Singapore. In spite of Leeson's campaign statement that he would be an exhibit in a show trial, and would receive unusually harsh treatment in a Singapore prison, his lawyers accepted that he did not have much choice, and set about limiting the damage.

By the autumn, the Singaporean government had decided that it had nothing to gain from a long trial that might draw attention to some of SIMEX's imperfections as well as Leeson's. Once that had been decided, a deal was on. A Singapore lawyer named John Koh had already been briefed by Pollard, not because he had a flashy courtroom manner, but because, as a former deputy director of the commercial affairs department, he would know the people who were preparing the case against Leeson.

Leeson had until 4 November to appeal in Germany against his extradition to Singapore. Before a final decision had to be made, however, there was a faint flicker of hope in London. Leeson was summoned to appear before a City of London Magistrates' Court to answer eight counts of deception and false accounting under the Theft Act. This clever diversion, thought up by the Baring bond-holders' campaign, appeared to work: the magistrate ruled that Leeson should appear on 30 October 1995. Only the full force of the reserve powers of the British government's law officers barricaded that avenue. Since there was now no choice left to them, Leeson's lawyers announced on 27 October that there would be no appeal. Leeson flew from Frankfurt to Singapore on 23 November 1995, having spent almost nine months in jail.

Speculation was rife that a deal had been done between Koh and the Singaporean prosecutors: Leeson would receive a lenient sentence in return for evidence that would enable charges to be brought against Peter Norris, James Bax and Simon Jones. Within days, that speculation was being treated as fact, but the deal that was being done in reality related to the number of charges that would be brought, and the length of the potential sentence. Leeson's claim that he could receive up to eighty-four years was always an exaggeration for public consumption only: the maximum sentence that could be imposed according to the original charges was fourteen years. Koh, assisted by Pollard, who had travelled with the Leesons to Singapore, negotiated a reduction in the charges to two, which carried a maximum sentence of seven years.

Once the charges were agreed, both sides were anxious to proceed quickly, and the date set for a decision about Leeson's fate was 1 December 1995. Before the case was heard, however, newspaper and television journalists became so swept up by their own speculation that they declared they knew already how long Leeson would get: two years, maximum; maybe only one. By all reports, Leeson himself was feeling pretty confident, too.

The Subordinate District Court stands on Havelock Road on the edge of what is still, a generation after the end of colonialism, called Chinatown. The twenty-six courts normally draw a decent audience of local people, although the lawyers wonder if the main attraction isn't the air-conditioning. There was no room in the public gallery of Court 26 on that Friday, however. Since there were only eight seats on the press bench and 100 journalists had gathered from home and abroad, the press queued for numbered seats in the gallery two hours before the court sat at 9 a.m.

Leeson was neatly but informally dressed: no jacket, white long-sleeved shirt, maroon tie. The judge was Senior District Judge Richard Magnus, a disciplinarian poised for promotion to the Supreme Court. That was bad news; Singapore judges do not get preferment by showing judicial liberality. The deputy public prosecutor, Lawrence Ang, informed the judge of the deal he had struck, but added that the nine charges that had been dropped could be taken into consideration.

Leeson, standing up straight with his hands behind his back, was asked how he pleaded. 'I am guilty, Your Honour,' he replied. After this twenty-minute session the court adjourned until 2 p.m. The only fresh news of the morning was Leeson's lunch – the late-twentieth-century version of the condemned man's last meal: two Big Macs and a large Coke.

Although he is still only in his late thirties, Lawrence Ang is a veteran of high-profile cases brought by the Singaporean government against opponents of the regime. Well groomed, with highly polished shoes, Ang is the model of a modern Singaporean apparatchik; histrionics are forsworn; the emphasis is on a ruthless exploitation of the facts. In his prosecution statement, Ang's Leeson was a cooler, more calculating figure than the Leeson in John Koh's plea of mitigation, which followed as soon as Ang sat down.

John Koh is about forty, heavy-set with thick spectacles. His hour-long plea of mitigation was fascinating, and told us a good deal about Leeson, and about Singapore. From Koh, we learned of Leeson's defence in the specific counts on which he was charged, and in the wider story of the collapse of Barings. In the following account of the proceedings, my commentary on the defence is printed in italics.

Koh conceded that Leeson's efforts to rectify his losses were misguided, and that he did break the law. But this was not all his fault: 'Proprietary trading is a ruthless business. The inexperienced, ill-equipped traders who do not have a sophisticated system of support, like our client and Barings, find it impossible to devise or execute a strategy to prevent trading losses.'

It is true that Barings did lack a sophisticated system to support an inexperienced trader, but that was not what Barings needed. What it needed was a system that would detect a sustained fraud.

Koh's next point was that Leeson saw himself as 'a dynamic, but, in the final analysis, insufficiently experienced trader'. This explained, Koh said, two misguided acts which were aimed at staving off the trading losses that had had the unintended consequence of bankrupting Barings. 'The first act was an act of simple cheating designed to throw off the auditors (which design was shared by certain superiors at Barings). The second act reflected the desperate attempt of a judgement-impaired young man in panic trying to eliminate the ballooning losses. In the ruthless free-market forces of trading, Barings' trading competitors punished the bank for its negligible controls and left Leeson with the responsibility of appearing before this court to determine his punishment.'

It was the fault of ruthless markets, then, that Leeson was on trial.

The next line of defence was the most brazen. Koh asserted: 'It has been accepted that our client originally established this [88888] account as a genuine account to post errors of Baring Futures (Singapore)'s inexperienced staff that occurred because of pressure by volatile trading conditions.'

But it has not 'been accepted'. The evidence does not support Koh's claim.

Koh denied that Leeson had cheated the auditors by forging documents relating to the SLK receivable. 'Our client's actions were to deflect attention from the losses caused by his trades, rather than to cover up any illegal act,' said Koh.

In fact, the losses were themselves the result of illegal acts.

Koh's next target was the auditors. 'With a balance-sheet discrepancy of [£50 million], they should have investigated it differently ... Why would any reasonable auditor accept photocopies given by the person queried? ... It should have been clear to the auditors that they could not rely on the fax [headed "From Nick and Lisa"].'

Koh was suggesting that Leeson committed a criminal act because the auditors were not 'reasonable'.

The prosecutor's second charge was that Leeson had cheated SIMEX by falsifying his accounts so that he would be liable for lower margins. For this charge, Koh altered his tone. SIMEX and the MAS were treated as sagacious, diligent bodies. 'SIMEX quite rightly, unlike Barings' management, was not prepared to rely purely on our client's representations or actions ... As the trades were beginning to look suspect [SIMEX] queried Baring Futures (Singapore) and Barings' management, not our client ... SIMEX and the MAS more appropriately sought and relied on assurances from the Barings Group.'

This made it appear as though the offence was committed by Barings, not Leeson.

Later in his speech, Koh stated: 'SIMEX has demonstrated its resilience and the effectiveness of its safeguards.'

Resilience, certainly.

Koh's view of SIMEX caught the flavour of all his comments on Singapore. These rewrote history and flattered the institutions of the state in language suggestive of a comic version of the show trials organised by dictators in the 1930s and 1940s.

On Leeson's suggestions that he would not get a fair trial, Koh said: 'He was wrongly influenced by the reports of a handful of irresponsible journalists, none of whom I believe are in this court. These reports suggested that in certain cases, especially politically sensitive ones involving the Singapore authorities, one could not hope for a fair trial in Singapore. He mistakenly believed these rumours. He has apologised at the earliest opportunity after obtaining appropriate advice.'

Leeson shifted in his seat, apparently trying not to smirk; the press gallery guffawed; Prosecutor Ang smiled – but it was he who had insisted on Leeson's recantation, as part of the deal. Judge Magnus glared sternly at the court.

Koh concluded his plea of mitigation by talking about money. Defendants in criminal trials in Singapore are expected to make a contribution to the prosecution's costs. Leeson offered S$150,000 (£70,000) to defray the expenses he had caused by fighting extradition. 'He has borrowed from third parties against his interest in London properties owned by his wife,' Koh explained. The use of the plural for 'properties' came as a surprise.

That was a prologue to Koh's peroration. 'Contrary to speculation,' he said, 'there are no secret profits. Our client has no assets . . . There is no Hollywood movie with Hugh Grant . . . Any Hollywood movie is also highly improbable. The likelihood of his profiting from his notoriety is remote, as a writ of summons has been served on him in England to strip him of any possible gain . . . Our client's conduct . . . did not involve personal benefit . . . He is not the normal criminal, and this is not the normal criminal offence . . . What do the facts show? Recklessness, foolishness. Our client is not a crook.'

Once Koh had finished, Judge Magnus adjourned the court until 9.30 a.m. the following morning, a Saturday, when he would deliver the sentence. Unlike the British journalists, who were still telling their editors in London that a short sentence was probable, Stephen Pollard was cautious. He judged a sentence of four to four and a half years more likely, though he thought that, with time deducted for the months spent in Frankfurt, and for good behaviour, Leeson ought to be free in less than three years. But Pollard had reckoned without Judge Magnus's concern for the integrity of Singapore's institutions.

Magnus's judgement concentrated on the principal victim of Leeson's crime. This was not the bond-holders, nor even his former employers, but the Singapore International Monetary Exchange. Judge Magnus's grim summary stated: 'There was manoeuvring of the transactions . . . in question . . . intended to give the auditors and SIMEX an impression of superficial reality. It was deliberately designed to beguile them. More critical is the effect of the accused's deception of SIMEX. His deeds placed the integrity of SIMEX at risk.' Leeson, who had arrived in court wearing a formal dark suit and looking relaxed and rested, had begun to swallow hard and look at his shoes.

The Judge proceeded to the matter of the SLK receivable. 'If it were not for this web of deceit, SIMEX would have known the true situation and it would either have suspended the trading activities of Baring Futures or liquidated the positions held by the company.'

Judge Magnus said that the direction and tone of the

mitigation plea had caught the eye of the court – but it did not appear to have much effect on him. 'The sentence must be sufficiently substantial to indicate to the public the gravity of the particular offence,' he said, before sentencing Nicholas William Leeson to six and a half years' imprisonment, backdated to 2 March 1995. In Magnus's judgement it seems, the facts clearly showed that Leeson was a crook.

Pollard and Koh looked grimly, first at each other and then across to Leeson, who was blinking repeatedly and biting his lip. Six and a half years was better than the lawyers had originally feared, but worse than they had eventually come to hope. As he was driven off to Tanah Merah Jail to begin his sentence, Leeson gave a broad grin to the cluster of photographers. For him, it was the end of the story.

17

The Bitterest of Tastes

Although John Koh's extravagant defence of Nick Leeson was shrewdly constructed to appeal to local manners and morals, it contained one statement that was entirely credible. When things got out of hand after the Kobe earthquake, Koh said, 'our client would have welcomed discovery'. Had he been exposed, 'it would have become equally the responsibility of Barings to manage the positions he had taken, and to rectify the situation'. The strain finally became intolerable.

Leeson had shown ingenuity and bravado in perpetrating his fraud and carrying out his forgeries, but there was no endgame; no hidden bank account that could have financed a fugitive existence. He knew that he would be found out. He told Stephen Pollard that, if he had tried the same game at his previous employers, Morgan Stanley, he would have been exposed within two months. He might not have lasted that long.

At Barings, he kept the ball in play for thirty-two months, and, much as he longed to be caught, his prevarication delayed his final exposure by Tony Railton for one further week. Only his disappearance finally set all the alarm bells ringing.

Leeson's grand fraud had taken place in an extraordinarily fertile environment. Barings lacked the cynicism about human nature, the relentless management style and the advanced computer systems to catch him. The Bank of England placed too much reliance on Barings' good name, and lacked the know-how of preventative regulation. SIMEX was willing to bend its rules to take business from its main competitor in Osaka.

Leeson was lucky, too. The failure of Lynn Henderson in 1993, James Baker in 1994 and Tony Hawes in 1994 and 1995 to insist on a full reconciliation of his business helped him to keep on going. The episode of the SLK receivable deserves a place in management-studies textbooks as an example of the perils of wilfully ignoring a broad hint of impropriety: Bax and Jones both knew the alleged trade was unauthorised.

Indeed, the management style of Barings was so inadequate that it is hard to believe that the bank could have survived much longer as an independent entity. It required new capital, but, more than that, it needed executive flair. Senior directors had told Andrew Tuckey as much, before 23 February 1995.

Leeson was a fraud in the right company, in the right place, at the right time. But to argue, as John Koh did, that he was not guilty because his bosses failed to stop him is a threadbare defence. Now the story has been investigated and told, the conclusion must be that, no matter how vulnerable Barings had become, Leeson was the man principally responsible for bankrupting it. He was given the opportunity – but why did he take it? What was his motive?

Money must certainly have been a motive. Leeson wanted to be a trader because traders make big money. His own career was proof of this. His 1992 bonus of £35,746 rose to £130,000 for 1993. Had he not been exposed – or had his profits been genuine – Leeson would have earned, on top of a decent salary, £450,000 for 1994. These bonuses add up to more than £600,000, a sum which many dedicated criminals would feel proud to get away with.

Yet Leeson was not a great spender. His sister Victoria reported that 'he doesn't exactly throw his money around', though whenever the family needed help, he gave it. His flat in Anguilla Road was not luxurious; relaxing at home, he liked watching football and movies on the video. He and Lisa travelled widely, but the firm often paid for that. He appears to have had no expensive habits. But spending is not necessarily the main motive for earning. Leeson's earnings were a status symbol: they did indeed amount to 'shagloads' – a great deal more than his former schoolmates at Parmiter's were getting.

Even so, it is hard to believe that money could have been his only motive. Popularity must have come into it, too. The Boy Scout in Leeson wanted to be liked as a good and caring colleague. Giving favourable prices to the traders in Tokyo, and taking losses into the 88888 account so that he could remit profits to Barings in London, undeniably succeeded in creating a dazzling reputation for him.

Pleasing Lisa is another plausible motive. His wife had replaced his mother as the person whose approval he sought. 'She's a very strong lady,' he told David Frost. When the sale of the rights to his autobiography were being discussed, one of his preoccupations was that there should be enough money for Lisa to live on, and to finance her travel to visit him in jail. For some months, I thought she must have known about his fraud: it is the kind of secret that is difficult to hide from a wife. Now I believe I was wrong. Leeson's ability to conceal the part of him that perpetrated the fraud enabled him to deceive Lisa, too.

None of these partial motives fully explains the premeditated nature of Leeson's crime. His plan was conceived before Barings started to trade on SIMEX, and set in motion at the first possible opportunity. What he had learned in the settlements office and the business development group at Barings made him believe that he could pull off his great deception. As we have seen, he told Pollard, his lawyer, that Morgan Stanley would have exposed him in two months. That being so, he would have been less likely to start it in the first place. After three years at Barings, Leeson seems to have decided that the odds against a speedy discovery were long enough. In no other case, ever, has an employee's scorn for his bosses proved so costly.

Class resentment? The only evidence of strong class feeling within the family comes from Victoria Leeson. After the collapse, she said: 'They seem to be saying that if you're working class, you should be working as a dustman or a shop assistant. They're trying to belittle him.' In the early 1990s, there was still plenty of belittling of the clerks by the toffs at Barings. Leeson may, like most Baring Securities people, have had no time for the stuffy bankers, and, as a yuppie, he may have felt contempt for the privileged class. But he aspired to membership of the moneyed class.

A therapist would also look for a motive in the dark, hidden part of Leeson's nature. The analysis might go something like this: Barings would take on the attributes of a parent – feeding Leeson, training him and nurturing him. In return for this, the 'parent' would expect obedience and loyalty. Leeson's resentment of this would lead him to bite the hand that fed him.

Having examined Leeson's years of deception, what strikes me most strongly is the way he was able to present himself as open and genuine. He was admired by his colleagues, and trusted by them. Nobody ever said he was shifty; nobody thought him likely to be a liar. When he prevaricated and dodged questions, he was always given the benefit of the doubt. The shadowy side of his nature was completely eclipsed, even from his wife.

In Singapore, Leeson lived out a fantasy life. He wanted to be the big, swinging dick, a legendary money-maker, like Christopher Heath – the man whose huge profits swelled the bonuses. And for thirty-two months he committed fraud and forgery to sustain this 'golden boy' image of himself. The part of him that must have known it couldn't last was suppressed to the bitter end.

The answer to the absorbing question about motive must lie in all, or some, of these explanations. I doubt whether Leeson could give a full answer himself.

In reply to a letter of commiseration, Peter Baring wrote that the episode showed how mistaken the management had been to give too much responsibility to a clerk. In saying this, he made Barings look like the Bourbons, who forgot nothing and learned nothing. The modern City cannot be run without giving responsibility to 'clerks'. Recognising this is an attribute of good management.

The *Daily Telegraph* declared that if Leeson went to prison and the former board of Barings went to Glyndebourne, the saga would leave the bitterest of tastes. And so it did. Peter Baring did not relinquish his chairmanship of the Glyndebourne Arts Trust. A fellow trustee reports that the summer season was almost over before a ghost of a smile was seen to cross his face, but his life went on. There was no interruption to the extensive refurbishment of the Victorian rectory near Hungerford.

In the months after the collapse, the Baring family appeared to hold together – although, by all reports, they did so by not speaking of the collapse at all. But as the evidence of gross incompetence piled up, their fortitude crumbled. No Baring would think of commenting in public, but in private they began to blame Peter. Sir John Baring, now Lord Ashburton, confessed to friends that he could not believe so much money could have gone to the Far East without anyone at the bank knowing what it was for.

Peter Baring was due to retire in the autumn of 1995. How he must have wished he had handed over to Andrew Tuckey a year earlier. Tuckey still sat in a box at the Royal Opera House, where he remained on the board. The chairman, Sir Angus Stirling, was nearing the end of his term, and Tuckey's name had been on a shortlist to succeed him – until Barings went bust. But despite this little setback, it soon became plain that the one person who had survived the debacle intact was Andrew Tuckey.

Along with Peter Baring, Tuckey submitted his resignation to ING on 3 April 1995. But he left through a revolving door, and came straight back again as a 'consultant' to the corporate-finance department. ING wanted him, and the Bank of England raised no objection, as long as he had no responsibility for controls or systems.

ING claimed that, as a consultant, Tuckey would not be

doing his old management job. So it came as a surprise when he turned up in the role of executioner in May. Eleven of his former colleagues in London were asked to 'resign', and told that if they would not do the decent thing, they would be fired. (Ron Baker and Mary Walz refused to go without a fight; Tony Hawes took the retirement that was due to him in 1993.) The *coup de grâce* in these cases of resignation and dismissal was administered personally by Tuckey. One victim reported that Tuckey looked so ill at ease that he felt sorry for him. Such sympathy was rare.

Tuckey explained to enquirers that he had stayed on at Barings because his presence ensured stability and continuity there. He had felt strongly about his duty to resign, but he felt even more strongly about his duty to the new owners. By the end of 1995, he was boasting that Barings was the top bank in the mergers-and-acquisitions business in the City of London. He appeared to be a completely guilt-free zone.

But Tuckey was also becoming accident-prone. On 22 October the headline in the tabloid *Sunday Mirror* read: 'WORLD EXCLUSIVE: As Nick Leeson was breaking the bank, top boss was Baring his other assets. THE £800m BONKER.' Tuckey's mistress, Tracy Long, had been hired in August 1994 as a media specialist in Barings' corporate-finance department. Previously she had worked in the public-relations department of Classic FM, a radio station. The *Sunday Mirror* reported that within the bank the couple was known as the 'Music Lovers'. The article was cruelly embarrassing, but little sympathy was expressed among his former colleagues for Andrew Tuckey. He had been the architect of the merger of Baring Brothers and Baring Securities, which was seen as a cause of the collapse. It had, indeed, left the bitterest of tastes.

Victims came from inside as well as outside the bank. Twenty-one men and women who were judged responsible for Leeson's fraud were 'summarily dismissed' in July, whether or not they had 'resigned' in May. For some, this was too much to bear. On receiving the hand-delivered dismissal letter from ING, one senior manager locked himself in the lavatory and wept. Some could not stop picking obsessively over the pieces; others immersed themselves in conspiracy theories. The lives of many were blighted, and the effect on their families was profound. Leeson had made fools of them all.

But the principal victims of Leeson's fraud were the bond-holders. Late in 1993, Barings had raised £100 million by issuing a perpetual loan at 9.25 per cent. Normally perpetual loans of this kind are bought by insurance companies and pension funds, but, with interest rates beginning to fall, the Barings bond offered an unusually attractive return. Brokers bought chunks of the loan and divided it up, selling it on to individual clients. So the creditors included such people as a south London doctor, a vicar in north Wales and a retired army officer. Many had invested part of their retirement savings. ING offered to pay only 5p in the pound, with the possibility of another 20p at some future time.

Nicholas Ritblatt was one of the bond-holders. The son of the chairman of British Land, one of the biggest property groups in the country, Ritblatt organised legal representation and began to collect the names of the bond-holders, forming them into a protest group. Contesting the decision to sell Barings to ING, rather than to liquidate it and raise money from the sale of assets like Baring Asset Management, was only the first of a series of legal skirmishes engaged in on behalf of the bond-holders' group.

The group's strategy is being organised by an energetic, experienced solicitor named Jonathan Stone, a veteran of previous campaigns of this kind, and a man with the persistence of a short-tempered terrier, who can be relied on not to compromise or give ground. Stone has set his sights on the brokers and bankers who underwrote the loan issue. Unfortunately, redemption is a lengthy process. Before Stone achieves a result, some of the bond-holders will almost certainly be dead.

The global financial market tried to shrug off the collapse of Barings. The reassuring message was that the company might have been historic, but it was only a small London bank whose failure had not shaken the system. The world's bank regulators didn't buy that. Within a month of Barings' failure, these regulators, pushed hard by Mary Shapiro from the CFTC in Washington DC, had met to discuss new standards for international co-operation. Within a year, British, American, Hong Kong and Australian regulators had agreed to share information about large positions held on their exchanges. Singapore did not sign up, however. 'They're cryptic about it,' Shapiro said.

For Eddie George, governor of the Bank of England, the one bonus of the affair was Barings' role as a dreadful example to the industry at large. In the ensuing days and nights, City banks worked overtime checking their risk-management and control systems. 'I think the collapse has done more durable good than all the efforts of the world's regulators laid end to end,' says George.

Volume slumped on derivatives exchanges as company treasurers digested the lessons of disastrous affairs like Bankers Trust and its OTC derivatives trade with Gibson Greetings Inc., as well as those of Barings. All of a sudden, companies were made acutely aware of the risks as well as the profits of derivatives-trading. Caution became fashionable again. There was only one exception to this global downward trend: trading on SIMEX went up.

But the danger foreseen by Henry Jarecki, the New York derivates dealer, in Chapter 3 – that, some day, wild gyrations in prices will bankrupt a major derivates-dealer, and that spreading contagion will plunge the banking system into chaos – still hangs over the world's financial markets. Jarecki's pessimism is based on experience as well as his nature.

Banks, especially in the City of London, learned one lesson and forgot another. Barings' collapse showed that banks should be either small or big: there is no security in the middle ground. A small bank trades with its clients' money and lives off the fees it earns. Proprietary trading is a game only for big banks that have deep, deep pockets. When these banks take huge daily positions in foreign-exchange markets, they are gambling: they cannot know whether the price is going to rise or fall.

And if there is an endemic risk in derivatives markets, the great British clearing banks are taking a share of it, along with the banks and securities houses in New York, Tokyo and elsewhere. The only people who benefit from the proprietary positions taken by the big banks are the staff and the shareholders, who receive bonuses and dividends. The customers whose interests are at risk receive no benefits at all.

Will the lessons that have been learned prevent the recurrence of a disaster like the collapse of Barings? Consider this observation in one report of inquiry.

> In part because of the importance to the firm's business, this department appears to have insulated itself from its other departments ... In this atmosphere, as his apparent profitability increased, he himself was able to put up a front of unapproachability and secrecy when enquiries about his trading activities arose. Throughout the firm, scepticism about his activities was often dismissed or left unspoken.

This is not a comment on Barings. The subject is Joseph Jett, who, as head of Kidder Peabody's government-debt trading-desk in New York, claimed a wholly false profit of $350 million. Jett's fraud was exposed in April 1994, after he had been doing it for two years. At the time, Leeson's losses were already rising fast.

During the summer of 1995, Eddie George was more sanguine: as a result of the Barings collapse, he thought it was unlikely that a similar catastrophe would occur. 'I'd be quite surprised to find, at any time in the next ten years, that somebody was allowed to be in charge of trading and the back office.'

By coincidence, I was on the floor of SIMEX late in September when news flashed up on the screen above the trading-floor that a Daiwa trader named Iguchi had lost $1.1 million in 30,000 unauthorised trades that had taken place in New York over eleven years. Like Leeson, Iguchi had been running both the front and the back offices, even after Leeson's fraud had made headlines around the world and had shaken trading-desks in every market.

Will an event like the collapse of Barings happen again? Of course it will. Somewhere, it – or something like it – is happening now.

A Note on Sources

The City of London has failed to inspire a rich body of literature. The bibliography for a book like this is never long. Even now, the City's history belongs principally to a strong oral tradition. Some City grandees are accomplished story-tellers. Most, but not all, of their recollections are off-the-record.

The history of Baring Brothers is better documented than most, but its official history, which was published in 1988, ends in 1929. After that, it is necessary to rely on what people say, and the Baring family is notoriously reluctant to speak about the business. Fortunately, not all of them are utterly discreet. I should like to mention those who did help, but a request for anonymity was a customary prelude to my conversations with members of the Baring family.

Although Leeson's case was never argued in full in court, there is, none the less, plenty of evidence in the reports produced in London by the Board of Banking Supervision, and, in Singapore, by the inspectors appointed by the minister for finance.

Bankers and traders in the United States are more confident about expressing opinions for publication than their London counterparts. New York is the best place to start an education in futures and options; Roger Geissler and Henry Jarecki are fine primary teachers. This education was continued in Chicago by skilful and experienced figures; by name, Leo Melamed, Bill Brodsky and Jack Sandner.

The history of the first decade of Barings Securities is told by Christopher Heath, Andrew Baylis, Richard Greer and Ian Martin, all of whom left Barings in 1993. The subsequent story is told by many of the characters who took over from Heath's people and ran the bank until the collapse of Barings, and their departure in 1995.

To begin with, all of them were reluctant to talk. As the months went by, some decided that, in the interests of accuracy and fairness, it was better to speak than to remain silent. I was able to interview nearly half the Barings employees who were victims of Leeson's fraud. In alphabetical order, they are Geoffrey Broadhurst, Tony Gamby, Fernando Gueler, William Daniel, Tony Hawes, Peter Norris and Mary Walz. Ron Baker came to the telephone a few times.

Some of the survivors at Barings spoke too, but never for attribution. The new Dutch owners, ING, would speak only through a spokesman in Amsterdam.

The Bank of England is a remarkably generous source of information. This tradition of openness began with Brian Quinn, the retiring executive director in charge of banking supervision. The bank's senior officials speak openly, and for the record. The Bank also provides historical lists of changes in currency values. In this book, the value of Japanese yen in terms of US dollars and sterling is altered to reflect month-end prices. When the dollars referred to are Singapore dollars, this is mentioned in the text.

Because Leeson's defence was conducted in Frankfurt and Singapore, his lawyers were not constrained by the *sub judice* rules of the English courts. Consequently, they were able to conduct a public defence. This created an uncommon inclination among the lawyers in the case to talk openly. The judicial authorities in Singapore made available the full details of the prosecution case. Brian Miller provided an account of Leeson's trial and conviction.

Because there are no footnotes, I have tried to direct the reader to the source of information in the body of the text.

Bibliography

BOARD OF BANKING SUPERVISION, *Report of the Inquiry into the Circumstances of the Collapse of Barings*, HMSO, London, 1995.

CROMER, ESME, *From This Day Forward*, Thomas Harmsworth, Stoke Abbott, 1991.

KYNASTON, DAVID, *The City of London: Volume 1, A World of Its Own*, Chatto and Windus, London, 1994.

LEWIS, MICHAEL, *Liar's Poker*, Hodder & Stoughton, London, 1989.

MINISTRY FOR FINANCE, SINGAPORE, *Baring Futures (Singapore) Pte Ltd: The Report of the Inspectors appointed by the Minister for Finance*, 1995.

RAWNSLEY, JUDITH, *Going For Broke: Nick Leeson and the Collapse of Barings Bank*, Harper Collins, London, 1995.

ROBERTS, RICHARD, *Schroders: Merchants and Bankers*, Macmillan, London, 1992.

WECHSBERG, JOSEPH, *The Merchant Bankers*, Weidenfeld and Nicolson, London, 1967.

WOLFE, TOM, *The Bonfire of the Vanities*, Farrar, Straus, Giroux, New York, 1987.

ZIEGLER, PHILIP, *The Sixth Great Power: Barings 1762–1929*, Collins, London, 1988.

Photographic Section
Acknowledgements

Associated Press/Topham, plate 2
Express Newspapers, plate 15
INS News Group, plate 17
Barny Jones, plate 24
Desmond O'Neill features, plates 5, 7, 10, 11
Press Association, plate 6
Reuters/Popperfoto, plates 3, 9, 12, 18, 22, 25, 26, 7, 28, 29
Rex Features, plates 4 (photo Sipa Press), 19 (photo James Morgan), 20
Sky TV Broadcasting, plate 13
Frank Spooner Pictures, plate 23 (photo Ian Jones)
Sygma, plates 1 (photo Mathieu Polak), 8 (photo Dillon Bryen), 14 (photo
   Voja Miladinovic), 16, 21 (photo MSI)

Index

Abbey National 203, 206, 216, 217
Abbott, Diane 248
ABM-Amro, Amsterdam 209, 229
Andrews, Neil 127
Ang, Lawrence 181–2, 276–7, 283–4, 285–6
Ang Swee Tian 133, 138
Argyropoulous, Danny 108, 194, 272
ALCO (Asset and Liability Committee, formerly BS Risk Committee) 166, 122, 126, 127, 155–7, 174, 182, 187, 194, 263

Baker, James 123–6, 127, 128–30, 131, 136, 139, 170, 269–70, 290
Baker, Ron 54, 115, 116; character 115, 121; and internal rivalries 118, 173; meets Leeson 123; champions Leeson 135–6, 185; 139–40, 143, 144, 155, 156, 159, 164, 169, 196, 255, 257, 269; BBS Report 253, 257; Singapore Inspectors Report 268; 294, 300
Bangkok 34, 195, 237
Bank of England 5, 11, 18, 45–6; Court of 12, 16, 67, 110, 207; Governors 11, 13, 16, 17, 18, 21, 213; worries about BSL 62, 64; 186; grants 'informal concession' 113; mounts rescue attempt 202–21; on Leeson's losses, 99, 183, 224, 231; new relationship with City 221–2, 242; relationship with Treasury, 213, 242–3; criticism of Bank 222, 243, 244–50; see Board of Banking Supervision
Bank Herstatt 221
Bank for International Settlements (BIS) 157, 187, 203, 255

Bankers Trust, New York 22, 44, 45, 54, 115, 211, 221, 296
Banque National de Paris 168, 256
Barclays Bank 102, 202, 212, 215, 216
Baring, Alexander (1st Lord Ashburton) 8, 9, 48
Baring Asset Management 54, 56, 102, 209, 219, 229, 295
Baring Brothers: arrogance 5, 11, 214; 'risk averse' image 5, 11–12, 16, 23, 63, 267; royal bankers 1, 5, 12, 17, 18, 91, 223, 229; 'first merchant in Europe' image 6–11; relationship with Bank 11–12, 18, 109–10, 242; Bank rescue attempt 202–20, 248; possible buyers 208, 209, 219–20, 229–30, 231; plight of the bond-holders 295
Baring Brothers & Co Ltd 11; in 20s and 30s 12; partnership reconstituted 13; in 50s and 60s 16–18; in 70s and 80s 15–17, 23, 27–9, 30; hire Heath 23, 27–8, bankers versus brokers 32, 52–3, 54, 56–7, 60–1, 63, 64, 67, 68, 103, 117–18, 267–8; consider closure of BSL 62; solo-consolidation 103–4, 111–12, 113, 114, 115, 118, 119, 121
Baring, Calypso 12–13
Baring, Cecil (3rd Lord Revelstoke) 12
Baring, Edmund (1st Lord Revelstoke) 9–11, 14
Baring, Evelyn (1st Earl of Cromer) 9
Baring, Evelyn B. 13
Baring Foundation 13–14, 23, 208, 232, 269
Baring, Francis (founder, d. 1810) 6–7, 9, 15, 48, 233
Baring, Francis (d. 1940) 18
Baring, Sir Francis (1st Lord Northbrook) 9

Baring, Francis (5th Lord Northbrook) 233–4
Baring Futures (Singapore) Ltd (BFS) 80, 85; 88888 account opened 92–3; client account anomalies noted 113–14; 1994 internal audit 123–6, 127, 128–31, 139; wins SIMEX Trader of the Year Award 140; challenged by SIMEX 149–53, 265; Hawes' Singapore Project 153, 172–3, 175, 180; fails to meet margin calls 156, 158; Leeson instructed to curtail trading 156, 157; SLK receivable 159–76; Leeson disappears 194–200; calculating the losses 213–14, 217; cock-up theory 253, 266–7; cover up theory 2, 254–5, 262, 264–5; conspiracy theory 253–4, 256, 257–9, 260–1, 262–4, 271; sackings 294
Baring, Hugo 18
Baring Investment Bank (BIB) 67, 117, 120, 121, 123, 153, 199
Baring, Johann (John) 6–7
Baring, John (2nd Lord Revelstoke) 9, 12
Baring, Sir John (Lord Ashburton) 14, 15–17, 18, 19, 20, 21, 23, 27, 28, 33, 110, 120, 293
Baring, Michael 54
Baring, Nicholas 18, 19, 23, 27, 63
Baring, Peter 17; character 18–19, 20, 204; becomes chairman 19–20; 54, 60, 62, 63, 64, 66; fires Heath 65; reassures Bank 109–10; 158, 186; learns of disaster 200; at Bank rescue attempt 203, 204, 206–7, 214, 217, 220; asks advice on sale 208; press interview 223–4; responsibility 246; BBS Report 253; 269, 292, 293
Baring, Rowland (3rd Earl of Cromer) 13–14
Baring, Samantha 63
Baring Securities Ltd (BSL): prospers 27–34; Japanese stock market coup 51–2; 1992 reorganisation 60–4, 102–3; sacking of Heath 65; optimism of 1993 109; BIB merger (1994) 116, 121
Baring Securities (Holdings) Inc. New York 189–90
Baring Securities (Hong Kong) Ltd 29, 30, 32, 33, 58, 62
Baring Securities International Holdings Ltd (BSIHL) 55
Baring Securities (Japan) Ltd 30–1, 33, 35, 52, 90, 105–6, 133, 134–6, 139, 140, 142, 186, 197, 199, 225, 265, 268, 272, 275
Baring Securities (London) Ltd (BSLL) 112, 160, 183

Baring Securities (Singapore) Ltd: capitalisation debate 54–7, 59; 80, 85, 90, 109, 173; obtains 'informal concession' 113, 246, 247, 250; BIB merger (1994) 116, 121
Baring Securities Risk Committee see ALCO
Baring, Theresa 19
Baring, Thomas 9, 10
Barnett, Geoffrey 118, 184, 253
Bates, Joshua 8
Bax, James 84, 85; criticises Leeson's reporting lines 86–8, 89, 90; 104, 109, 140, 152, 157, 164; resentment of head office 127, 130, 153, 176; the SLK receivable 169, 173–4, 254, 256, 257, 259–60, 261–2, 263, 264, 290; promises to split Leeson's front and back office responsibilities 170, 172, 263; supports Leeson 172, 173, 175; and Leeson's disappearance 195, 196, 198, 200; BBS Report 253; Singapore Inspectors' Report 258, 259, 260, 277; 283
Baylis, Andrew 29, 32, 34, 35, 36, 50, 51–2, 57, 59–60, 66, 68, 96, 97, 300
BCCI collapse 204, 222, 250
Bennett, Alan 280–1
Berlins, Marcel 277–8
Bettelheim, Eric 228
Big Bang (1985) 16, 20, 21, 22–3, 205, 222, 269
Birch, Peter 206, 217
Bischoff, Win 208, 209
Black, Fischer 41
Black Monday (19 Oct 1987) 29, 53, 57
Board of Banking Supervision 2, 109–11, 118, 129, 186, 203, 209, 213, 244; BBS Report 86, 88, 100–1, 109–10, 113, 123, 129, 139, 154, 158, 173, 175–6, 246
Bolsover, John 54, 64, 219
Bond, John 212
Bonnefoy, Phillipe 143–4
bonuses 14, 30, 31, 32, 35, 52, 55, 59, 63, 67–8, 73, 95, 104, 117, 135, 145, 214, 217–18, 233, 256, 262, 269–70
Borneo Times 235
Bowser, Gordon 86, 88, 89–90, 98, 100–1
Broadhurst, Geoff 114, 116, 118, 127, 128, 129–31, 167, 169, 174, 176, 190, 197, 198, 253, 254–5, 260, 263, 264, 300
British American Tobacco 17
Brodsky, Bill 299
Brunei Investment Authority 219, 220
Brunei, Sultan of 213, 219, 220, 229
Buenos Aires Water Supply and Drainage Co debacle 10

Index

Burns, Sir Terry 204
Buxton, Andrew 212, 213, 216–17, 218

Carlsson, Roger 272
Cazenove 230
Changi jail 239
Chase Manhattan Bank 45, 95
Chicago Board of Trade 226
Chicago Mercantile Exchange (the Merc) 39, 41, 43, 46, 91, 93, 180, 227, 275
Citibank 100, 107, 156, 164–5, 183, 257
City of London 21–2, 46, 73, 222, 270
Clarke, Kenneth 218, 244, 252
Clitheroe, John 235, 238
Commodities Futures Trading Commission (CFTC) 226, 228, 296
Coopers & Lybrand 60, 148, 149, 158, 159, 167, 168, 169, 173, 174, 176, 254, 264, 266, 268–9, 277
Courtaulds 17
Coutts Bank 73
Craven, John 24, 220
Crédit Lyonnais 248
Crédit Swisse First Boston 142, 215
Cromer, Esme Lady 13

Daily Mail 2
Daily Telegraph 246, 293
Daiwa 22, 44, 48, 205
Daniel, William 30–1, 76, 157, 225, 300
Dare, John 33
Dean Whitter 271
Denton, Nicholas 258
Deloitte and Touche 100–1, 149
Deutsche Bank, Frankfurt 23, 44, 205, 220
Dickel, Tony 86, 88, 90
Dillon Read 56
Donovan, Tom 226
Dresdener Bank 102
Duff and Trotter 59, 67, 256, 262, 281

Eastwood, Lindsay 72
Economist, The 205, 206
Edinburgh, HRH Duke of 223
88888 account 93–4, 97–8, 100, 101, 107, 108, 115, 122–3, 134, 141, 148, 150, 152, 156, 159, 164, 181, 183, 193; exposed 198; 255, 257, 260, 261, 264, 265, 268, 272, 275, 279, 291
Elardo, Mark: The Complete Trader's Bag of Tricks 46–7, 137
Ernst and Young 228, 229, 231, 234, 272
European Bank & Trust Ltd 143

FCT (First Continental Trading) Chicago 107–8, 137, 194, 272
Federal Reserve Bank, Washington 210

Financial Times 223–4, 243, 246, 258, 260, 271
Fitzgerald, Duncan 167, 176
Foot, Michael 203, 204, 207, 210, 215, 219, 222
Fortune Magazine 83
Frankfurt 33, 236, 237–8, 239, 273, 279, 282; Book Fair 2, 281
Fraser, Andrew 29, 34, 52, 53, 61, 64, 66, 86, 117, 263
Frost Interview, The 85–6, 90, 93, 94–6, 97, 99, 101, 107, 108–9, 144–6, 178–9, 186–7, 191–2, 225, 236, 261, 263, 270, 278–81
FTSE 100 (the Footsie) 38
Fuchs, Benjamin 105
Fujita, Yukihusu 267

Gamby, Tony 116–17, 118, 128, 131, 133, 167–8, 169, 170, 184, 187, 189, 190, 192–3, 195, 196, 198–200, 213, 253, 255, 261, 268, 300
Gapper, John 258
Geissler, Roger 37, 41, 42, 43, 44, 45, 46, 142, 267, 272, 299
George, Eddie 17, 110, 203, 204–5, 208; character 213; puts ferrets down holes 210–11, 212, 215–16, 218, 219; declares Barings bankrupt 220; on consequences for Bank 221–2, 242–3; 224; and Treasury 213, 242; before Treasury and Civil Service Select Committee 244–6, 249–50; 247, 248, 251, 252, 296, 297
George V, King 12
Gilmore, Patrick 216–17
Glyndebourne Opera House Trust 18–19, 246, 293
Goldman Sachs 22, 34, 55, 58, 142, 144, 205, 211, 271
Goodison, Sir Nicholas 206, 207, 212
Granger Brenda 168, 169, 180–1, 183, 185, 189, 190, 195, 253, 255
Grant, Hugh 281, 287
Greer, Richard 30, 52, 59, 60, 196, 300
Guinness flotation (1886) 10
Gueler, Fernando 106, 115, 133, 138–9, 140, 141, 142, 143, 144, 147, 156, 157, 199, 270, 300
Guy John 68, 69, 74, 75, 77

Hardcastle, Sir Alan 244
Hawes, Tony: prepares for solo-consolidation 103, 111, 113, 114, 115, 118, 119; character 120–1, 173; harbours doubts about Leeson 124, 125, 126, 127, 128; 130, 131, 134, 138;

Hawes, Tony – *cont.*
    visits Singapore 140, 155–6; the
    Singapore Project 153, 159, 167;
    returns to Singapore 172–3, 175, 176–
    7, 180–1, 187, 194; 185, 186;
    Singapore showdown 197–8, 200, 265;
    253, 256, 258, 261, 268, 290, 294, 300
Heath, Christopher: builds BSL 23–31, 33,
    51, 269, 292; 'the burr under the
    saddle' 32–3, 52–3, 62, 64, 103, 115;
    character 34, 63–4, 67; joins main board
    54–5, 58; restructuring debate 59–60,
    61, 62, 63, 105, 109, 267–8; the
    Stabbath 65–7, 103, 104, 255;
    influence 67–8, 69, 88, 117, 251; 300
Heath, Edward 14
Heimann, John 209
Henderson-Baring 18
Henderson Crosthwaite 23, 25, 26, 27
Henderson, Lynn 114, 290
Hoare Govett 84
Hoechst prison, Frankfurt 238
Hogan, Richard 161
Hogg, Sarah 205
Hong Kong and Shanghai Bank 62, 76, 102
Hopkins, Ian 116, 118, 121, 127, 130, 153,
    170, 173, 174, 176, 185, 197, 253
Hu, Richard 260
Hughes, David 196
Hunt, Bunker, 2, 45
Hunt, Herbert 45

ICI 17, 25
Iguchi, Toshihide 267
Independent 237
Independent on Sunday 33–4
ING (Internationale Nederlanden Groep)
    229–33, 244, 247–8, 271–2, 293–4,
    295, 300
Ingrams, Leonard 14–15, 17, 19, 67, 120,
    233
Ingrams, Richard 14
International Financial Review 138
International Herald Tribune 83

Jacobs, Aad 230–3
Japan, Bank of 210–11, 215
Japanese stock market see Tokyo, Osaka
Japanese Government Bonds (JGB) 91, 122,
    134, 155, 157, 172, 188, 192, 193–4,
    206, 211, 272, 275
Japanese warrant market 26–7, 34, 52, 251
Jarecki, Dr Henry 37–8, 40–1, 43, 45, 49,
    50, 99, 296, 299
Jett, Joseph 131, 267, 297
Jones, Simon: resentment of head office 85,
    86–8, 89, 124, 127–8, 130, 133,

169–70, 172, 176, 187; 90, 95–6, 104,
    115, 127, 128; fails to separate Leeson's
    front and back office responsibilities
    89–90, 126, 170, 253–4; SIMEX letter
    of 11 Jan 95 150–2, 158–9, 257, 265;
    the SLK receivable 164, 165, 175, 195,
    259, 266, 290; and Leeson's note of 1
    Feb 95 168–9; SIMEX letter of 27 Jan
    95 172, 175; last meeting with Leeson
    194, 256; the hunt for Leeson 198,
    200, 255; Singapore Inspectors' Report
    259, 263, 265–6; 283
Johnson, Bruce 115
Johnson Matthey collapse 204, 220, 222

Kellock, James 240
Kelly, Diarmaid 29, 61, 66, 117
Khaled Abdullah, Prince 102
Kidder Peabody 131, 267, 297
Killian, Mike 80, 86, 90, 95, 97, 106, 139,
    140, 143, 155
Kingsley Napley 235, 238
Khoo Kun Wing 149
Kleinwort Benson 202, 208, 216, 248
Kobe earthquake 153–4, 180, 182, 289
Koh Ben Seng 227, 273
Koh, John 283–3, 284–5, 286–7, 289, 290
Kynaston, David 10

Lawrence, Sir Thomas 9, 15, 233
Lee Kwan Yew 81, 82, 83
Leeson, Anne 70, 71, 72
Leeson, Lisa 75–6, 78, 80, 96, 107, 144,
    158, 161, 188, 192, 194–5, 196, 235,
    236, 237, 240, 241, 273, 277, 285,
    291
Leeson, Nick: background 1, 70–2, 74–5;
    character and behaviour 2, 73, 74, 75,
    78, 79, 91, 137–8, 147, 191, 291, 292;
    early promise 75–7; joins BFSL 77–8;
    confused lines of reporting 86, 88, 89,
    90; front and back office
    responsibilities 80, 89, 106–7, 125,
    126, 131, 132, 159, 170, 176; in
    charge of BSFL SIMEX operation 86,
    88, 90–1; starts 88888 deception 94,
    97–8, 104; starts losing money 97–9,
    122; becomes proprietary trader 106,
    124, 136–7; commended in internal
    audit 125–6; given own position limits
    135; cross trades deception 134–5, 141,
    155; sells short straddle futures 142,
    183; ALCO instructs to reduce trading
    positions 156, 187; the SLK receivable
    160–77; questioned by Hawes 175;
    presses for more funds 182–4, 186;
    meeting with Norris 188, 255–6, 258–

9, 261; meeting with Railton 192–4;
flight 194–200, 225, 235–7; arrest
237–8; attempts to get UK trial, 236,
239, 240, 277–8, 281–2; trial 182,
283–8
Leeson, Sarah 70, 253
Leeson, Richard 70
Leeson, Victoria 70, 290, 291–2
Leeson, William (Harry) 70, 71
Leigh-Pemberton, Robin (Lord Kingsdown)
242
Lewis, Michael: *Liar's Poker* 46, 48
Liddell, Guy 12
Lidderdale, William 11
Lim, Michael 258, 259
Little Brown 281
Lloyds Bank 216
London International Financial Futures
Exchange (LIFFE) 43, 45
Long, Tracy 294
Loveday, Mark 230

Maclean, George 104, 116, 118, 155, 197,
253
MacMahon, Sir Kit 45, 49
Macmillan, Harold 13
Magnus, Judge Richard 283, 286, 287–8
Mail on Sunday 281
Major, John 205
Mallinkrodt, George 203, 206–7, 208, 209,
217, 220–1
Marunouchi 222
Martin, Ian 29, 56, 59, 66, 68, 74, 77, 86,
88, 300
McIntosh Securities 188, 261
Melamed, Leo 47, 49, 91, 227, 299
Merrill Lynch 205, 209, 221, 227, 228
Midland Bank 49, 212, 215, 216, 229
Monetary Authority of Singapore (MAS) 84,
92, 209–10, 215, 227, 228, 273
Moody's 249
Moore, Charles 212
Morgan Grenfell 23, 24, 220
Morgan, J. P. 48, 215
Morgan Stanley 22, 34, 45, 55, 57, 69, 73,
74, 75, 95, 187, 199, 205, 211, 229, 270,
289, 291

National Westminster Bank 5, 78, 216, 229
Nelligan, Mark 172
Nelson, James 25–6
Nelson, Lucy 25
Nisa (Singapore settlements clerk) 149, 165,
182, 188, 276–7
Nomura 22
Norhasalinda Hassan (Linda) 140, 148, 149,
165, 276

Norman, Montague 213
Norris, Peter 32–3, 57–9; character 59,
118, 256, 263; and Heath 60–2, 64–5,
117, 267, 269; chief executive officer
BSL, 66, 67, 109; and solo-consolidation
104, 105, 115; 110, 116, 155, 157, 158,
170; and the SLK receivable 169, 172,
174, 254, 261–2, 263, 264;
conversation with Leeson 188–9,
255–6, 258–9, 261; crisis meeting in
London 195–200; rescue attempt at
Bank 204, 214, 220; admits share of
blame 225; BBS Report 253; Singapore
Inspectors' Report 255, 256, 258–60,
262–3, 277; 283, 300

Osaka Securities Exchange 37, 88, 92, 94,
106, 111, 113, 118, 121–2, 125, 134,
135, 136, 139, 153–4, 157, 175, 178,
211, 220, 246, 271

Pang Mui Mui 149, 159
PCFC 76–7
Peacock, Edwin 12
Peers, Jim 187
Pennant-Rea, Rupert 202, 203–8, 210, 218,
243
'Philippe' 143–4
Phillip Bros 45
Phillips, Willie 32
Pollard, Stephen 71, 72, 74, 78, 238–9,
240–1, 277–8, 281, 282, 287, 288,
289, 291
Postbank 230
Price Waterhouse, Singapore 258

Quinn, Brian 109, 110, 204–10, 211–12,
213, 249–51, 300

Raffles, Sir Stanford 81–2
Railton, Tony 169, 170, 174–5, 176, 179,
183, 184, 187–8, 189–90, 192–4, 195,
197, 255, 289
Rees-Mogg, William 224
Reid, David 210
Reid, Sir Edward 12, 13
Richards Butler 265
Ritblatt, Nicholas 295
Rivett-Carnac, Miles 15, 54, 56–7, 60, 66,
104–5, 117
Rothschilds 11, 23, 208
Rothschild, Sir Evelyn 209
Rothschild, Jacob 27
Rubin, Howard 267

Sacranie, Sajeed 116, 124, 167, 196, 197,
198, 255

Salomon Brothers 22, 45, 46, 48, 53–4, 55, 63, 205
Sam, Elizabeth 274
Sandner, Jack 299
Savundra, Emil 279
Scholey, Sir David 207–8, 215, 220, 221
Schroders 26, 187, 202, 203, 208, 209, 216, 217, 220, 221
Scott, Sir Richard 228, 232
Securities and Exchange Commission (SEC) 189
Securities and Futures Authority (SFA) 60, 62, 79, 112, 228, 251
Securities and Investment Board 228
Sedgemore, Brian 244–5, 250
Seet Wee Teong 149, 159, 160–4, 165
Sergeant, Carol 112
Sergeant, Sir Patrick 212
Serious Fraud Office 239, 240–1, 257, 263, 279, 282
Shapiro, Mary 226, 227, 228, 296
Singapore 80–4, 137–8, 191
Singapore Commercial Affairs Department 181, 239, 262, 273, 282
Singapore Inspectors' Report 97, 100, 107, 127–8, 134–5, 145, 175, 182, 192, 258–60, 262, 263, 266, 272, 274–5
SIMEX (Singapore International Monetary Exchange) 37, 39–40, 69, 80, 84, 86, 88–9, 90, 91–2, 93, 106, 107, 108, 114–15, 121–2, 123, 124, 133, 134, 135, 136, 138, 140, 148, 149–50, 151, 152, 156, 158, 159, 174, 178–9, 180, 181–2, 186, 188, 193, 198, 214, 220, 226–7, 257, 260, 264, 265–6, 271, 272, 274–6, 282, 286, 287, 290, 291, 296, 297
SLK (Spear Leeds & Kellogg) receivable 107, 137, 160–9, 172, 173–4, 176, 195, 198, 254, 255–7, 258–61, 262, 263, 264, 265, 266, 277, 286, 287, 290
Slaughter and May 200
Smith Barney 229
Soo Yu Chuan 150–2, 158, 172, 257
Soros, George (Quantum Fund) 49, 143, 215
Spear Leeds & Kellogg see SLK
Standard Chartered Bank 45, 216–17
Standard and Poor 249
Staple, Christopher 240–1

Stone, Jonathan 295
Straits Times 84, 137
Sun 240, 271
Sunday Mirror 243, 294
Sunday Telegraph 212
Sunday Times 212, 281
Swiss Bank 145
Su Khoo 105, 115, 141

Tan, Nicky 258, 259
Tanah Merah jail, Singapore 288
Thompson, Christopher 64, 110, 112–13, 185–6, 246, 247, 250
Times, The 224, 236, 243
Tokyo Stock Market 29, 30, 34, 36, 50, 51, 92, 94, 105–6, 133, 135, 139, 153–4, 155, 157–8, 178, 185–6, 187, 198, 211, 220, 225–6, 255
Trustee Savings Bank (TSB) 206, 212, 216
Tuckey, Andrew 15; background 17–18, 205; 19, 20, 24, 33, 52–3, 54, 55, 58, 59; clashes with Heath 59–60, 61, 62, 64–5, 66, 267; solo-consolidation 67, 116; 102, 103, 105, 117–18, 158, 186; alerted to collapse 197, 200; crisis meeting in London 204; rescue attempt at Bank 214, 220; talks to Jacobs 230; BBS Report 254; 269, 290; survival 293–4
Tuckey, James 17
Tuckey, Hon Mr Justice Simon 17
Tugendhat, Christopher 203
Tyler, Rodney 239–40

Union Bank of Switzerland 229

Watford Observer 72, 253
Walz, Mary 121, 134, 139, 144, 147, 155, 156, 157, 159, 169, 185, 196–7, 199, 253, 255, 258, 294, 300
Warburg, S. G. 16, 20, 23, 202, 207, 208, 221, 248
Waxman, Jerome 63
White's 17–18, 67
Wilson, Harold 13
Wolf, Eric 93
Wong, Dr Edmund 93–4

Yong, Rachel 152, 165, 182, 195, 276